Maria Theresa of Austria

BY

J. ALEXANDER MAHAN

AUTHOR OF
"VIENNA YESTERDAY AND TODAY"
"FAMOUS WOMEN OF VIENNA"
AND
"MARIE LOUISE: NAPOLEON'S NEMESIS"

THOMAS Y. CROWELL COMPANY
PUBLISHERS   -   NEW YORK

COPYRIGHT 1932
BY THOMAS Y. CROWELL COMPANY

All rights reserved—No part of this book may be reproduced in any form without permission in writing from the publisher.

MARIA THERESA AT FORTY

To
ELSBETH

PREFACE

In this brief biography of Maria Theresa of Austria, the author addresses himself to general readers who are assumed to be unfamiliar with the details of European history. Care has been used to explain associated characters and events as they are mentioned in the narration, and two explanatory chapters have been introduced dealing with the Holy Roman Empire of the Germans, the Austrian Monarchy, and the contemporaries of the queen. We have aspired to make this book such that the average American reader may be able to understand and enjoy the text from beginning to end without the use of reference books.

But the author also hopes this work may be deemed worthy of a place in the libraries of historians. Due attention has been given to accuracy in the statement of facts, and all inferences drawn from them have been carefully considered. Many citations of authorities have been given and their use made as practical as possible by supplying a complete list of the works mentioned, with full data concerning publishers and dates of publication. This seemed necessary to avoid confusion, since many of the works cited have been repeatedly printed in editions which are not uniform in volumes and pages. To save space nearly all the citations are given in an abbreviated form of the complete entries placed at the end of the text. For the most part, letters have been referred to by names and dates so they may be easily located in any publication containing them. Perhaps we should explain that the references are given not merely to support the author's statements, but also to indicate where further information may be found, and to enable the reader to learn how the subject under discussion has been regarded by other writers; in a few instances, it may be discovered that the citations present views which diverge from those of the author.

We believe the House of Hapsburg is looked upon too unfavorably by the English-speaking race, especially in the United States of America. We are prone to forget that this, the greatest ruling dynasty in modern history, spanned the long period from the Crusades to the World War, and that during much of that time it formed the main bulwark which held back the rising tide of Mohammedanism threatening to engulf Europe and sweep Christian culture from the face of the earth. The Hapsburgs were not only strong, but also appeared upright and honorable when compared with most of their contemporaries. Even when the House, after six centuries of power, went into decline, it never sank to the low level of degradation and impotency occupied by most of the dynasties of Europe when approaching extinction.

Maria Theresa was the only ruling queen of the House of Hapsburg and many—we think very justly—regard her as the most capable, honorable, and conscientious ruler of the entire dynasty. For the author, she has always had a peculiar charm because of her supreme courage, lofty aspirations, and good common sense in the presence of apparently overwhelming difficulties, debased contemporaries, and erratic advisers.

To write her biography has been a pleasant task, in spite of the fact that many of her convictions seem to have been fundamentally wrong.

This biography departs somewhat from the stereotyped form, in that the details of military campaigns and political discussions, which may be read in almost any history of Europe, have been curtailed to make room for personal matter appearing here almost for the first time in the English language.

J. ALEXANDER MAHAN

Vienna, Austria
July 1932.

CONTENTS

CHAPTER		PAGE
I	An Unwelcome Daughter	3
II	A Blighted Romance	21
III	A Discouraging Accession	42
IV	The Empire and the Monarchy	61
V	Contemporaries of the Queen	76
VI	The First Contest	103
VII	Reforms in the Monarchy	170
VIII	The Change in Alliance	184
IX	The Second Contest	196
X	The Queen as a Woman	227
XI	The Queen as a Mother	266
XII	The Scourge of the Hapsburgs	315
XIII	Late Diplomacy	320
XIV	Death of the Queen	334
	Genealogical Table of the Hapsburgs	*facing* 340
	Chronology	341
	Works Cited in the Text	352
	Index	355

LIST OF PORTRAITS

Maria Theresa at Forty	*Frontispiece*
	FACING PAGE
Emperor Charles VI	6
Empress Elizabeth Christina	18
Maria Theresa When a Child	22
Maria Theresa When a Girl	36
Maria Theresa's Sister, Maria Anna	40
Prince Eugene of Savoy	44
Francis of Lorraine When a Young Man	50
Louis XV	86
Maria Theresa Shortly After Her Accession	104
Prince Charles of Lorraine	130
Count Wenzel Anton Kaunitz	163
Frederick II of Prussia	172
Madame de Pompadour	198
Field Marshal Daun	206
Baron von Loudon	218
Emperor Francis I	234
Maria Theresa After the Death of Her Husband	284
Marie Antoinette	304
Emperor Joseph II	310

MARIA THERESA OF AUSTRIA

I

AN UNWELCOME DAUGHTER

1

CHARLES VI, Archduke of Austria, King of Hungary, King of Bohemia, and Emperor of the Holy Roman Empire of the Germans, was asleep in his hunting lodge at Laxenburg, when, at three o'clock on the morning of May 13, 1717, a messenger arrived from the Hofburg, the imperial castle in Vienna, with very important news—Empress Elizabeth Christina was about to give birth to her second child. Dressing hastily, Charles rode the thirteen miles to Vienna and entered his palace at six, to find his *weise Liesel* in the final agonies of a confinement. The Emperor's emotions were a mixture of joy and suspense: joy at the prospect of an heir but suspense over whether the new arrival would be a boy or a girl. The birth of a son would make him supremely happy but the advent of a daughter would overwhelm him with disappointment.

The Emperor's feelings were shared by his entire household and all his subjects, for he was the last male representative of his line, and its extinction would probably be marked by another bloody war of succession, in which thousands of lives might be sacrificed and the peace of all Europe broken—perhaps for a generation—just as it recently had been by the long War of the Spanish Succession.

Vienna had not slept so soundly that night as to be totally unaware of what was taking place in the imperial palace. When the messenger set forth in hot haste for Laxenburg, he had been seen and questioned as he galloped away, so news that the long expected moment was near at hand spread like wildfire through the sleeping city. A crowd soon assembled before Kärntnertor and along the street from the city gate to the palace, eagerly awaiting the arrival of the Emperor; and as he rode by pell-mell, without halting, the throng closed in behind and followed him to the walls of the palace, where it settled down to receive the first news of the outcome of the fateful confinement. It was not strange that the people were so excited, for what was then happening meant as much to them as a national election means to us.

In whispered conversation the throng beguiled the anxious hours gossiping over the domestic affairs of the Emperor. Some spoke of the birth of Crown Prince Leopold, a little over a year before, and his recent death, expressing a fond hope that the Emperor and his subjects might have better luck this time. Others feared His Majesty had incurred the wrath of Heaven by marrying a girl who had pretended to be converted to Catholicism merely to become eligible to marry a Hapsburg. Several declared that the Empress had been seen secretly reading Lutheran books. Perhaps the Emperor was to be cursed with deaths and female

An Unwelcome Daughter

children for having united his Holy Catholic House with the Protestant House of Brunswick. Such remarks met with indignant *Pfuis!* (fie, for shame) from His Majesty's admirers, who reminded the traitors that the son of an Emperor could do no wrong.

Suddenly, at half-past seven, the tones of the great bell in Stephansdom swept across the city, and all knew the child had been born. No one could explain how the signal had passed from the Hofburg to the high tower, but the fact that the bell rang before any message was spoken to the crowd before the palace was not encouraging—bad news was more likely to be purposely delayed than good news. Some ran to the church, hoping to receive the first information there, but others remained motionless and almost speechless before the castle, straining eyes and ears for the expected trumpeter. Presently the great iron gates swung and a messenger rode through crying, "Hear ye! Hear ye! An archduchess is born to Their Apostolic Majesties, the Emperor and Empress!"

The announcement was received in silence, except for a few sighs of "Too bad! Too bad!" But no people on earth are more certain to discover small blessings in the wake of great disasters than the Viennese. "What if it is a princess?" they soon began to say. "The Emperor is only thirty-one and the Empress is but twenty-five; they had a baby last year, another this year, and next year there will be still another. We shall at least make a glorious holiday! To the *cafés!* To the beer halls! Let us eat, drink and be merry!"

The castle was soon bustling with activity, making ready for the baptism which was to occur on the evening of the same day. Of this event we have many long and very detailed accounts, in the *Wiener Diarum*, in the documents of the Austrian Archives, and the writings of several contemporaries; nothing is left to our imaginations. In the baptismal font were five drops of water from the River Jordan and one thorn from the very crown the Roman soldiers pressed on the head of Christ. One statement appears several times in the descriptions of this august ceremony: in the baptismal procession the infant was carried ahead of the daughters of the preceding Emperor Joseph I—"right before the eyes of Joseph's widow, Wilhemina Amalia"—thus boldly announcing that the new-born princess was to outrank the daughters of the preceding Emperor.

When the Bishop baptized the infant he pronounced the name, "Maria Theresa Walburga Amalia Christina," that being almost the only time in the whole life of the princess that the last three names were ever mentioned.

Through all this trying ceremony, Charles did his best to conceal his emotions, but many spoke of the sadness of his countenance, the difficulty with which he restrained his tears, and other involuntary evidences of grief and disappointment. His only consolations were a hope for more children and the decree he had made four years before.[1]

II

It was Prince Liechtenstein who carried the infant on a soft pillow in the baptismal procession of May 13, 1717. The Prince could have reeled off the ped-

---

[1] The authority for much of this story of the birth of Maria Theresa is Bermann, 1-15.

igree of this baby with the same ease that we name the days of the week, and given the traits of her ancestors as readily as the qualities of his favorite hounds. Had his hobby been genetics instead of collecting paintings, he might possibly have foretold just what sort of woman the baby would be when she reached the age of twenty, for like begets like and certain inherited attributes, subjected to specified environment, yield fairly definite results just as flour, mixed with yeast and water and placed in a hot oven, produces bread. The Prince held in his arms that evening many potential germs of wars, alliances, reforms, and royal marriages, destined to grow and be harvested at the price of much blood and suffering, and no end of joy, grief, and bad temper.

A most interesting pastime in the study of celebrated men and women is to pick their characters to pieces, in much the same spirit that a boy takes his moving toys apart to see what makes them go. One finds pleasure in searching out the coiled springs of power, and the hidden wheels of emotion that enabled such men and women to accomplish so much more than others engaged in the same line of work. When we do this we are often surprised to discover that most individuals of renown drew their elements of strength from ancestors who were not accounted very great. Certain qualities, properly combined and subjected to favorable influences, may make one person eminent; the same qualities, differently grouped and placed under other conditions, may leave another mediocre.

We shall find that Maria Theresa drew her unusual ability from her attributes of perseverance, courage, patriotism, piety, conscientiousness, intellectuality, and her most exceptional physical charm. There were brilliant flashes of the same attributes in her father and mother, who but for their enviable positions—by birth or marriage—would have gone straight to oblivion, so it is interesting to pause, before beginning Maria Theresa's story, and scan the lives of her parents, searching especially for the origin of those strong traits of character just enumerated.

Emperor Charles VI, Maria Theresa's father, succeeded his elder brother, Joseph I, who died of smallpox at the age of thirty-three after a brief reign of six years. Charles and Joseph were the only sons of the renowned Emperor Leopold I, whose reign lasted forty-seven years. For the present we shall not follow her ancestry farther than this celebrated grandfather.

Leopold I died in the midst of a war for the crown of Spain, which had been left without a direct male heir by the death of Charles II, son of Philip IV. Leopold had married Philip's daughter, and upon the death of Charles II, claimed the Spanish crown, but it so happened that Louis XIV of France had also married a daughter of Philip IV, and likewise claimed the crown for a relative. The issue was being fought out in the War of the Spanish Succession but Leopold seems to have been confident that Austria, in alliance with England, would win; hence he reckoned Spain among the possessions to be divided between his two sons, Joseph and Charles.[2]

---

[2] Coxe, III, 2.

For an explanation of the Roman and Arabic figures used in the citations, see list of "Works Cited in the Text," to be found immediately before the index.

The reader's attention is also directed to the list of important dates supplied in the "Chronology" at the end of the text.

Joseph, being the elder, was naturally given the home dominions of Austria, Bohemia, and Hungary, together with several distant provinces in Italy, while the crown of Spain and her dependencies was bestowed upon Charles. Leopold further decreed that, in the event of the death of either of his sons without a male heir, the other should inherit the dominions of both. Also—and this is the most important provision of all for this story—in case both sons died without a male heir, the possessions should be inherited by a daughter, those of Joseph, the elder son, being given preference over those of Charles, the younger. In order that there might be no dispute between the two sons, the father had them both sign this decree and swear to abide by it.[3] Soon after this Leopold I died, no doubt fully convinced that he had provided for all possible contingencies that might arise in connection with the accessions of his descendants. But Leopold was a bad prophet; the War of the Spanish Succession proved to be a very long and bloody one, and, combined with an epidemic of smallpox, completely wrecked the old Emperor's well-meant provisions.

Charles was proclaimed King of Spain, under the title of Charles III, at Vienna in 1703, and immediately set forth to complete the conquest of his kingdom.[4] He first visited his ally, England, going by way of Holland, where he was received by the Dukes of Marlborough and Somerset. From Holland he was conducted by the King of Denmark to visit Queen Anne at Windsor. Of this visit we have the printed account of Tindal, well worth quoting because it brings

[3] Struvius, II, 1442, cited by Coxe.
[4] Coxe, II, 2.

out certain qualities of the young King which were later so well exemplified by his distinguished daughter. Tindal wrote: "The court was splendid and much thronged; the Queen's behavior toward the King was very noble and obliging. The King charmed all present; he had a gravity beyond his age, and wonderfully tempered with modesty. His behavior was in all points so exact, that there was not a circumstance in his whole deportment that was liable to censure. He paid extraordinary respect to the Queen, and yet maintained a fine dignity. He had the art of seeming well pleased with everything, without so much as smiling once all the time he was at the court, which was three days. He spoke but little, and all he said was judicious and obliging." [5] Later on, we shall find very similar tributes paid to his daughter, Maria Theresa, who inherited all the good qualities of her father—together with a few which were rather questionable.

We have many accounts of Charles' conduct in Spain. He landed in Catalonia, where he soon won the devotion of a band of natives under the command of the Earl of Peterborough, who wrote a full description of the events in which he also participated. Affairs were in such a desperate state that the British commander was about to embark his troops and sail away, abandoning all attempts to capture Barcelona, but this determination was overruled by the spirited resolution of Charles to "stay and die with his brave Catalans." Accordingly the siege began, and it terminated in the triumphant entry of Charles and his "plucky Catalans"

---

[5] Tindal, Chap. XV, 569, cited by Coxe.

into the city where he was proclaimed King. But very soon Barcelona was besieged by the French and Spaniards, and the condition of the garrison became most desperate. Charles remained firm in his resolve to stay in his capital, and according to all accounts, showed much more concern for the security of the garrison than for the safety of his own person.[6]

For twenty-two days the city was surrounded by overwhelming numbers, but the besiegers were so intimidated by the reckless adventures of the young King and his brave followers that it was not taken by storm, as it could have been at almost any period of the siege. Walpole, who witnessed the relief of Barcelona, wrote: "Not a speck of blue appeared to offer the least hope for the preservation of the city, nor even the King's person." On one side was what seemed to be an irresistible army, on the other a strong French fleet completely blocking the harbor, but still the courageous garrison refused to surrender. Finally, British ships appeared on the horizon, the French fleet sailed away, reinforcements landed, and the siege was over. The stubborn determination of the young King to perish rather than surrender, saved the city.

The deliverance of Barcelona was followed by a long series of alternating triumphs and defeats. Twice Charles sat on the Spanish throne in Madrid, and twice was compelled to flee to avoid capture. Sometimes he was master of nearly all Spain, and at others limited to the narrow boundaries of Catalonia. It was during this period of turmoil that he married and settled down to

---

[6] Coxe, III, 2, citing Peterborough's Conduct in Spain 101

win the Spanish crown, even though it required a lifetime.[7] His seven years in Spain won him a glorious reputation, which was largely lost during his after life in Vienna. Perhaps only adversity could bring out the strong traits of his character, but his conduct at this period of his life proved that he had such traits, at least when a young man, and we may reasonably expect them to reappear in his daughter Maria Theresa.

In 1711 came the sudden death of Joseph I, and Charles set out for Vienna. He was now entitled to all the inherited dominions of the House of Hapsburg and likely to be elected Emperor of the Holy Roman Empire of the Germans.

On the way to Vienna he was notified that he had already been elected Emperor, and almost at the same time, he was chosen King of Bohemia and King of Hungary. All the other dominions of the Hapsburgs were his without question and since he had not abandoned his right to the crown of Spain he seemed in a fair way to become as powerful as the great Charles V, who once held more than half the Christian world in the hollow of his hand. But such a future was not in store for Charles VI. By the Treaty of Utrecht in 1713, a treaty which the Germans dubbed *Unrecht*, Charles was forced to abandon the crown of Spain and limit himself to the dominions previously ruled by his brother Joseph.[8]

Five years of married life passed and Charles had no children. During all these years he was confronted by the two daughters of his brother Joseph, the elder being the heir apparent to the thrones of the Haps-

---
[7] Coxe, III, 4–5.
[8] *Ibid.,* 19.

burgs. The sad fate of dying without heirs appeared on the horizon of Charles' destiny, first as a tiny cloud no larger than a man's hand, but it grew year by year until it completely filled his skies. What should he do? What could he do? All day long he wrestled with such questions and at night they haunted his dreams. Gradually he concluded that the provisions of his father's decree were unfair, especially in one particular respect: should Charles fortunately have a son, his heir would inherit the crowns, but, if he had only daughters, they would be preceded by those of Joseph. If he could make his own daughters take precedence over those of Joseph, it would double the probability of a continuation of his own line, but he had signed his father's decree and sworn to abide by it, and any such an alteration would be a violation of his pledge to his dead parent and brother.

Now and then, quite involuntarily, the thought of changing his father's decree suggested itself to Charles. It was an alluringly tempting idea and he permitted it to return again and again, until it remained constantly in his mind. Next he began to excuse it and before long to justify it. He reasoned that his father could not have foreseen the loss of the Spanish crown; had he thought of that he would not have made such an unfair decree. Also, if the father, Leopold I, could make rules for the succession of his house, the son, Charles VI, could alter them.

Finally Charles yielded to temptation and on the morning of the nineteenth of September, 1713, assembled his ministers and had a secretary read a new decree governing the accession of the House of Hapsburg. It almost repeated the words of the decree of his father, with the exception of one very important alteration—it gave the daughters of Charles VI precedence over those of Joseph I. At this time Charles had neither sons nor daughters and no flattering prospects of either, so the new edict seemed quite purposeless.[9] It was regarded as the result of nervousness on the part of the Emperor, who was known to be brooding over his ill fortune in remaining childless.

Compared with the manner in which we change our fundamental laws under a modern republican form of government, this action on the part of Charles VI seems very simple and easy. All he did was to dictate his decree to a penman, then assemble his ministers, seat himself comfortably on the throne, and have it read. There were no messages to Congress or Parliament, no annoying amendments, and no submission to the people for ratification. The fundamental law of the land was altered in one forenoon.

But the alteration was by no means completed. Charles knew there were relatives and potential pretenders all over Europe, and if the decree was to become effective, it must be ratified by the inherited dominions, the princes and electors of the Empire, and almost every power in Europe. It was a tremendous undertaking and he labored at it continuously, in spite of all sorts of discouragements, almost until his death in 1740. It cost him much territory—more than his advisers thought it was worth—but the Emperor never once faltered or abandoned his purpose. The efforts of his whole reign were swallowed up in securing ratifications of his pet scheme.[10]

[9] Arneth, I, 4.
[10] Coxe, III, 105–108; Arneth, I, 5; Guglia, I, 42.

The edict was given the name of Pragmatic Sanction, and although it seemed senseless and of no significance at the time it was issued, Charles made of it one of the most important pieces of parchment in European history. It might have been written many million times in the blood it cost the people of that and the succeeding generations. In three years after it was issued the Empress gave birth to a son, whereupon it became more useless than ever; but the son died the same year and the next spring a daughter arrived. Then the Sanction became supremely important, for it placed her ahead of her cousins in the line of accession.

The Pragmatic Sanction became a floating mast to which Charles clung, with the desperation of a drowning sailor, to save his line from perishing. He was always hoping to be rescued by the appearance of a son, when he meant to abandon his makeshift entirely.

Passing to other accomplishments of Maria Theresa's father, we find that the greatest physical monument to his reign is the beautiful Karlskirche, still standing in Vienna and familiar to all tourists.[11] The story of its erection brings out certain very marked characteristics of the monarch. In 1713 Vienna was visited by a dreadful epidemic of the plague, which seemed on the verge of exterminating the whole population. In a similar epidemic in 1679, Leopold I, Charles' father, fled for safety to a country town. Charles did nothing of the kind; he staid faithfully by his people and did all in his power to relieve their suffering. In the midst of the epidemic he formed a procession and carried the relics of Saint Borromeo to the altar of St.

---

[11] Malleson, *Vienna Yesterday and Today*, 233.

Stephan, where he publicly prayed and vowed to erect a church upon the cessation of the scourge. This vow he kept and the result is Karlskirche, built at a great sacrifice, and dedicated only two years before the Emperor's death.[12]

Perhaps we have told enough of Charles VI to show that he had brilliant flashes of most of the qualities that later lifted his daughter to eminence. His persistence at the siege of Barcelona, and the stubborn fight, lasting nearly twenty years, that he made for the ratifications of his Sanction, were conspicuous marks of perseverance. His courage against disheartening odds was several times clearly demonstrated in Spain; his piety and patriotism shone like beacon lights during the epidemic of the plague in 1713, and in the manner in which he held his vow afterward; while his shrewd discernment—perhaps we might call it intellectuality—was exemplified in the way he issued his Pragmatic Sanction at a period when it appeared senseless to others, but at just the proper time to put it over without encountering too much opposition.

Then we must not fail to call attention to Charles' ability to bend a stiff, cumbersome conscience to fit the rough exigencies of several emergencies with which he was confronted, and to do it so dextrously that he appeared almost justified. The manner in which he squeezed his elder brother's daughter out of the line of accession and his own daughter in, in spite of his oath to his dead father and brother, is a wonderful example of how principles may be cleverly twisted to fit the demands of stern expediency. We shall find that

---

[12] *Oesterreichischer Erbefolge-Krieg*, I, 897.

An Unwelcome Daughter

Maria Theresa inherited every grain of her father's ability in this respect; perhaps she even surpassed him on one or two occasions. In fact, when we take her character to pieces, we find that most of its wheels and springs are identical with those used by her father.

III

It is no less interesting to analyze Maria Theresa's mother to see what the daughter derived from that source. Fate seems to have hesitated before deciding who should be honored with the motherhood of the one destined to be the only reigning queen of the House of Hapsburg. Charles almost married Caroline of Ansbach—the union was abandoned only because she refused to forsake the Lutheran faith and become a Catholic. She married the Prince of Wales, and later, as the wife of George II became a queen of England.

Elizabeth Christina, the granddaughter of Antony Ulrich, Duke of Brunswick-Wolfbüttel, was next considered, and the same difficulty arose,[13] for Elizabeth likewise refused to change her religion until strongly urged by her grandfather, to whom all faiths were alike. Her parents strenuously opposed the union on religious grounds, but the grandfather flouted the idea of refusing to marry a Hapsburg for such flimsy reasons. He convinced Elizabeth that it was easy to change religions, by himself abandoning the Lutheran faith and becoming a Catholic. He told his granddaughter she could ease her conscience when attending masses by repeating to herself the creed of the Lutherans.[14] Such

---
[13] Coxe, III, 223; Sir Robert Walpole, *Memoirs*, I, 274.
[14] Bermann, 21.

arguments and demonstrations overcame Elizabeth's scruples, and she joined the Catholic Church for no other reason than to make herself eligible to marry Charles. All her life the genuineness of her conversion was doubted in Vienna and she was often accused of secretly clinging to the Lutheran faith.

In April, 1707, she set out from Wolfbüttel and reached Vienna in May. The next year she was married to Charles by proxy, Emperor Joseph I substituting for his brother, who was then in Spain. Next she made the long and hazardous journey to meet her husband in Barcelona.

We have the testimony of several witnesses to prove that Elizabeth Christina was a woman of exceptional beauty. Upon meeting his bride Charles exclaimed quite involuntarily, "Well now, I never dreamed you were so pretty!" One of those present on this occasion wrote: "The King loves his Queen so tenderly that he cannot bear to allow her out of his sight; whenever he has a moment of leisure, he rushes to spend it with her. He seems to be just such a woman's man as was his father Leopold I." [15]

Immediately upon the Queen's arrival Charles wrote a joyous letter of thanks to old Antony Ulrich, of which we quote a part: "Although on all sides I was told beforehand of the exceptional and remarkable qualities of my angelic Queen and consort, yet now, when I have seen her, all that was said seems like a shadow which has vanished in the full light of the sun. Words fail me to express my exceeding happiness and satisfaction. I shall be eternally grateful to you for making it possible

[15] *Ibid.*

An Unwelcome Daughter

for this angel to become my Queen. I only wish she had a consort worthy of her merits, but I shall do my best to be to her a faithful and loving husband. The rare treasure entrusted to my care will be most carefully guarded." [16] Lest the reader may jump to the conclusion that Charles was a perfect husband, we add that his idea of faithfulness did not prompt him to sever his relations with the beautiful Countess Althans, who before and after his marriage, served him in the capacity of a semi-official mistress.

Another writer of the times, who frequently saw Elizabeth Christina, said: "She was very intellectual and steadfast. She took an active part in all the affairs of the court, and bestowed upon them a charm which otherwise would have been entirely wanting."

Lady Montagu, the wife of the British Ambassador to Constantinople, visited in Vienna, where she met Empress Elizabeth Christina, and was so impressed by her personality that she wrote the following: "I was perfectly charmed by the Empress; I cannot, however, say that her features are perfectly regular; her eyes are not large but have a look full of sweetness; her complexion is the finest I ever saw; her nose and forehead are well made, but her mouth has ten thousand charms that touch the soul. When she smiles 'tis with a beauty and sweetness that force adoration. She has a vast quantity of fine fair hair; but her person!—one must speak of it in poetry to do it justice; all that the poets have said of the mien of Juna, the air of Venus, comes not up to the truth. The graces move with her; the famous Venus de Medici was not formed with more delicate proportions; nothing can be added to the beauty of her neck and hands. Till I saw her hands, I did not believe there were any so perfect, and I was sorry that my rank did not permit me to kiss them, but they were kissed sufficiently, for every one who waits on her pays homage at entrance and departure." [17]

Lady Montagu's tribute is especially noteworthy because she wrote so much that was uncomplimentary of other women she saw in Vienna. In speaking of Viennese women in general, she said, "They are the ugliest women God ever made," and she described their morals as being so loose that Vienna might be called a "city of free adultery."

From such glowing descriptions, even after discounting them because the writers may have been somewhat overawed by the high station of the lady of whom they were writing, we may reasonably believe that Elizabeth Christina was a charming woman, who had the power to win the admiration of all who came into her presence. Surely in this beautiful mother, the captivating Empress, we have the source of those physical attractions and winning manners that later served Maria Theresa to such wonderful advantage; it was largely what she inherited in this line that boosted her safely through a great crisis, the most perilous one of her whole life, as we shall presently see. The germs of strength and beauty that Prince Liechtenstein carried in his arms in that baptismal procession on the thirteenth of May, 1717, enabled the baby to become one of the most remarkable queens in history.

---

[17] Lady Montagu, Letter of Sept. 14, 1716.

II

A BLIGHTED ROMANCE

I

WE may be sure that Charles VI never looked upon his daughter Maria Theresa with any high degree of satisfaction, for he saw in her the source of too many embarrassments and disappointments which he might have been spared had she been a boy. He could never quite satisfy his conscience for having broken his pledges to his brother and father by advancing his own daughter to the place which rightfully belonged to one of his nieces. Then too, the difficulty of securing her acceptance as his heir to the hereditary dominions proved to be much greater than he had supposed at the beginning, and to have her elected Emperor of the Holy Roman Empire was quite impossible. Charles toiled diligently at his task of clearing the way for her accession, but with the same spirit in which a carpenter shapes a bad piece of timber while hoping and expecting to be provided at any moment with a better stick. Since he always expected a son, he did not bother to have his daughter instructed in many subjects most essential to the ruler of a great empire. When the son arrived, the daughter would be married to some important ruler of Europe and become the queen of a brilliant court. For such a position she would need to be able to sing, play the spinet, dance, paint, ride, wear diamonds, speak half a dozen languages, dress in the latest fashion, receive courtiers, flirt with diplomats, and squelch them without giving offense when they were about to cross the line of toleration. When compelled to reconcile himself to the idea of a daughter as his heir, would be soon enough to begin teaching her the sterner subjects of mathematics, law, diplomacy, military tactics, commerce and finance.

This psychology of Charles was clearly reflected in the education of his daughter. She was instructed in drawing and painting by Anton Bertolli, one of the best art critics of his day. At the age of twelve she was making pictures, some of which are still preserved, to bear eloquent testimony to her talent and industry. George Christopher Wagenseil, an assistant of Johann Fuchs, the *Kapellmeister* of the court, taught her music, and her progress in singing and dancing were so rapid that at the age of six she sang in an opera of the *Hof* while her father directed the orchestra. In behavior and etiquette she was in charge of Countess Charlotte Fuchs, to whom she became so greatly attached as almost to excite the jealousy of the Empress. The little girl's devotion to Countess Fuchs was so strong that it endured for life, and when the Countess died, in 1754, Maria Theresa had the body of her beloved teacher placed in the Capucine Church, where it remains to this day among the coffins of the Hapsburgs.[1]

In such surroundings and with such talented instructors, Maria Theresa developed into a most delightful,

---
[1] Bermann, 257.

MARIA THERESA AT THE AGE OF THREE
FROM A PORTRAIT IN THE HOFBURG, VIENNA

light-hearted princess, endowed with all the graces of her mother. We have several interesting pictures of her and her sister Maria Anna who was born just a little more than a year after Theresa. Theresa and Anna looked as much alike as two peas; both were slender, doll-like little girls, with blond hair and large wistful blue eyes that seemed to look out upon the world in wonder and amazement, not quite understanding how and why they differed from other children.

There is one painting of little Theresa that almost rouses our pity. The three-year-old tot stands all tricked out in a drawing-room gown, fashioned after those of the ladies of the court. The bodice is tightly laced and the full skirt sweeps the floor. In her right hand she holds a garland of roses, while her left arm tilts stiffly out from her body in such a strained position that it almost wearies us to look at her. Her thick hair is parted precisely in the middle, over a forehead rather too full to be natural. Her countenance seems almost painfully fixed, as if she might be posing for a very important photograph, but it is her eyes that arrest and hold the attention; we hardly know whether she is about to burst into tears or wink at us and say, "Hello there! You don't know me in this outfit, do you?"

II

Courtiers visited the court of Charles VI, met Maria Theresa, and went away to advertise her beauty until her fame resounded throughout Europe. Naturally every one was asking about her betrothal; in reality, no sooner was she born and baptized, than the court of Vienna busied itself in arranging for her marriage, and we may be sure that she, also, thought of marriage very early in life, for the mating instinct was strong in this demure little maid. Very soon all eyes turned in the direction of Lorraine, where there was a young Prince Clemens, nine years older than Theresa.[2] His suit was urged by the most influential courtiers, among whom was Prince Eugene of Savoy, who had delivered Austria from the menace of the Turks, carried the Austrian standards to victory on so many battlefields, and secured the imperial crown for Charles VI.[3] If any one was entitled to make suggestions concerning the intimate affairs of the Emperor's family, it was surely Prince Eugene.

Under the eyes of a Duke of Lorraine, Prince Eugene first served in the Austrian army—at the time of the great Turkish siege of 1683—and won his first distinction in battle. The two men had always been comrades and fast friends. This Duke of Lorraine was Prince Clemens' grandfather and a stepbrother-in-law to Leopold I, the grandfather of Maria Theresa. It seemed only fair and just to the Lorraines that the little Princess be given to a representative of the Duke's house in marriage. Apparently Charles consented to this arrangement quite willingly, for when Maria Theresa was six the fourteen-year-old Prince Clemens was invited to come to the court of Vienna to complete his education and get acquainted with the little girl who was to be his wife. But instead of the Prince, a messenger, clad in mourning, came from the father to announce that Prince Clemens had just died of the small-

[2] Arneth, I, 6; Guglia, I, 32.
[3] Coxe, III, 7.

pox, so little Theresa, who regarded herself as already mated for life, imagined she was a widow.[4]

But Leopold of Lorraine, the father of Prince Clemens, had another son, Francis Stephan, who was now heir to the dominion and eight years older than Maria Theresa. Leopold immediately offered to substitute Francis for Clemens, and soon won the support of Prince Eugene to the project, but in the meantime Charles seems to have altered his mind. Probably, upon reflection, he concluded that his eldest daughter might be needed to win an alliance with one of the more important powers of Europe, and that he should not be in a hurry to dispose of her merely to please old friends of the family; yet he did not object to extending an invitation to Francis Stephan to come to the court to finish his education. Thus it seemed as though the young Prince was to be received on a sort of probation. He arrived in Vienna at the age of fourteen, and was assigned to quarters in the Hofburg.[5] This immediately gave the impression that he was to be betrothed to Maria Theresa, an impression Charles neither affirmed nor denied.

The lad was most pleasant and well-behaved. We do not know precisely when he was introduced to Maria Theresa—possibly they first met on a hunting excursion as represented by a celebrated artist—but we do know that before long both Theresa and Anna were much pleased with him and seemed to regret that they could not both marry him. He also found favor with the Emperor and Empress, for he was a good entertainer and very fond of hunting, which was a passion

[4] Arneth, I, 8; Guglia, I, 32.
[5] Arneth, I, 9.

with Charles VI.[6] As time passed and the long-wished-for boy failed to arrive in the imperial family, the father hesitated more and more over yielding his consent to the betrothal of the daughter. In 1724, the Empress gave birth to another girl, Maria Amalia, very much to the disappointment of the parents, and Charles was again most forcibly reminded of the fact that only the Pragmatic Sanction and his daughters stood between him and the extinction of his line. Francis Stephan continued at the court and Maria Theresa fell deeper and deeper in love with him, but while the father could not bring himself to consent to a betrothal, he did not have the courage to send the lad away.

Once Charles thought of arranging a marriage between his daughter and the Crown Prince of Portugal, but soon abandoned the plan because he feared the Prince of Portugal was too much under the influence of France, the traditional enemy of Austria.

Then, in 1725, marriage negotiations were opened with Elizabeth Farnese, and Charles signed a secret pact to marry Theresa and Anna to Elizabeth's sons, Don Carlos and Don Philip. Rumors of this arrangement reached the keen ears of Maria Theresa, then but eight years old, and she grieved so much over it that she lost her appetite and grew pale. But news of this pact leaked out, and the leading nations of Europe, seeing the balance of power about to be destroyed, prepared for war.[7] Charles was compelled to renounce the betrothals, and little Theresa sprang to life like a withered garden flower after a refreshing rain.[8]

---
[6] *Ibid.*
[7] *Ibid.,* 16–17; Guglia, I, 33.
[8] This betrothal was strongly opposed by Prince Eugene.

A Blighted Romance

Next, Seckendorf, the Austrian Ambassador at Berlin, conceived the idea of strengthening Prussia's loyalty to the Emperor by arranging a marriage between young Frederick, afterward Frederick the Great, and the eldest princess of the House of Austria. When Theresa heard of this she again wilted and became actually sick. Prince Frederick was likewise much displeased, not because he had any strong objections to wedding Maria Theresa, but because he did not wish to be betrothed to any one until he was much older. In spite of all the protestations of the prospective bride and groom, this marriage probably would have taken place but for the fact that Frederick was a Lutheran and stubbornly refused to become a Catholic, so it was finally abandoned.[9] In breaking off the marriage negotiations with Frederick's father, Charles sought to ease the blow by giving Elizabeth Christina, a relative of Maria Theresa's mother, to Prince Frederick. This was the unhappy marriage of the future King of Prussia which will be discussed more fully a little later. One cannot help wondering what might have been the result had Frederick married Maria Theresa. Could Europe have been saved all the bloody wars over Silesia? In the light of subsequent events we are tempted to answer this question in the affirmative.

III

In 1729, Duke Leopold of Lorraine died and Francis left Vienna to take charge of his realm.[10] The young man, who was now twenty, had been at the court of

[9] Guglia, I, 33; Goldsmith, 41.
[10] Arneth, I, 18.

Charles VI for five years, and had completely won the heart of Maria Theresa, who was then twelve. He was still waiting, full of hope, and with as much patience as he could command, for what seemed to him a stubborn father's consent to marry his daughter.

After putting the affairs of his realm in order, Francis set out to see the world, visit the courts of the principal powers of Europe, and enlarge the horizon of his influence by becoming personally acquainted with important sovereigns and their prospective heirs, in order that he might be a more useful husband to the future Empress. He seems to have made this prolonged journey with the official approval of Charles VI, who supplied him with credentials and sent General Neipperg—Francis' instructor in Vienna—with him. In every capital he was met by an Austrian Ambassador who received and introduced him as if he were some sort of an Ambassador-extraordinary from the court of the Emperor. The semi-official capacity in which he traveled was based, not on his position as the Duke of Lorraine, but on the understanding that he was to marry the heir to the throne of the Hapsburgs.

This prospective marriage endowed Francis with tremendous importance in the minds of the various rulers he visited. Maria Theresa was known to be a most charming archduchess, but no one supposed she would be of much consequence as a monarch. All visualized her as presiding over a brilliant social court, but submitting to the better judgment of her husband in important matters of state. She could never be elected Emperor of the Germans, but it was assumed that this high honor would probably fall to her husband, since it had become almost a perquisite of the Hapsburg family. While Emperor Charles had never officially promised anything to the young Duke, his actions indicated to the world all that has been mentioned, and his silence corroborated it. Francis of Lorraine was looked upon as one of the most potentially powerful princes in Europe.

Francis first visited the court at Versailles, where he had some important business to transact concerning one of his possessions. Then he went to The Hague, where he was met and much charmed by the British Ambassador, Philip Dormer Stanhope, afterward Lord Chesterfield. Stanhope seems to have induced Francis to join the Freemasons.[11] This little statement almost makes us gasp for a moment. Why did Francis, who expected to be the consort of a Catholic queen, and even hoped to be the next Emperor of the Holy Roman Empire of the Germans—an empire completely committed to Catholicism—ever consent to become a Mason?

The answer is very simple; the Freemasons were not then regarded as anti-Catholic.[12] Masonry is supposed to have originated at the building of King Solomon's temple, but the organization which we now know, and which Francis of Lorraine joined, really dates from 1717—strange to say, the year of Maria Theresa's birth. In that year the Mother Lodge in London, the ancestor of all the lodges of today, was founded. From it the order spread rapidly through England and Scotland, but the lodge at which Francis was made a Mason was probably the first ever assembled on the Continent of Europe. It was opened by Englishmen who

[11] Bermann, 295.
[12] *Ibid.*, 295-296.

came for the very purpose of conferring the degrees upon the Duke of Lorraine. Its membership was limited almost entirely to eminent people, most of them connected with the British nobility and the army. The British Masons were eager to get their order started on the Continent and to make it an exclusive world society. Francis foresaw that it would spread rapidly among the nobility, and believed it would be of the greatest service to him in conducting the diplomatic affairs of his future Queen.

But Francis did not foresee that Freemasonry would be banned by Pope Clement XII in 1738, that it would bring him into disgrace with the Catholic House of Austria, and become a source of friction between himself and his wife. Had he known all this he probably would not have joined the order. We may be pretty sure that Charles VI and his daughter Maria Theresa both knew that Francis had become a Freemason and were not displeased. Neither of them had any premonition of the impending conflict with Catholicism. The fact that Francis was the first Freemason to receive the first and second degrees on the Continent—he received his third in England—gave him a sense of proprietorship and special zeal in Freemasonry; he considered himself as somewhat of a father to the order on the Continent.[18] More will be said of this when we come to discuss the domestic affairs of Maria Theresa.

Francis visited England and was received at the court of George II with great honor, as a brother Mason, as Prince of Lorraine, and especially as the future ruler of the Germans. He went hunting with the

---

[18] *Ibid.*, 301.

A Blighted Romance

Prince of Wales and hobnobbed with the royal family for weeks. He was an excellent mixer, a clever gambler at cards, and a skillful hunter and horseman, good-natured, handsome, and well-dressed—in fact, he was a hale fellow and a "jolly good" sportsman. He charmed the British court, and when he left King George wrote him a sort of a recommendation in which he said, "Nothing could have given me a greater satisfaction than your sojourn in this country." Charles VI heard all this and was pleased; Maria Theresa heard it and was delighted. They looked upon their Prince as an ambassador of good will whose visit would do much to promote friendship between the two great powers.

From England, Francis went to Holland, and later to Berlin, where he hunted with Crown Prince Frederick who then was, or very soon afterward became, a Freemason.[14] Strange to say, Frederick was at that very time on the verge of marrying Elizabeth Christina of Brunswick, the betrothal having grown out of the tangle, already noted, involving Frederick and Maria Theresa. This caused no unpleasantness between the two princes, for Frederick had never wished to marry Francis' sweetheart.

During all this time Francis was sending semi-official reports back to the court of Charles VI, and regarded himself, with good reason, as certain to marry Maria Theresa. The matter was also happily and completely settled in the mind of the young Archduchess, who, with all the pinings and yearnings of a true lover, followed her Prince Charming in his travels and sighed for the happy day when he would return to entertain

---

[14] Carlyle, III, 93.

the imperial family with his tales of adventure in foreign lands. To Maria Theresa, Francis was a great man of the world, intimately acquainted with all the crowned heads of Europe and master of the diplomatic questions of the day. Above all, he was her very own, had always been hers, and could never be anybody else's.

Francis, having completed his triumphant parade to all the great courts, thought it time to return to Vienna and claim his bride, who was almost fifteen—old enough, according to the traditions of the House of Hapsburg, to get married. But just as he was about to start from Berlin, he received a message from Charles VI, instructing him to visit Mayence and settle a difficulty which had arisen between the Emperor and the Elector. Francis was delighted to receive this important commission, for he thought it meant that he was being groomed for the high office of Emperor. Yes, apparently Charles VI intended his daughter to inherit his dominions under the Pragmatic Sanction, and her husband to be elected King of the Romans, so that there would be no question over retaining the title of Emperor in the family when Charles died. Francis gladly delayed his return to Vienna to perform a duty connected with the Empire.

When he had finished his task at Mayence he joyously set out for Vienna, but on the way received notice that he had been appointed representative of the Emperor to Hungary. He did not understand this and was not especially pleased over it. He neither knew nor cared much about Hungary, and feared the new office would require him to live in Pressburg when he wished to be in Vienna with his prospective bride. He would have declined the appointment but for the fear of offending the Emperor.[15]

Upon arriving at Vienna he was warmly received by Maria Theresa, and was surprised to see how she had developed during the two and a half years he had been away. She was no longer a little girl but a young woman, tall, well-formed, and appealingly conscious of her sex. The Emperor and Empress also gave him a pleasant reception, but remained strangely silent upon what was uppermost in Francis' mind—the betrothal of their daughter. On the very day of his arrival, he was informed that the Emperor had arranged a grand reception for him at Pressburg in two weeks. The Emperor talked much of this reception and of the necessity of getting ready for it. To Francis it seemed that Charles was hurrying him away, as if eager to have him removed from the presence of Maria Theresa; hurrying him very politely, of course, but rather significantly.

The truth was that Charles was worried. He was about to engage in a war with France. He had promised to bestow the crown of Poland upon the King of Saxony in return for another ratification of the Pragmatic Sanction, a very important one in the mind of Charles, because the King was married to Maria Josepha, the elder daughter of Joseph I. Louis XV also claimed the crown for his father-in-law, Stanislaus Leczinska, so Charles was entering another war of succession.[16] Presently there would be a peace conference at which diplomacy would be played for high stakes, and in such a game, the Emperor's eldest daughter

[15] Arneth, I, 20.
[16] *Ibid.*, 22; Guglia, I, 24.

might become an ace of trumps. He did not think it wise to play such a valuable card without winning something more than a petty principality, already numbered among his inherited dependencies.

In this War of the Polish Succession, the fortunes of Charles went from bad to worse, and he was eventually compelled to sue for peace. Louis XV took advantage of the Emperor's helplessness to impose the most humiliating terms. France yielded the crown of Poland—for which Louis XV cared very little because it was not hereditary—but demanded the rich province of Lorraine as a possession for Stanislaus Leczinska, with the provision that at his death it should become one of the hereditary dominions of the French crown. As a compensation for this traditional German province, Louis XV was willing to give the Lorraines a quitclaim deed to the province of Tuscany, to be taken over at the death of the reigning Grand Duke who was the last of the Medicis. Louis naturally did not call the Emperor's attention to the fact that the Spanish Bourbons also claimed Tuscany, and would contend for it whenever they were able.[17]

Such terms were very hard for Charles to accept, but as they were backed by a preponderance of the French at arms, and a desertion of his allies, he was compelled to entertain them. They meant not only disinheriting Francis of Lorraine, whom he had permitted to promenade all over Europe as his prospective son-in-law, but also the loss of a rich dominion and a degradation of the House of Lorraine, to which the House of Hapsburg had been deeply indebted ever since the

---

[17] Arneth, I, 23; Coxe, III, 156, quoting from a letter of Robinson.

siege of Vienna by the Turks, in 1683. When the conditions were announced to Count Sinzendorf he exclaimed: "What a severe sentence is passed on the Emperor; no malefactor was ever carried to the gibbet with a harder doom!"

An embarrassing feature of the sacrifice was that Louis XV demanded that the exchange of territories be confirmed in writing by the Duke of Lorraine, and the very unpleasant task of securing the Prince's signature rested with the Emperor. Charles was probably glad that he had held back his consent to Maria Theresa's betrothal, for now he had something tangible to offer in return for the Duke's cession of his birthright, a fine domain which had belonged to the Lorraines for seven centuries.

We can easily sympathize with Charles VI on account of the extremely disagreeable position in which he was placed, but can hardly excuse him for the manner in which he extricated himself. Instead of summoning the Duke and explaining the whole situation to him before asking him to sign away his heritage, Charles turned the task over to the hardest man in his ministry, John Christopher Bartenstein, who brusquely demanded the Duke's signature in return for the hand of Maria Theresa in marriage. When Francis hesitated, Bartenstein delivered a cold ultimatum by saying, "If you refuse to yield your possession, you shall not marry Maria Theresa; no signature, no Archduchess." [18]

In this cruel, brutal manner the finest courtship in the history of the House of Hapsburg was terminated. A real love affair, tender and sweet as a garden flower,

[18] Arneth, I, 24; Robinson to Lord Harrington, Dec. 31, 1738, quoted by Coxe, III, 164.

was bruised and crushed until all its romance oozed out, evaporated and vanished, leaving a devotion stripped of all its beauty and poetry. Charles VI, instead of graciously bestowing his daughter upon a pleading lover, tossed her across the counter to Francis of Lorraine, begging and urging him to accept her as the price of something sorely needed to save the dynasty. Maria Theresa was thrown into the arms of a man in exchange for his kingdom, much in the same spirit as the ancient Greeks fed their maidens to the Minotaur. The only redeeming feature of the transaction was that the purchaser happened to be the man she loved.

Maria Theresa's love survived this harsh treatment and continued very much as before. It was at this time that the British Ambassador wrote: "She is a princess of the highest spirit, and regards her father's losses as her own. She sighs and pines for her Duke of Lorraine all day and all night. If she sleeps it is but to dream of him, if she wakes it is but to talk of him to her lady in waiting." [19]

But we have reasons to believe that the love of Francis for Maria Theresa received a shock from which it never completely recovered. His nature was not so deep and constant as hers, and his love was put to a harder test. He declined to sign the cession of his territory before the terms were modified to allow him to retain Lorraine until the death of the Grand Duke of Tuscany enabled him to take possession of that province. When the modified treaty was received in Paris, Cardinal Fleury, the French Minister, refused

---

[19] Robinson to Lord Harrington, July 5, 1735, quoted by Coxe, III, 154.

to accept it, and France prepared to continue the war. The original treaty was returned to Charles VI and he again gave Bartenstein the task of securing the Duke's signature. Three times Bartenstein silently but sternly placed the pen in Francis' hand, and three times Francis threw it to the floor, but the fourth time he wrote his name.[20]

IV

When we wish to write of the sentiments and emotions of the Hapsburgs—with the exception of Maria Theresa—we are often driven to use inferences or the letters of contemporaries, such as those of Lady Montagu and Sir Thomas Robinson. Rarely did the Hapsburgs frankly and honestly put their sentiments into writing, and the *Wiener Diarum* and documents of the Archives of Austria are almost as devoid of emotion as official deeds and charters of corporations. But when we wish descriptions of ceremonies, we are completely flooded with details. We could reproduce every step of the betrothal and wedding ceremonies of Francis of Lorraine and Maria Theresa, even the exact words spoken, the hour of the day, the place, decorations, and costumes. One chronicler wrote as follows: "On the thirty-first of January, 1736, Duke Francis Stephan of Lorraine, accompanied by Niklas Freiherr von Jaquemin (born 1671, died 1748), his private secretary and Minister to the Court of Vienna, drove in a six-spanner to the Hofburg. He was followed by the Emperor's chamberlain, Johann Casper Graf Cobenzl (born 1664, died 1742), and the Emper-

[20] *Ibid.*

or's equerry, Heinrich Johann Joseph Graf Auersperg (born 1696, died 1783), each in a separate six-spanner. It was eleven o'clock in the forenoon." [21]

Next we have a description of the Duke's clothes in minutest detail, followed by the manner in which he bowed himself into the private chambers of His Holy Imperial Majesty, the number of steps he made forward and backward in front of His Majesty before speaking, what was said, and how he bowed himself out. Much in the same manner he called upon Empress Elizabeth Christina and the Dowager Empress Amalia Wilhelmina.

After the betrothal, in compliance with the etiquette of the court, Francis left Vienna, not to return until the day of the wedding, February 12, 1736. This brief interval he spent in Pressburg, and it was during this time that Maria Theresa wrote him the love-letters, still preserved, and so often quoted. One of them may be translated as follows:

"Dear Sweetheart,—I am under endless obligations to you for having sent me news concerning yourself, because I was uneasy, like a little dog, about you. Love me and forgive me that I do not write more, for it is ten o'clock and the messenger is waiting. Adieu, my little mouse, I embrace you with all my heart. Take good care of yourself. Adieu, Sweetheart! I am your happy bride." [22]

This letter, scribbled on the back of a more formal one probably supervised by her governess, conveys the idea that Maria Theresa thought of herself as a little

---

[21] Bermann, 275.
[22] Archives of Austria. This letter was exhibited at the *Maria Theresia Austellung* in Schönbrunn in 1930.

A Blighted Romance

dog trying to catch Francis of Lorraine who was a mouse. This was probably but an exaggeration of the truth. From the day the little seven-year-old Archduchess met the fourteen-year-old Duke, he was her Prince Charming.

Francis answered this exuberant outburst on the part of his sweetheart rather formally. His answer read: "I have this moment received my dearest's gracious letter, and it is no small comfort to me, separated as I am from her. I assure you the days on which I do not hear from my dearest bride seem almost unendurable. I would be very downcast if I did not constantly remember our coming union on Sunday at the St. Augustine Church. Thereafter my happiness will be complete." [23] This is said to be the most affectionate letter Francis ever wrote to Maria Theresa, and, under the circumstances, he could hardly have been excused had he displayed less emotion.

The wedding is described as a perfectly happy one,[24] but we are certain this is a misrepresentation. The event was blighted by the manner in which Francis had been compelled to sacrifice his birthright and that of his family. The gloom flowing out of this sacrifice did not settle upon Francis alone. His mother was still living, and came in with a scathing tirade against her son and the Emperor, pointing to the fact that Francis had been untrue to his ancestors and had robbed his descendants. She called down the wrath of Heaven upon him for the heartless manner in which he had sold his heritage to wed the daughter of a Cæsar. Duke Charles, Francis' brother, was also at hand to wail over

[23] Archives of Austria.
[24] Arneth, I, 26; Bermann, 275-278.

how he had been "sold out" by a "traitor to the family." It was in the midst of such criticisms and charges of guilt that Francis of Lorraine and Maria Theresa were married, and we may be sure that for the groom the joyous occasion was immersed in sadness and misgivings. The bride also felt the disgrace of her husband and continued to feel it for years. Several times we shall find her striving with all her might to recover his dominion in order to vindicate herself for the injury she felt had been inflicted upon him in connection with her marriage.

Tuscany was a beautiful possession, but it was Italian and not German. Also the title was defective, for it was still claimed by Spain, then under the control of the Termagant who was seeking dominions for her two sons. There was no telling when the Duke of Tuscany would die and in the meantime the House of Lorraine had no home and no income.

While Charles VI, through his gruff secretary Bartenstein, had demanded this sacrifice of his prospective son-in-law, he felt very badly over having been compelled to do so. He would gladly have continued the war had he not been so completely deserted by his allies. He did what he could to recompense the family for their loss; appointed Francis Governor of the Netherlands and promised Duke Charles the hand of Maria Anna in marriage. Such favors put an end, for the time being, to the disagreeable complaints of the Dowager Duchess.[25]

Incidentally, we may remark that this cession of Lorraine to France, a little less than two centuries ago,

---

[25] Arneth, I, 33.

lit a firebrand of contention between the French and the Germans which is still glowing. From the Franco-Prussian War of 1870 to the end of the World War, the monument to Strassburg stood in mourning at the Place de la Concorde in Paris, and today a wreath decorated with crape hangs over the emblem of Lorraine in the monument to *Herr-mach-uns-frei* in Munich, while similar reminders of the hate springing out of this cession of German territory to the French are to be seen in other German cities. Perhaps only a few who see these portentous emblems associate them with the marriage of Francis of Lorraine and Maria Theresa in 1736.

III

A DISCOURAGING ACCESSION

WHATEVER joy Vienna may have felt over the marriage of the Archduchess to the Duke of Lorraine was soon submerged in the deep sorrow precipitated by an event occurring on the night of the twenty-first of April, 1736—it was the death of Prince Eugene of Savoy. This Prince meant so much to Austria, and his passing had such great influence upon the future of Maria Theresa, that it is worth while to review briefly the story of his adventurous life.

Prince Eugene, one of the most renowned soldiers of fortune in all history, was of Sardinian parentage, but born in Paris in 1663. His mother, Olympia Mancini, a niece of Cardinal Mazarin, was seduced in her youth by Louis XIV, who almost immediately abandoned her to make a declared mistress of her sister Marie. To rescue Olympia, Cardinal Mazarin married her to Eugene Moritz of Savoy, who became the father of the celebrated Prince. The name suggests that Prince Eugene was a Jew and this is true in part; his father was a Jew.

As a child Eugene was so delicate that the father, who had turned Catholic, educated him for the priesthood, but the lad was interested in nothing but the army. When he was nineteen he joined a French regiment, but owing to his small size and solemn face, the soldiers tauntingly called him "the little Abbot," and almost laughed him out of the service. This greatly angered him and in his rage he exclaimed, "If I cannot fight with you, I will fight against you!" and immediately left France to offer his services to the Germans.[1] Many believe his lifelong hatred for the French was partly due to the fact that he heard how Louis XIV had made a concubine of his mother. Be that as it may, we know that later Prince Eugene scorned all overtures from the French King suggesting a return to the flag of his native land; when he said good-bye to his allegiance to France, it was forever. He arrived at Vienna during the trying time of the siege of 1683, and, since no one then willing to fight the Turks was denied an opportunity, he was promptly placed in command of a small company under the Duke of Lorraine, the grandfather of Francis Stephan.

He was present at the fierce battle in which the Duke and John Sobieski drove the Moslems from the walls of Vienna, and with the Duke, Eugene followed them down the Danube. During this campaign he distinguished himself in several actions and won the admiration of his commander.[2] In a few short years he was generalissimo of the Austrian army and the most successful commander it had ever had. It was he who

---

[1] Arneth, *Prinz Eugen*, 1, 9; Bermann, 279.

After her marriage, Olympia, whose husband was known as the Count of Soissons, returned to the court of Louis XIV and became much enmeshed in scandal. Many gossipers asserted that Louis XIV was the father of Prince Eugene. Olympia was also accused of having poisoned her husband, and later she was likewise accused of having poisoned the Queen of Spain. She died completely impoverished in Brussels in 1708, leaving five sons, only one of whom became famous.

[2] Arneth, *Prinz Eugen*, I, 16-19.

rendered the valley of the Danube—we might almost say all Europe—safe for Christianity by making the Turk forever afraid to attack Vienna. From any quarter where Prince Eugene commanded an Austrian army, there came news of glorious victories. He was the hero of Zenta, Belgrade, Blenheim and numerous other battles won by the Austrians and their allies.

That his services were highly appreciated by his adopted land is proved by his two wonderful homes in Vienna, the one on Himmelpfortgasse and the magnificent palace and grounds of Belvedere, the latter being the finest in all Austria, with the single exception of Schönbrunn. It is also proved by the fact that when he died he was one of the richest men in the monarchy.[3]

Lady Montagu, in one of her letters, speaks of visiting Prince Eugene. She said: "Bonneval told me that the General has many books on the art of war, leather-bound in the skins of janissaries and spahis, and that the sight of them always brings a smile from this Jew, who is a most famous warrior. Prince Eugene showed me with particular pleasure his famous collection of portraits, formerly belonging to Fouquet, and recently purchased at an excessive price. He has augmented it by a number of new acquisitions, so that he now has one of the finest collections of portraits in all Europe. If I told you the exact number, you would say I am making an indiscreet use of the license to lie, granted to travellers by the indulgence of the candid."[4]

In spite of his immense popularity and great influence, Prince Eugene was always loyal to his emperors, although on certain occasions they must have tried his

[3] *Ibid.*, III, 77.
[4] Lady Montagu, Letter of Jan. 2, 1717.

patience to the limit. He was the genius of the Austrian army for nearly fifty years, and on his monument in Heldenplatz we may now read, "The True Servant of Three Emperors."[5]

In speaking of the emperors, he once said, "Leopold I was my father, Joseph I, my brother, but Charles VI is my master." This saying, so often quoted, conveys the idea that Charles VI did not appreciate Prince Eugene for his full worth. The blessing of the great General's genius had been showered upon Austria for so long that it was regarded as one of the gifts of Heaven, which came as a matter of course, and was likely to be continued regardless of the ingratitude of recipients. Charles probably came to regard himself, rather than Prince Eugene, as the source of Austria's strength, and wished the General to understand that he, the Emperor, was master of his own country.

Prince Eugene really ruled Austria, but in such a respectful and unobtrusive manner that Charles VI was unconscious of it. In steering the ship of state Charles stood in full view at the wheel, but behind him crouched Prince Eugene, almost unnoticed, guiding the Emperor's hands, and not until Eugene's sight began to fail and his arms became unsteady from age did the old ship head for the rocks. Frederick the Great once said: "Prince Eugene was the real Emperor of the Germans."

Some claim that the idea of the Pragmatic Sanction originated in the mind of Prince Eugene, but he soon saw that with Charles VI it had become a fetich, and frequently warned him not to depend upon its ratifica-

---

[5] Mahan, *Vienna Yesterday and Today*, 196.

tion by rulers who were sure to forget their pledges as soon as Charles was in his coffin. Once the old General exclaimed: "Bah! two hundred thousand soldiers are worth more than all the sanctions in the world." [6]

Prince Eugene was President of the Council of War, and passed in and out of the Hofburg almost daily. He became very fond of little Maria Theresa who was born the very year he won his great victory over the Turks at Belgrade. Eugene brought his comrade, John Palfy, to visit the infant Archduchess, and later they both longed to see her married to the grandson of their old commander, the Duke of Lorraine. During the last years of his life, Eugene seemed to be kept alive by the hope of seeing this marriage consummated. After the wedding ceremonies he began preparing for death, and it is more than probable that his departure was hastened by grief over the degradation of the Lorraines when they were deprived of their ancient heritage by France.[7] Prince Eugene died the night after he attended a meeting of the Privy Council at which the principal subject discussed was the abdication of Francis of Lorraine.[8]

II

The death of Prince Eugene left a painful vacuum in the Privy Council of Charles VI, one which the Emperor was at a great loss to find a suitable person to fill.

---

[6] Whitman, 227.
[7] Arneth, *Prinz Eugen*, III, 485.
[8] Prince Eugene went to bed apparently in good health on the evening of April 20, 1736. The next morning he did not appear as usual and an investigation revealed that he had died in bed during the night. The exact cause of his death was never determined.

A Discouraging Accession

The man who succeeded in substituting himself in a large degree for the Prince was John Christopher Bartenstein, a very unusual character. Like many men who owe their eminence to sheer ability, Bartenstein had a very high opinion of himself, and very little patience with ministers whom he was able to dominate by his wonderful command of language and display of bad temper. He possessed a strange talent for flattering the Emperor and finding fault with the other ministers. He pried into all the departments of the government and ran to his master with tales of scandal, thus enabling Charles to confront his ministers with criticisms based on pretended shrewdness. Bartenstein became very influential with the Emperor and was greatly feared by other officials, not a few of whom were dismissed because of the secret disclosures of this tattler. He also taught the Emperor to lay the blame for mistakes upon others and this was most agreeable, since Charles made so many for which he did not care to assume the responsibility.[9]

No one was spared by Bartenstein; he even criticized Prince Eugene and blamed him for the stubbornness of Francis of Lorraine in hesitating to sign away the rights of his house. Despite the fact that Bartenstein was not of "the elect" because of his lowly birth, he was the most feared man in all Vienna, not even excepting the Emperor.

Under the command of Prince Eugene Austria had been so often victorious over the Turks, that Charles thought it would be very easy to win territory in the east to compensate for his heavy loss—to France and

---

[9] Coxe, III, 161; Arneth, I, 71–75; Guglia, I, 52–58.

Spain—in the west and south Russia was at war with Turkey and Czarina Anne appealed to Charles for assistance, with the unexpected result that Austria immediately declared war on the Turks. So eagerly did Charles rush into this conflict that he almost took the leadership away from the Czarina. He turned his back to France, in the full confidence of recouping his fortunes in the Orient, because there he believed he would be relieved of the baneful opposition of Cardinal Fleury, whom he had learned to dread. Little did he realize that the specter of this aged minister of Louis XV haunted every capital in Europe, and was nowhere more potent than in Constantinople. In making war upon the Turks Charles was confronted with the Cardinal's brains directing Mohammedan soldiers.

Nearly all the Emperor's advisers opposed entry into this war, since they realized that Austria's army was in a very reduced state and the monarchy's finances almost exhausted, but Charles rashly overruled his ministers because he thought the Turks such easy antagonists. He excused himself, as usual, on religious grounds, stating it to be his Christian duty to exterminate the enemies of the Church of Christ, as he had been exhorted to do by his father confessor. The insincerity of this excuse was manifest when he placed Seckendorf, a Lutheran, in supreme command.[10]

Space does not permit us to introduce all the details of this disastrous war, but the events most important to the welfare of Maria Theresa and her husband will be noted. Seckendorf, largely due to religious cabals in the ministry at Vienna, conducted a most unfortunate

[10] Coxe, III, 166–167.

A Discouraging Accession

campaign, terminating in his arrest and in imprisonment in a castle at Gratz until the death of the Emperor. Over his conduct all Austria became divided into two hostile camps, one Catholic and the other Lutheran, each bitterly charging the other with responsibility for the failure of the campaign. The Catholics vowed the favor of Heaven had been withdrawn because of the employment of heretical commanders; even the Empress was once more charged with plotting against the Catholics. The Emperor yielded to this distracting clamor in a strange manner; he appointed Francis of Lorraine, a Catholic Freemason, commander-in-chief of the Austrian army, in spite of the fact that Francis had had no practice whatever in the command of armies at war. Apparently fearing that he might be making a mistake, he then gave Königseg, a more experienced warrior, the power to countermand the orders of the young Prince, so that Francis shouldered the responsibility but was at the same time seriously limited in authority. A better recipe for bringing on a complete failure of the campaign and degrading the Prince could hardly have been contrived.[11]

In the first encounter, by a streak of good luck, Francis won a small victory and was soon proclaimed in Vienna as another Prince Eugene. But very shortly afterward he was badly defeated, and under the pretense of being sick, left the army and returned to Vienna. Against his wishes, but very likely with the co-operation of Maria Theresa, Charles sent him back to the front where he soon led the army to a terrible disaster. Poor Francis was then recalled in disgrace, and

[11] Letter of Robinson to Lord Harrington, Dec. 8, 1742, cited by Coxe, III, 177.

immediately a great hue and cry was set up against him in the capital. He was accused of cowardice in leaving his army, of spending his time at the front in hunting and dissipation, of being a foreigner, and finally of being a Freemason. The poor distracted Emperor was urged to marry Maria Anna, already promised to Prince Charles, the brother of Francis, to the Elector of Bavaria, and change the order of succession to the Bavarian house. Public indignation against Francis reached such a high pitch that he finally thought it wise to retire to Tuscany, where the last of the Medicis had recently died, under the excuse of taking possession of this province; so only two years after her marriage Maria Theresa found herself preparing to follow a disgraced husband into exile.[12]

Francis and Maria Theresa left for Tuscany on the seventeenth of December, 1738. They traveled, with a two-months-old baby, in great discomfort through the deep snows of the Tirols, frequently harassed by rumors of an epidemic of the plague. On the twentieth of January, 1739, they reached Florence, but were not enthusiastically received, for the news of Francis' disgrace had preceded them. By discreet conduct they managed to escape open hostilities.[13]

Their life in Florence was far from pleasant, so it was with much joy that they set out on the twenty-seventh of the following April to return to Vienna.[14] On the return trip they met Francis' mother at Innsbruck, and once face to face with her mother-in-law, Maria Theresa soon won a complete reconciliation.

[12] Coxe, III, 180; Arneth, I, 45; Guglia, I, 36.
[13] Arneth, I, 46.
[14] Guglia, I, 37.

Francis Stephen, Emperor of Germany, Duke of Lorrain & Grand Duke of Tuscany.

A Discouraging Accession 51

There had never been any just reason for the Dowager's ill will toward her daughter-in-law, for Maria Theresa had not been a factor in the loss of Lorraine; she was merely injected into the controversy by her father.

Charles VI had been greatly disturbed by the absence of his daughter. He feared, that in the event of his own death, France might aid some of the pretenders in preventing the return of the heir to the throne. He even had visions of Maria Theresa spending years in some secret French or Bavarian prison while her throne was occupied by a foreigner. Finally the Emperor could endure the suspense no longer and arranged for the return of the disgraced son-in-law, which was accomplished very quietly, and almost secretly.[15]

The war with Turkey still continued, with its endless train of disasters for the Austrians, and the quarrels at home became more and more distracting to the Emperor.[16] Eventually Charles was compelled to sue for peace, only to have the Turks spit in the face of his plenipotentiary and threaten to execute him. Charges and countercharges in the army and ministry continued worse than before. Belgrade was lost, the army completely disorganized, and many of its best commanders thrown into prison. In the end Charles was only too glad to make peace at the cost of Belgrade and a large part of Servia. Not for centuries had the fortunes of the monarchy sunk to such a low level, and perhaps never before had Vienna been the scene of such bitter disputes among those in authority. The whole atmos-

[15] Robinson to Walpole, Aug. 22, 1739.
[16] Coxe, III, 194.

phere was charged with disaster and despair, as if the monarchy were in the last agonies of dissolution. For this state of affairs, the ministers blamed one another and Charles blamed them all.[17]

In a letter to the Czarina, the Emperor wrote: "While I am writing this letter to Your Imperial Majesty, my heart is filled with anguish. The history of past ages reveals no vestige of such ruinous events. I was on the point of preventing the fatal and too hasty execution of these preliminaries, when I heard that they were already concluded, even before the designs had been communicated to me; thus I see my hands tied by those who should glory in obeying me. All who have approached me since that fatal day, are but so many witnesses of my grief; and, although I have many times experienced adversity, I was never so afflicted with anything as with these events. In this dismal series of misfortunes, I have but one comfort left, which is that the blame cannot be thrown on me." This was one of the times when a Hapsburg put his emotions on paper, but we may very well doubt if he was telling what he believed to be the truth.

Charles seems then to have forgotten that he had engaged in war against the advice of his ministers, and for the stated reason that he hoped to secure some compensation, at the expense of the Turks, for what he had lost to France and Spain in the west and south.

At this time the Austrian Monarchy was in financial ruin, its army had become impotent and its ministry gone up in the smoke of a spontaneous combustion; famine, from a failure of crops, was gazing like

---

[17] *Oesterreichischer Erbefolge-Krieg,* I, 897 seq.

a gaunt specter at the capital, and the heir to the throne was married to a disgraced husband. The Emperor was sick with despair. Had the Turks but realized the truth, they might have advanced once more to the walls of the city they hated, but when they looked up the Danube they imagined they saw the shadow of Prince Eugene, and drew back in terror.

On the nineteenth of August, 1739, Sir Thomas Robinson wrote to Walpole: "Everything in this court is running into the last stages of confusion and ruin; there are signs of the worst folly and madness that ever afflicted a people whom Heaven has determined to destroy, no less by domestic divisions than by the more public calamities of repeated defeats, defenselessness, poverty, famine and plague." [18]

At another time Robinson wrote: "The Turks seem to the Viennese to be already in Hungary and the Hungarians themselves in arms against Austria. They imagine the Saxons are in Bohemia, and the Bavarians at the very gates of the city, while France, the very soul of their opposition is everywhere." [19]

In the midst of all this tumult, confusion, and misfortune, the Emperor's health began to fail. The cause of his illness was very well stated by a Mr. Porter, who happened to visit Vienna at that time, and afterward became British Ambassador to Constantinople. He wrote: "The haughty behaviour of France, joined to the natural hatred the Emperor bore for that nation, the internal combats with which he was beset, and the servile compliance to which he was reduced, preyed

---
[18] Robinson to Walpole, Aug. 19, 1739; *Oesterreichischer Erbefolge-Krieg*, I, 896.
[19] Robinson to Lord Harrington, Oct. 22, 1740; Guglia, I, 47.

upon his mind, and was the proximate cause of that ill habit of body which at last put a period to his life. And, if his most confidential physician may be depended upon, it was not so much the loss of Belgrade as the manner in which it was surrendered, and the usage of the French, that bore so heavily upon the Emperor, and threw him into a profound melancholy." [20]

On the tenth of October, 1740, Charles VI was seized with indigestion after eating heartily of mushrooms, and on the morning of the twentieth, very much to the surprise of his physicians, he died. The doctors had disagreed over the diagnosis and treatment of his disease, and Charles, who had heard too many disputes in his last years, exclaimed: "Cease your wrangling; you may open my body after my death and settle your quarrels!" [21] In the language of Voltaire, "A pot of mushrooms changed the history of Europe."

The reign of Charles VI was one long tragedy ending in a stupendous climax. If we attempt to seek the cause of his trouble, we can hardly avoid the conclusion that he was the victim of too much faith in humanity. He seemed to be convinced that the rulers of Europe and the pretenders for the crowns of the Hapsburgs would consider themselves firmly bound by their agreements. Had Frederick the Great wished to promulgate a Pragmatic Sanction he would have issued an edict, but instead of asking all Europe to agree to it, he would have built up a powerful army to enforce it. Charles labored all his life, and squandered his resources, to secure ratifications which were absolutely

---

[20] Mr. Porter to Walpole, March 29, 1741, quoted by Coxe, III, 220; *Oesterreichischer Erbefolge-Krieg*, I, 896 seq.

[21] Coxe, III, 221.

worthless, but at the same time, allowed his army to become completely disorganized.

We shall see that this simple faith in the honor of nations was passed on to his daughter, but that she was speedily disillusioned.

III

On the twentieth of October, 1740, a sadly romantic scene was enacted in the throne room of the Hofburg. Maria Theresa, in the presence of her husband and surrounded by the ministers of the dead Charles VI, approached the platform supporting the throne, placed one foot on the first step, then halted, and for a moment glanced back and wept. She was in her twenty-fourth year and looked every inch a queen as she stood, with her classic face and tall athletic figure, like some statue dug from the ruins of ancient Rome or Athens. One of the ministers said to another in a whisper, "Oh, if she were only a man endowed with all that she possesses!" Her keen ear caught the remark and she replied, "Though I am only a queen, yet have I the heart of a king!" [22]

We have many glowing descriptions of Maria Theresa's appearance at that time, and after reading them, we may easily conclude that she was not so delicately beautiful—not so doll-like—as her mother had been at the same age. Her form was more stately and majestic, and her face showed much more strength of character. Sir Thomas Robinson wrote of her: "Her person was formed to wear a crown, and her mind to give luster to the exalted dignity of her position; she

---

[22] Arneth, I, 296.

possessed a most commanding figure, great beauty, animation and sweetness of countenance, a pleasant voice, feminine grace with a remarkable strength of understanding, and an intrepidity above her sex." [23] Another eyewitness said: "Had one been given all the women of the world from whom to choose a queen, yet would the choice have fallen upon Maria Theresa." [24]

This meeting, within a few hours of the trying ordeals of listening to her father's final admonitions, and witnessing his death, must have required great courage and self-control on the part of a young woman; yet those who were present said she was calmer than the aged ministers, and only for a moment yielded to her emotions. She presented a striking omen of her coming greatness.[25]

In spite of all Maria Theresa's ambition, noble intentions, and firm belief in her call from on High for the work she was undertaking, that must have been a very sad hour, for she knew only too well that she was bidding farewell to a life that appealed most of all to her. Just for a moment she clung fondly to the thought of being a German wife and mother, whose whole existence is measured in rounds of births, baptisms, confirmations and weddings; first with her own, and later with her children's children. Now she was to be a queen, which almost necessarily implied the neglect or abandonment of her duties as a mother. Such sweet joys must be curtailed when she ascended the throne of the Hapsburgs, for before her were the imposing trials and responsibilities of the ruler of a great mon-

---

[23] Robinson, quoted by Coxe, III, 225.
[24] Wraxall, II, 299, quoting from an eyewitness.
[25] Arneth, I, 86.

A Discouraging Accession

archy, burdens that had proved too heavy for her father who now, at fifty-five, lay stretched on his bier, dead of a broken heart. She realized, at least in part, the difficulties confronting her and the weakness of her senile ministers. If she could call to her service another Prince Eugene how much easier it would be, especially in the beginning.

She thought of Chancellor Sinzendorf, very old, indolent and easy-going, and always embarrassed with his private debts; she could hope for little real assistance from him. Then there were the two Harrachs, likewise old and inert. Seckendorf, one of her ablest statesmen and generals, was imprisoned in distant Gratz; Neipperg, whom both she and Francis liked, partly because he had been Francis' teacher, was also in prison. She visualized no one to whom she could turn for counsel in an hour of need.[26]

At the time of her marriage she had looked forward to receiving much assistance from her husband, whom she regarded as almost infallible, but since his disgrace and their exile, the very thought of which made her shudder, doubts of his ability had risen unbidden in her mind. Over all her counsellors loomed the vindictive Bartenstein, the only man in the ministry under seventy years of age. She disliked him for the cruel manner in which he had dealt with her husband in her betrothal, but feared she could not dispense with him at first.[27]

She must have been embarrassed and oppressed by her physical condition, which prevented her from appearing at her best either physically or mentally, for during the four years and a half of her married life

---

[26] *Oesterreichischer Erbefolge-Krieg*, I, 898.
[27] *Ibid.*, I, 898 seq.

she had given birth to three children, and the fourth was due to arrive in a few months. Already she had seen one of her children placed in its little coffin, while another was in feeble health on account of exposure during the wintry flight to Italy. Most women, under similar circumstances, would have considered themselves completely incapacitated for any undertaking outside the home.

She knew there was trouble brewing in Vienna, where the people were clamoring for food and killing the wild animals in the game preserves on account of a famine resulting from failure of the harvest. She also knew the Viennese had no confidence in her ability, and were spreading rumors that the Elector of Bavaria would soon arrive to take over the government and deliver them from their woes.[28]

Maria Theresa was not totally unprepared for the duties of a great ruler. For several years she had been a deeply interested observer of the conduct of her father, concerning which she had often expressed her approval or disapproval most vigorously. She had frequently discussed politics with her husband, and from him had learned of the many intrigues of the various ministers. The last few years of her father's reign had been a period during which politics had been uppermost in the minds of all, and we may be sure she knew all about the leading questions of the day. Unlike her father, who never seemed to believe that his daughter would really succeed himself because he always had strong hopes for a son, Maria Theresa had felt sure, for several years, that she would some day be at the

---

[28] Arneth, I, 61; Coxe, III, 226.

head of the monarchy, and had endeavored to acquire at least a smattering of what she would need to understand in the discharge of her duties. She had mastered Latin, the official language of Hungary, and read European history with great interest. She spoke French almost as fluently as German, and often used it in conversation with Francis, to whom it was a mother tongue.

In spite of the weakness of her ministers, Maria Theresa had no intention of "trading horses in the middle of the stream." She thanked them all for their devotion to her father—a tribute which must have made some of them blush for shame—and begged them to continue at their respective posts. That seemed to be the only way to get the new government going and gain time to take her bearings. Bartenstein, who fully expected to be dismissed, was much surprised when she asked him to continue as before.

The next day there was another meeting of the ministers and the first duty performed was to get off messages to the dominions and foreign lands, asking them to recognize her government and confirm their pledges to support the Pragmatic Sanction.[29] She scarcely hoped for a favorable answer from the Elector of Bavaria, who was known to be determined to renounce his ratification of the Sanction and set up a claim to the throne, but she had little fear of him unless he secured the assistance of France, and she still held faith that France would keep the promises purchased at such heavy sacrifices on the part of the dead Emperor. Maria Theresa, at first, failed to comprehend that

---

[29] Arneth, I, 87.

there was one standard of morals for individuals, and an entirely different one for nations. This error she inherited from her father and it was destined to cause her no end of trouble.

The new Queen performed another official act that day, and in doing so did not please her ministers; she appointed John Palfy as her representative in Hungary.[30] She trusted, almost loved Palfy, because Prince Eugene had told her the old Hungarian patriot was her true friend, so she asked no one about the appointment but made it in obedience to her intuition.

Having performed these simple duties of state, Maria Theresa adjourned the meeting to join her family and ministers in mourning for the departed Emperor. As the Archduchess of Austria, and Queen of Bohemia and Hungary, she had set up her first government. She may have realized that it was a weak one, but probably felt that it was better than nothing and would tide her over until she could recover from her grief and set her affairs in order.[31]

[30] *Ibid.*, 90.
[31] *Oesterreichischer Erbefolge-Krieg*, I, 905; III, 1.

IV

THE EMPIRE AND THE MONARCHY

I

BEFORE beginning the story of the reign of Maria Theresa it seems appropriate to offer brief explanations of two political organizations which have since passed into history. We refer to the Holy Roman Empire of the Germans and the Austrian Monarchy, both of which are tedious, uninviting subjects covering a much longer time than the reign of the Queen. They must be mentioned very often as we proceed, and unless we have a fairly clear idea of their nature and significance, we shall not be able to understand the position of Maria Theresa, especially at the time of her accession, when her tasks were so very complicated and arduous.

The Holy Roman Empire of the Germans was a sovereign power—at least we shall call it such for the moment—made up of more than three hundred commonwealths scattered over the present territories of Germany, Czechoslovakia, Austria, Hungary, and a part of Switzerland and Italy. It had an emperor elected for life by seven electors, who were the rulers of seven of the leading principalities,[1] and a diet of three houses: a House of Electors, a House of Princes, and a House of Imperial Cities, the bodies

[1] Bryce, 225 seq.

ranking in importance according to the order named. Some of the units were ruled by the Catholic Church, while in others the prevailing religion was Protestantism, usually Lutheran. Each little unit made its own laws by means of some sort of a local council or by the edicts of princes.[2]

The nature of this political organization suggests that it was probably a great empire on the road to disintegration. This was true; hence it can be understood only by examining its history, for it was what it was solely because of what it had been. When we seek the beginning of this empire we soon discover that we must go back very far—in fact we must keep going until we arrive at the founding of the Roman Empire under Cæsar Augustus, twenty-seven years before the birth of Christ. Then, by roughly tracing its evolution down to the time of Maria Theresa, we get a fair idea of its immense significance to her.

The Roman Empire was very large, powerful and durable, but its northern boundary in Europe was never firmly established beyond the Rhine and the Danube, which mark almost a direct line from the Black Sea to the North Sea. North and east of that boundary dwelt the barbarian tribes of the Germans, who were never conquered by Roman arms but yielded to Roman institutions and Roman culture.

No doubt Rome could have conquered these tribes and extended the Empire to the Baltic, but in ancient times this northern country was regarded as a frozen wilderness incapable of supporting a commercial civilization. How strange it seems that the very land

[2] Higby, 29-30.

The Empire and the Monarchy 63

Rome considered unworthy of her arms, eventually seized the Roman government and preserved its laws, architecture, art, and religion for centuries after the old Empire had passed from existence. In history, what is least to be expected is usually what happens.

According to the belief of many German historians, the so-called fall of Rome has been greatly exaggerated. They say Rome never fell because the Germans did not wish it to fall. For centuries the barbarians of the north mingled with the Romans, absorbed Roman laws, architecture, art, and science, and above all, were converted to Roman Christianity. Many Germans served in the Roman army and the two races amalgamated by frequent intermarriages. Germans were often seen on the streets of Rome, gazing in awe at the imposing public buildings constructed of chiseled blocks of stone, held together by a strange paste which itself turned to stone under the magic of Roman science. Germans travelled over paved roads which swung across rivers on spans of masonry apparently resting on nothing but air. With what wonder these simple sons of the north gazed at the stupendous dome of the Pantheon, the Coliseum, and the great edifices surrounding the Column of Trajan. To them the city seemed supernatural, solid as the mountains and eternal as the world.[3]

But it was not with awe and wonder alone that the Germans contemplated Rome; they revered it, for Rome had given them a religion bringing the gift of life beyond the grave. They did not hope or wish to destroy such a city; they feared its destruction.[4] Pres-

[3] Bryce, 16–17.
[4] *Ibid.*, 17 ff.

ently they largely replaced the Romans in the imperial army and began to feel their own power. With this sense of strength there developed, among the more intellectual Germans a desire to possess Rome and at the same time a wish to preserve its ancient institutions. When Odoacer captured the city in 476 A. D., he sent a messenger to the Emperor at Constantinople acknowledging the supremacy of the eastern ruler, and to the extent of his ability, saved the principal buildings of the fallen city from destruction at the hands of his savage soldiers. As long as the Emperor at Constantinople was able and willing to protect Roman institutions and the Christian religion in the west, he was accepted by the Germans as the highest authority of the whole Empire.[5]

But in 797, a woman, one of the worst in history, established herself on the throne of the Cæsars in Constantinople, and in order to secure absolute power, deposed and blinded her son Constant VI. Although she is known as "Wicked Irene," it was probably not her sins but her sex that, in the minds of the Germans, disqualified her to occupy the throne of the Cæsars. To the Germans the idea of a female ruler was repulsive, without precedent, and contrary to the teachings of St. Paul, the Roman Apostle—in fact, a female Emperor was an impossibility. They considered the throne of the Cæsars to be vacant.[6]

[5] *Ibid.*, 25.
[6] The question of a woman on the throne of the Cæsars had been raised twice before. Pulcheria, the sister of Theodosius, was hailed as Augusta, but only because she was to marry Marcian immediately. Martina, the widow of Heraclius, tried to pose as a Cæsar, only to be hooted down with cries of "God forbid that Romans should ever be ruled by a woman!"

The Empire and the Monarchy 65

Coincidentally with this usurpation, Charlemagne conquered nearly all the lands belonging to the ancient Western Empire, and conceived the idea of making himself Emperor of Rome. In spite of Irene's unsavory record he proposed marriage to her, hoping thus to unite the two Empires and become ruler of all the lands of ancient Rome. But as usual under such circumstances, the Catholic Church managed to insert itself at the opportune moment.

On Christmas Day, 800, while Charlemagne was praying in St. Peter's at Rome, Pope Leo III placed on the conqueror's head the diadem of the Cæsars and proclaimed him Emperor.[7] The results of this incident were tremendous. The long line of Cæsars, extending continuously from the time of Cæsar Augustus, then broken by the female Irene, was picked up by Charlemagne, who from that day claimed to be Emperor of the Romans, a claim freely acknowledged by the Western Empire but denied by the Eastern.[8] The political capital was then changed to Aix-la-Chapelle, which was not illegal since Constantinople had already furnished a precedent for shifting the seat of civil power.

In this somewhat questionable accession of Charlemagne there was but little weakening of the title of Emperor of the Romans, either theoretically or practically, except in one respect; the pope had greatly emphasized himself by choosing and crowning the emperor. Having done this once, he claimed the right to continue. Had he been able to assert this right the emperor would have become a creature of the pope,

[7] Bryce, 48–49.
[8] *Ibid.*, 51 seq.

but the pope was not able to exercise the prerogative except in a limited degree, and for a limited time. That the pope continued to claim the right to dictate in the selection of emperors was often manifest. As late as 1273, Pope Gregory X ordered the German princes to meet and elect an emperor to end an interregnum, backing his command by a threat to appoint one himself if they failed to obey. We may add that the princes obeyed his orders, apparently very much against their inclinations. That the pope divided authority with the emperor was frequently revealed.

The Empire of Charlemagne went to pieces very quickly. In less than a century it had disappeared, but the title of Emperor of the Romans continued right along, almost without a break. It shifted precariously from one land to another, still preserved by the influence of the popes, until seized by the Saxon kings and eventually by the German Hohenstaufens, who held it permanently until the coming of the Hapsburgs.[9]

In the meantime the popes had almost lost out politically, and were scarcely consulted in the selection of emperors. The German princes thought it no longer essential that the emperors be named and crowned by the popes, but they were always eager to have the approval of Rome. Only two Hapsburgs were crowned by popes, but many of them gratefully received the sanction of the head of the Catholic Church. In some manner the popes managed to tack the word *Holy* to the title, which was eventually rounded off to "Emperor of the Holy Roman Empire of the Germans,"

---

[9] *Ibid.*, list of emperors and popes, pp. XIX–XXIX.

although it was no longer either holy or Roman.[10] From 1438 until the death of Charles VI in 1740, the tenacious Hapsburgs managed to keep this precious title in their dynasty, and it became one of the cornerstones of the Austrian Monarchy. Charles VI was able to cast his eyes backward and boast of being a Cæsar, but, when he looked forward, he saw the ancient line about to be broken by the accession of his daughter Maria Theresa, somewhat as it had been broken by the wicked Irene at Constantinople. No Pragmatic Sanction could assure her an election to the throne of the Cæsars, for that would never be tolerated by the stubborn German princes.

Such a brief *résumé* scarcely brings us to realize how, in "looping the loops" from land to land and dynasty to dynasty through nine centuries, the august title had lost nearly all its original qualities. The Holy Roman Empire of the Germans was but a ghostly shadow of the Roman Empire of the ancient Cæsars. It had degenerated into a loose confederation of the German princes, deriving its real strength from whatever hereditary holdings the emperor possessed, together with such other lands as he could beat and bluff into subjection. Instead of the old dignified Roman Senate, it had a diet of German princes meeting irregularly in different cities at the call of the emperor. Aside from this, it was supplied with but feeble imitations of the machinery necessary to maintain a strong central government. It had no fixed capital, no standing imperial army, no well-established courts, and no efficient means of taxation. Whatever military strength it pos-

[10] Bryce, 196.

sessed was recruited, for the most part, from the Emperor's hereditary dominions and by appeals to the princes. Hence only a strong power, such as Austria, was able to maintain the prestige of the ancient title.[11]

It is true that one or two German princes declined the imperial crown, Frederick of Saxony for example, in 1519, but generally speaking, we may declare that from the beginning to the end of the Holy Roman Empire, in spite of all the weaknesses and imperfections noted, there were few monarchs of Europe who would not have crawled on their hands and knees to receive the crown of the great Empire founded by Charlemagne. Rudolph I was broken-hearted because he was unable to secure the election of his heir to succeed himself. The greatest kings of England and France longed to be emperors. Henry VIII and Francis I both strenuously sought the honor in 1518 and 1519.[12] In later years the brow of Napoleon Bona-

---

[11] *Ibid.*, 394-402.

[12] How the imperial crown was coveted by the great rulers of Europe is well illustrated by this notorious campaign beginning early in the year of 1518 and terminating with the election of Charles V in June, 1519. Emperor Maximilian I, believing himself so near death that he was afraid to leave Vienna without carrying his coffin with him, undertook to have his grandson, Charles of Spain, elected as his successor. Regardless of the fact that neither France nor England belonged to the Holy Roman Empire, both Francis I and Henry VIII became active candidates. Of the seven electors, all but Frederick of Saxony were for sale to the highest bidder, but so corrupt as not to remain true after receiving their prices. Henry VIII, either too stingy or too wise to follow the game to its conclusion, soon withdrew from the race, leaving the contest to be fought out between Francis and Charles. Francis thought himself richer than Charles, and vowed he would sate the electors with bribes until they could not refuse to vote for him. Accordingly he drained the treasury of France into the pockets of the

The Empire and the Monarchy 69

parte itched most annoyingly for the imperial crown, but he was afraid to assume it because of its association with Catholicism. Undoubtedly he meant to restore the Empire when he gave his son the title of King of Rome.

The Emperor of the Holy Roman Empire of the Germans had social and political prestige surpassing that of any other monarch of his day. It was he who could raise the title of princes from Elector to King, as Leopold I did for the Elector of Brandenberg. In processions his place was always the one of highest honor, his consent was required in forming family pacts among the princes by marriage, and he alone was addressed as "His Holy Imperial Majesty." His influence extended into ecclesiastical realms and was exerted in the selection of bishops and abbots; often he almost dictated at the elections of popes. He held the most ancient and honorable title in the world, possibly

electors, who, as subsequent events proved, had no intention of permitting him to be elected. On the first ballot Francis and Charles each received three votes, Frederick of Saxony refusing either to vote or end the tie after the ballot. Next Frederick of Saxony received six votes, and, many believe according to a prearranged plan, declined in favor of Charles, declaring him to be "a real German prince and scion of the noble House of Hapsburg to whom the throne rightfully belongs." Charles was then unanimously elected. The defeat rankled in the breast of Francis I until it drove him to war with Charles V. During the war, Francis I was captured in battle, carried away as a prisoner to Madrid, and the French nation brought to the very verge of extinction. After his ransom Francis continued a lifelong enemy of Charles V, and the two rulers embroiled all Europe in strife for a quarter of a century. Francis even went so far as to form an alliance with Suleiman the Turk, and encouraged him to invade the Danube and attack Vienna which he almost captured in 1529, thus seriously endangering the very existence of Christian civilization.

excepting some of the titles of the Orient, and his office placed him at the head of the German principalities by right, and all the kingdoms of Europe by common consent.[13]

When we remember all this, it is not difficult to understand with what dismay Austria, whose monarchs had held this proud distinction for centuries, looked upon the accession of Maria Theresa who was clearly ineligible to this high honor, and whose husband was in so much disgrace as to render his election to the imperial crown improbable. No wonder the Viennese preferred the Elector of Bavaria who was already favorably mentioned as a candidate for emperor. Fortunately for herself, Maria Theresa scarcely realized the significance of her fundamental disqualification to sit on the throne of the Cæsars, but she was destined to learn it by bitter experience. The loss of the imperial crown would have been a very severe blow to the Hapsburg dynasty had it fallen upon an archduke; it was surely very disheartening to an archduchess.[14]

II

The Austrian Monarchy was made up of the so-called hereditary dominions of the Hapsburgs, insecurely spliced into a nation by a strong ruling house and the Catholic Church. These hereditary dominions must be carefully distinguished from others of the Empire, for the former were ruled more or less di-

---

[13] *Ibid.*, 256–261.
[14] *Oesterreichischer Erbefolge-Krieg*, I, 902 seq. Up to the time of Maria Theresa, England had had queens, and France many queen-regents, but Austria had never been ruled by a woman.

rectly by the monarch and would have been his to govern even if the imperial crown had passed to another dynasty. The power of the Hapsburgs was much greater and more directly applied in Austria, one of the hereditary dominions, than in Bavaria, a separate unit of the Empire with its own prince. When the Holy Roman Empire of the Germans was dissolved in 1806 by Francis II, he still retained his own dominions, out of which he formed a new Austrian Empire.

The Archduchy of Austria with its subsidiary provinces was the nest egg of the Hapsburgs; they always claimed it and the claim was seldom denied. It included all the present Republic of Austria, together with large additions around the head of the Adriatic and in the Tirols, both now belonging to Italy. The next best possession of the monarchy was Bohemia which, with its outlying provinces, almost coincided with the present state of Czechoslovakia and a slice of German territory known as Silesia; the latter included the important cities of Breslau and Glatz. Bohemia had its own diet which met at Prague, and each of its separate units also had some form of legislative body. It also had its own crown; it was a proud kingdom within the Hapsburg Monarchy. The third possession —the largest and richest of all—was Hungary, spread across the whole valley of the Danube from a short distance above Pressburg to Belgrade. Hungary was also a proud monarchy which boasted of a crown, a constitution, and a separate nationality seven or eight centuries old.[15]

[15] For this reason we write the words *crown* and *throne* in the plural when using them in connection with the Hapsburg rulers, who were entitled to the crowns of Hungary and Bohemia, and also had come to

In addition to these territories the monarchy possessed, at the accession of Maria Theresa, the Austrian Netherlands, roughly coincident with the present state of Belgium, Lombardy with the important metropolis of Milan, and Tuscany with the ancient city of Florence—held by Francis of Lorraine. It also claimed the rich little duchies of Parma and Piacenza.

During the unfortunate reign of Charles VI, Austria had lost Lorraine, whatever claims she had to Spain, all of the Italian Peninsula southeast of Rome, together with the Island of Sicily, and an immense stretch of the lower valley of the Danube below Belgrade. All this territory, and certain important trade rights in the east, had been sacrificed in securing ratifications of the Pragmatic Sanction, and in the last disastrous war with the Turks.

But even after such losses, Austria was still one of the most powerful nations on the Continent, at least in appearance. In reality, it was so loose-jointed that it rattled whenever jarred. There was no national feeling in the monarchy. The Austrians spoke of the Bo-

---

regard the crown of the Holy Roman Empire of the Germans as a part of their heritage. The full title of Francis Joseph ran thus: "Emperor of Austria, King of Hungary and Bohemia, King of Lombardy and Venice, of Dalmatia, Croatia, Slavonia, Galicia, Lodomeria and Illyria; King of Jerusalem, Archduke of Austria, Grand Duke of Tuscany and Cracow, Duke of Lothringen, of Salzburg, Styria, Carinthia, Krain, and the Bukovinia; Grand Prince of Transylvania, Margrave of Moravia, Duke of Upper and Lower Silesia, of Modena, Parma, Piacenza, and Guastalla, of Auschwitz and Zator, of Teschen, Frioul, Ragusa and Zara; Princely Count of Hapsburg, Tyrol, Kyburg, Görz, and Gradiska; Prince of Briden; Margrave of Upper and Lower Lausitz; Count of Hohenembs, Feldkirch, Bregenz, Sonnenberg; Lord of Trieste, Cattaro, and the Windisch Mark."

The Empire and the Monarchy 73

hemians and Hungarians as *draussen im Reich* (outside in the Empire). The Bohemians did not consider themselves as belonging to the same nation as the Austrians; a Hapsburg was not regarded as their king until he came to Prague and was crowned, and he was not supposed to come until invited. The same feeling was more pronounced in Hungary; the Hungarians had refused to ratify the Pragmatic Sanction except with a provision that they be allowed to elect a king of their choice in the event of the extinction of the male line of the Emperor. This independent national spirit persisted to the end of the Austrian Monarchy; the Hungarians did not invite Francis Joseph to be crowned in Budapest until after he had occupied the throne in Vienna for twenty years, and the honor was finally bestowed largely to please Empress Elizabeth who, as they thought, was being mistreated by the Austrians.

Almost too often to enumerate, the Hungarians had made war against Austria, and a friendly feeling between the two peoples was practically unknown.[16] The Hungarians had descended from Mongolians, and were unable to speak the German language of the Austrians. The Bohemians were mostly Slavs, and likewise unable to speak German; neither could the Bohemians and Hungarians understand one another. Then in the Tirols, Tuscany, Lombardy, and about the head of the Adriatic were Italians, unable to converse with any of the races mentioned. Nor was this all. Down the Danube were the Roumanians, Croats, and Serbs,

[16] Bright, 14.

all unable to understand any of the rest. In religion, the inherited dominions were also badly divided; there were Catholics, Protestants, and Mohammedans, mixing Latin services, halleluiah choruses, and prayers to Allah and the Prophet.

In consequence of all this confusion and jangle of hatreds the Austrian Monarchy had fearful epidemics of falling to pieces, and one of the worst of these scourges occurred just at the close of the reign of Charles VI, who had completely lost his grip upon the people of his dominions. His grasp had been weakening throughout his troubled reign, and was almost entirely broken by his last war with the Turks.

The nobility and clergy of the provinces held a powerful club which they very often swung at the head of the monarch. He had to go to them annually, like a supplicant, and beg them to tax themselves to raise and support an army to defend the commonwealth, and before they granted his requests they usually demanded something in return. In this manner they had made themselves exempt from taxation, and bit by bit pinched off the authority of the crown, until they almost ran the government. In Hungary every meeting of the assembly developed into a bartering convention between the monarch and the kingdom, for the Hungarians, having no national sentiment, were not likely to put themselves to any great trouble to defend Austria or Bohemia.

The Hapsburg Monarchy was a lumbering old craft which moved smoothly only when piloted by a master, and now it was facing a storm brought on by a tremendous innovation in the form of a female ruler. It was necessary to square the sails to new winds, and it was doubtful if the old ship of state could outride the gale.[17]

[17] Much of the material concerning the Hapsburg Monarchy was derived from Gürtler's *Volkszählungen*. See list of reference books at the end of text.

V

CONTEMPORARIES OF THE QUEEN

I

THE reign of Maria Theresa was cast on the flood tide of the monarchial form of government in Europe. The republics of Greece and Rome were remembered only as experiments which had ended in failures. There were a few republics on the Continent, such as Holland, Genoa and Venice, but they were then countries of secondary importance, not really independent, and considered as erratic instances in which small groups had been permitted to usurp the divine rights of kings and queens; none of them had proved to be very successful. The feudal system had passed, leaving in its wake immense landed estates and a clergy, both invested with tremendous power and endowed with wonderful privileges, all of which they were most jealously endeavoring to retain and even enlarge. So bad was the condition of the masses, who were living but little better than slaves, that dark clouds of revolution were gathering over all Europe, and sovereigns realized that the preservation of their crowns depended upon their ability to withdraw exemptions and prerogatives from the estates and the clergy.

Rulers then thought of their possessions very much as we now view farms and city lots; they could transfer them in trades, yield them in treaties, and seize others in war with almost no regard for inhabitants. A large part of Europe was considered as free to be bought and sold, or taken by force of arms at any time. This was true of almost all the present state of Italy, the Netherlands, many of the German principalities, and the territory on the lower Danube. Such a condition naturally produced a period of shifty monarchs, who sought to enlarge their domains by diplomacy, marriage alliances, and very often by war. They became greedy, crafty, and unscrupulous. It was a time when the strong survived and the weak perished. A ruling house might rise to great power, or sink to utter helplessness, in one reign.

Prior to the accession of Maria Theresa there had been a certain sense of honor among the kings and princes of Europe. They robbed and plundered, but did it according to fixed rules and customs, and always had a care for the preservation of their much vaunted good names and reputations among their contemporaries. When they wished to seize a province, they searched archives for claims, or shrewdly provoked some condition which might be regarded as a justification for what they purposed to perform. Each monarch had a lively desire to be thought of as playing the game according to the rules.

With the advent of Frederick the Great, all such rules were virtually abolished. Territories were seized without any attempt to establish claims, and wars were begun without the formality of diplomatic notes, or even declarations. Frederick took what he could, when he could, and in any manner that he could, and other monarchs, to a large extent, followed his example.

Frederick was honest in that he did not disclaim dishonesty; other rulers soon learned that when possible, he would do whatever was to his interest, which was nothing more than they had been doing under the cover of diplomatic shams.[1] The monarchs of Europe became like wolves, and no one can accuse a wolf of being dishonest.

Under such an arrangement the Queen's contemporaries were of the greatest significance. Her success or failure rested entirely upon her ability to cope with them, since the fact that she was young and inexperienced rendered her all the more certain to be attacked.

To understand and appreciate the greatness of Maria Theresa, it is necessary to know something of the character of her competitors, for the difficulties of her position were directly proportional to their strength and ability. Before beginning the story of her reign, we must pause for a moment to glance at the principal rulers of Europe, with whom she was destined to contend.

II

Perhaps the most important, certainly the most interesting, of Maria Theresa's contemporaries at the beginning of her reign, was Frederick II of Prussia. He came to his throne a few months before the Queen's accession and continued to reign until her death. During almost all this long period he was uppermost in her mind; she never reached any important decision without carefully weighing its probable effects upon

---

[1] Bright, 6 seq.

Frederick, and nearly all her diplomatic acts were to a greater or less degree influenced by him.

Frederick was the third King of Prussia; his grandfather had been elevated from an elector to a king by Maria Theresa's grandfather, Leopold I. Frederick's father and grandfather were very proud of their new title, and showed both loyalty and gratitude to the Queen's father and grandfather.[2] Their homage, however, had been directed toward the Emperor of the Holy Roman Empire of the Germans, and since Maria Theresa was not to have this title, she was not destined to fall heir to Frederick's support. In his mind she was not superior to the German kings and electors, all of whose dominions he regarded as fair prey.

Probably Maria Theresa believed that she understood Frederick, and at first, did not regard him as very important. He was thought to be the weak, effeminate son of a brutal father who, as all Europe knew, beat and abused his children; some said he also beat his wife, the daughter of George I of England. It must have been from his mother that the boy inherited his passion for music and literature. Frederick William, the father, reveled in the rough life of the army, for which the boy had nothing but horror. He sought to change the disposition of his son by imposing upon him the hard life of a Spartan youth, ridiculing his music and poetry and administering all sorts of cruel punishments. Macaulay says Oliver Twist in his workhouse was a spoiled youngster compared with little Frederick, the heir to the throne of Prussia.[3]

At the age of seven the child was removed from

[2] Goldsmith, 20.
[3] Ibid., 29, 25 and 31.

his German governess and placed under the care of an officer of the army. A French woman was chosen to educate him in "book-learning," for the father realized that French was the language of diplomacy, and since the Hohenzollerns had become kings, the future ruler must be able to meet and converse with diplomats.[4]

This coarse father held his tutors responsible for the strictest discipline of his son. Frederick William believed the future of Prussia rested with the army, and wished his heir to be one of the sternest of soldiers.[5] Presently the lad rebelled and brought upon himself very severe punishments. There are many recorded instances of such severity, but we shall enumerate only a few of them. Once the father broke Frederick's flute, and threw the fragments into the fire, but Frederick found another flute, and formed the habit of visiting a young lady of Potsdam who accompanied him on the spinet. The father discovered this and had the lady led about the market by an executioner, after which she was publicly whipped—"right before Frederick's eyes."[6]

So impatient was Frederick under the bullying of his father that he decided to run away to his grandfather in England. In this enterprise he secured the assistance of a young army officer named Katt. News of the plot reached the father, and both Frederick and Katt were arrested and thrown into prison. On this occasion the father wrote to his wife: "I have had that scoundrel Fritz put in jail, and I shall treat

---

[4] *Ibid.*, 28.
[5] *Oesterreichischer Erbefolge-Krieg*, I, 934–935.
[6] Goldsmith, 50, quoting from Voltaire.

him as his crime and his cowardice deserve. I no longer acknowledge him as my son, for he has brought disgrace upon me and my house. The wretch does not deserve to live."

Frederick William then had his son, as well as Katt, tried by a court-martial, and pretended to be very angry because only one member of the court voted a death sentence for the son. Katt was not so fortunate; he received a death sentence, just as the King desired. The father had this cruel judgment carried out in the most horrible manner imaginable. A scaffold was erected before Frederick's window, and officers held the poor lad facing the scaffold while his friend was executed. As Katt was led to his death, Frederick cried, "Forgive me, forgive me, my dear friend!" [7]

"Death for such a charming prince is sweet," replied the brave, devoted Katt.

Before the execution was finished, Frederick fainted and fell to the floor. The whole performance was probably intended by the heartless father to be an object lesson for the prince, but Frederick never forgave such brutality on the part of his sire. After the execution Frederick William sent a minister to the prison to demand that his son sign, under oath, the following pledge: "I swear henceforth to obey the King implicitly, and to adhere strictly to my duty as his subject and son." Frederick signed the pledge, hoping, as he afterward stated, that his father would not live forever.

Frederick was inclined to be affectionate, and cherished a beautiful love for his sister Wilhelmine who was four years older than himself. Once, when he was visiting with his father at the court of the King of Saxony, where he was much amused at the King's many concubines and children, Frederick wrote to Wilhelmine: "Dear Sister,—In spite of so many diversions, I think of you constantly, and shall not forget you till I die. But wait a minute; let me cough, spit, and blow my nose. Now, what would you like to hear about?" Then he proceeded to tell her of the King's "mistresses and bastards." The boy's language was not very refined but most expressive. All his life, Frederick had the power of making witty remarks and pithy phrases.[8]

Frederick's greatest ambition was to be a poet; he idolized Voltaire with whom he finally ventured to open a correspondence. Later he wrote a book in French and sent the manuscript to his oracle to be criticized. He had no taste whatever for the life of the army; he hated the Germans, and despised their language; he often cursed the fate that had made him the Crown Prince of Prussia.

In spite of Frederick William's cruelty, he was a most pious Lutheran, and often preached long sermons in the cathedral. During his last illness he gave much attention to religion, but continued to rage over the worthlessness of his heir. At this time young Frederick wrote Wilhelmine: "Father's love of God is boundless, but he thinks very little of his son or the common people."

Frederick William had forced his son to marry Elizabeth Christina, of the House of Brunswick, of whom

---

[8] Goldsmith, 46.

Frederick wrote the following pungent description: "She is neither beautiful nor ugly, not entirely without brains, but very ill-bred, shy and without grace. She has a disagreeable laugh, walks like a duck, has bad teeth, dresses in poor taste, is nervous when she talks, but generally keeps silent. Apart from this she has a fair skin, a nice figure, nice hands, blond hair, and a good heart. She tries to be polite, but is always either too courteous or not courteous enough." [9]

When Wilhelmine saw her new sister, she wrote an equally unenthusiastic description. She said: "My sister is tall, but not slender; she sticks out her stomach, which ruins her appearance. The intense pallor of her face is emphasized by the vivid color of her cheeks; her eyes are a very pale blue and do not show much intelligence; her mouth is small and her features dainty without being beautiful. . . . Her hair is naturally curly, but all her outward charms are ruined by her ugly teeth which are black and irregular." [10]

Immediately after the wedding, Frederick accompanied his bride to her apartments, told her good-bye, and did not return except at long intervals.[11] "Thank God, it's over!" he wrote to Wilhelmine.

One day in May, 1740, Frederick William died, and young Frederick was King.

The announcement of his accession was greeted with anything but enthusiasm at home, with sympathy, almost akin to pity, in friendly states, and with restrained exultations among several kingdoms which were jealous of the enviable position Prussia had already at-

[9] Goldsmith, 77.
[10] *Ibid.*, 77.
[11] Carlyle, III, 170.

tained under the Hohenzollerns. It was believed that this poet, musician, and philosopher, who despised military service and was more at home among artists and sages than among warriors and statesmen, would make a bad mess of playing king to a people who had no literature and no art, and apparently no taste for either. He would be a man of many words and but little action. Other rulers regarded him as quite harmless, and imagined themselves now confronted with a kitten instead of the old lion they had previously known on the throne of Prussia.

Maria Theresa visualized in him somewhat of a kindred spirit, likely to become one of her best friends. They had similar tastes, were both inexperienced, and badly prepared to become rulers of important states. She knew that ever since her grandfather had elevated a Hohenzollern from an elector to a king, Prussia had been very loyal to her ancestors. She also knew that her father had purchased Prussia's ratification of the Pragmatic Sanction by ceding to Frederick's father the Duchy of Jülich-Berg, and she expected the son to recognize her as a ruler very promptly.[12] Charles VI had been dilatory in turning the Duchy of Jülich-Berg over to Frederick William, but she planned to attend to this immediately. She anticipated that the new King of Prussia would do more than merely recognize her; she believed he would be willing to support her husband for the honor of Holy Roman Emperor of the Germans, and did not hesitate to send a message requesting the King's aid at the coming election.[13] She believed that Frederick and Francis of Lorraine were good

[12] *Ibid.*, 446.
[13] Guglia, I, 45–46.

friends and brother Masons, and probably expected that to have a considerable influence.[14]

Frederick's character is a most interesting one from the standpoint of the psychologist. Here was a man of fine natural traits, who had been surrounded during childhood with an environment of cruelty which, although resented, was quite sure to modify his character. Would he follow the training of his father and become a cruel warrior, or would he be a peaceful ruler, devoting himself to music, literature, and the arts? He was likely to have a double personality because he would be unable to completely repress either his primary tendencies or his early training. That he was just such a man is proved by his conduct in war, his many poems, and his very tender devotion to his sister Wilhelmine.

III

Undoubtedly the power which Maria Theresa feared most of all was France. France had managed to get the better of the other powers in the Treaty of Westphalia. During the reign of Charles VI she had bullied Austria out of territories by threatening to renounce the Pragmatic Sanction, and just before his death had intimidated him by supporting the Turks in their raids on Austrian territory in the lower Danube.[15]

Maria Theresa probably realized that the King of Bavaria and the King of Saxony were likely to announce claims to the Hapsburg crowns, in the hope of extorting from her whatever they could, but she also

[14] *Oesterreichischer Erbefolge-Krieg*, I, 993-994.
[15] *Ibid.*, 906.

knew that neither of them would cause serious trouble unless encouraged by France. Austria and France had had many wars, and in spite of the fact that Charles had paid such a high price for the ratification of his Sanction, a recognition of the Queen by France was most anxiously awaited.

The situation in France was rather unusual. Louis XV was on the throne and he was almost no king at all. There are many who contend that if Louis XV had been brought up properly, he might have given a good account of himself to his subjects during his long reign from 1715 to 1774. As a child he was very sickly and not expected to live long enough to become king. His physicians directed that he be spared all worry and not required to do anything against his will. Cardinal Fleury, who had charge of his education, carried out such instructions to the letter, with the result that Louis grew up completely spoiled. At the age of fifteen he was married to Marie Leczinska, a daughter of the exiled king Stanislaus Leczinska of Poland. His wife was seven years his senior and neither clever nor beautiful.[16]

Cardinal Fleury had stuffed the boy's mind with fear of the awful consequences of sin, but had also given him to understand that a loophole for escape was provided by confessions to a priest. So Louis sinned and confessed quite freely until he was well accustomed to all sorts of transgressions except one; that one was a violation of his marriage vows. He was apparently ashamed to go to his priest with such a confession for the first time, and this timidity kept him virtuous for

[16] Williams, 1-4.

Contemporaries of the Queen 87

nearly fifteen years, during which his wife bore him two sons and several daughters. It began to look as though Louis XV was about to set a new record for the Bourbon kings of France.[17]

But at that time there were many scandalous intriguers in Paris, who thought the virtuous king might be plucked and devoured by a beautiful adventuress. There were also many charming young women only too eager to do the plucking and pass some of the emoluments, in the form of political prestige, back to the conspirators, who could plan and execute a successful *coup de main* resulting in the installation of a mistress in the King's palace. So it happened that the Duc de Richelieu managed to get the King intoxicated and presented him with the clever Comtesse de Mailly. The occasion marked the beginning of her career as a mistress to Louis XV but she was soon supplemented by the unsolicited assistance of a sister, whose services terminated most abruptly because she became *enceinte*. Louis, to save appearances, married her to a pliant nephew of the Archbishop of Paris, the Archbishop himself performing the ceremony.[18]

From that time forward Louis was rarely without an official mistress; whenever he sent one out of the love nest at Versailles he left the door ajar, and the women of the *noblesse* tumbled over one another to enter.

But, in 1745, one arrived from the *bourgeoisie*, and remained for nearly twenty years. She was given the melodious title of Madame de Pompadour and became the real ruler of France. She made treaties, appointed

[17] *Ibid.*, 4.
[18] *Ibid.*, ¶ 7.

and dismissed ministers, commanded the army, upset time-honored alliances, and became the queen of fashion in a court renowned throughout Europe for its wit and brilliancy. With Maria Theresa of Austria and Elizabeth of Russia, she eventually formed the most powerful female triumvirate Europe has ever seen.

It may seem almost immoral to call Madame Pompadour one of the great women of history, but her rare judgment and cleverness compel us to consider her as such. Since she was not of the high-born she was obliged to spend so much of her energy in holding her position against jealous titled competitors, that she accomplished little for France. Had her place been more secure, she might have made at least a part of the reign of Louis XV really constructive.

But we have outrun our story in order to introduce a character we shall have occasion to mention several times as we proceed. At the time of Maria Theresa's accession, France was under the control of Cardinal Fleury, an exceptionally capable minister. He was getting very old, but with the assistance of Marshal Belleisle,[19] whose head was always bursting with plots for the aggrandizement of France, Fleury embarked upon the scheme of limiting Maria Theresa to Hungary, and partitioning Austria and Bohemia between the Elector of Bavaria and the King of Saxony,[20] both of whom could resurrect old claims to the possessions of the Hapsburgs. All this was concocted in spite of the fact that Cardinal Fleury had extorted territory from Charles VI in return for a ratification of the Pragmatic

[19] Bright, 7.
[20] *Oesterreichischer Erbefolge-Krieg*, I, 907, 923-924, 994; Robinson to Lord Harrington, Oct. 22, 1740.

Sanction. So we see that the very move which Maria Theresa dreaded most of all was actually planned against her.

IV

This brings us to a discussion of Charles Albert of Bavaria, who, at the time of Maria Theresa's accession, was an elector. Charles was married to Maria Amalia, the younger of the two daughters of Joseph I, who, as we have seen, was the older brother of Charles VI. In the agreement which Charles had signed with his brother it was specifically stated that the older sister should take precedence over the younger, and since Maria Amalia had an older sister, Maria Josepha, the former was excluded from any rights under this agreement. Again, in marrying a foreign prince, Amalia—as was always demanded under such conditions—had renounced all her rights to the dominions of the Hapsburgs. But Charles VI, wishing to make his Pragmatic Sanction absolutely secure, had induced the Elector of Bavaria to ratify it, something Charles Albert claimed he had done with his fingers crossed and very strong mental reservations. In addition to all this, the Elector had a feeble claim of his own, since he was a distant relative of one of the bygone Hapsburgs.[21]

It was easy to see that the Elector of Bavaria had a very diluted claim, and under the circumstances it was not likely to be seriously asserted unless he secured the backing of one of the stronger powers. The only one which it was feared might join him in the enter-

[21] Carlyle, III, 443 seq.

prise, was the very one then scheming to do so—France.[22]

If all went well, France meant to make a puppet Emperor of the Holy Roman Empire out of the Elector of Bavaria, and thus win considerable authority over all the German states, as well as complete control in Bavaria, Bohemia, and probably Austria. It is uncertain whether this scheme first originated in the mind of Cardinal Fleury or Marshal Belleisle, but we may be sure it did not spring from the simple intellect of Louis XV. That it was definitely formed there can be no doubt, for we shall presently see it carried out in part.

Personally, the Elector of Bavaria was not badly adapted to take the ignoble part for which he was being groomed by the plotters in Paris. He was ambitious enough to be lured into the trap by having the prize of the imperial crown dangled before him, but not strong enough to become unpleasantly assertive after securing it. Of the greatest importance was the fact that he had at his disposal the resources of Bavaria, which, under the direction of Cardinal Fleury and Marshal Belleisle, could be used to immense advantage.[23]

V

Very similar to the claim of the Elector of Bavaria was that of the King of Saxony and Poland, although the latter was besmirched with more ingratitude and fraud. Frederick Augustus II of Saxony had married

[22] Robinson to Lord Harrington, Nov. 7, 1740.
[23] Bright, 6–7.

Maria Josepha, the eldest daughter of Joseph I, so that his claim almost duplicated that of the Elector of Bavaria except for one very important modification—the King's wife was older than the Elector's. Charles VI evidently feared the right of this elder daughter more than that of the younger, and took great pains to forestall any claim from the King of Saxony.[24] To compensate Augustus for ratifying the Pragmatic Sanction, Charles had won for him the crown of Poland against the contention of Stanislaus Leczinska, who had been exiled. The reader may recall that this unpronounceable name belonged to the father-in-law of Louis XV. Augustus of Saxony probably realized the worthlessness of his claim, and Louis XV cared little or nothing for his father-in-law; both rulers had been much overpaid already for their ratifications. Also, Josepha had renounced all her claims when she married Augustus, who was a foreign prince.

It would seem that Augustus should have been ashamed of himself when he revived such a flimsy claim to embarrass Maria Theresa, but he presented it, and prepared to wheedle as much as possible out of the young Queen.

Augustus was not fond of war and not likely to cause serious trouble unless tampered with by conspirators. He very much preferred to enjoy the amenities of life, with which he was surrounded at Dresden —his luxurious palace; his famous green diamond, for which he had paid four hundred thousand thalers; the opera, and his fine collection of paintings—than to risk the hazards of battle. When it came time to fight to

---

[24] *Oesterreichischer Erbefolge-Krieg*, I, 931–932.

substantiate his claim he was likely to arrive late and leave early.

VI

Of the greatest importance to Austria were the rulers of Russia, which had risen to the dignity of a power of the first class during the reign of Peter the Great who died in 1725. In 1730, the government had been seized by Anne, the daughter of Ivan, who was an imbecile brother of the great Czar. Czarina Anne was securely established on the throne at the accession of Maria Theresa. Russia had assisted Charles VI in his struggle to seat Augustus of Saxony on the throne of Poland against the claims of Stanislaus Leczinska. Czarina Anne hated the Turks, with whom she too had waged war, so her two enmities—the other was for France—prompted her to look favorably upon the new Queen of Austria.[25] Although the Czarina was sullen, ignorant, vindictive, sensual and immoral, Maria Theresa must have regarded her as a valuable asset, and was probably disappointed when she died, soon after the death of Charles VI. Then, in a short time, came Elizabeth Petrovna who was much more efficient.

Elizabeth was the daughter of Peter the Great and inherited much of her father's sense, but she was very peculiar. She had a careless, independent disposition, and was soon known as the woman who had fifteen thousand gowns but always appeared slovenly dressed. One of her first edicts was to abolish capital punishment. Under her encouragement Russian literature and music

---

[25] *Ibid.*, 986; Guglia, I, 43.

Contemporaries of the Queen 93

thrived and she founded the first university in Russia, at Moscow in 1755. She also built the celebrated Winter Palace, at a cost of ten million rubles—an expenditure which flattened her purse so badly that she was refused further credit by her French milliners.

At first Elizabeth was not unfriendly to Frederick of Prussia. She asked him to send her a suitable wife for the nephew who was to be her successor, and hinted that his sister Ulrike would be acceptable. Frederick ridiculed this suggestion; he had no intention of giving one of his sisters to "good-for-nothing" Peter. He sought out the most insignificant Prussian Princess he could find, Sophie Auguste of Anhalt-Zerbst, and sent her over to Elizabeth. Little did he think—little did any one think—that this obscure Princess Nobody would turn out to be Catherine the Great, and become a very sharp thorn in the side of Frederick the Great.[26]

Elizabeth was very jealous of her rights and prerogatives, and owing to her touchiness, became offended at some of Frederick's facetious remarks concerning the sphere of women in general, and Elizabeth's private life in particular. Their relations became strained and she joined Maria Theresa in a long and bitter war with Frederick, as we shall presently see.

When Maria Theresa came to the throne she considered Anne of Russia one of her friends. A little later she regarded Elizabeth in the same manner and expected the Czarina and Frederick of Prussia to come to her assistance if it became necessary to defend her crown against France and the Elector of Bavaria.

---

[26] Goldsmith, 150-154; Anthony, 60.

In this connection also we must say something more concerning a character already mentioned—one destined to play a very important part in the later life of Maria Theresa. We have already told how Catherine arrived in Russia. Little was heard of her until after the death of Elizabeth in 1762, when Catherine's husband, the silly Peter III, came to the throne. Peter completely reversed the policies of Elizabeth, and upon being opposed by his wife, threatened to divorce her. She went to the army with her troubles, and returned leading a formidable insurrection. Peter offered to compromise by sharing the power with her but was refused, whereupon he begged to be permitted to retire, taking with him only his dog and his fiddle. Shortly afterward Peter III was killed in a drunken brawl, many believe at the instigation of Catherine. Intellectually, Catherine was more than abreast of the times. She was fond of reading Voltaire's works, Blackstone's Commentaries, and Buffon's Natural History. Her court was brilliant but we are told that it was she who made it so. She had one male favorite after another, many of them being household pets whom she maintained merely for her own amusement. When she tired of one, she dismissed him for another, very much as Napoleon handled his mistresses. In this respect her court was an inversion of the one at Versailles.[27]

Catherine was troubled by the plots of many pretenders, probably because she was a foreigner. She dealt with such rivals most severely; some were sent to Siberia; others met with mysterious, violent deaths.

---

[27] Catherine the Great was mistress to at least thirteen men, and it is claimed that she spent upon them not less than one hundred and ninety million dollars. Anthony, 234.

She was cold, calculating, clever, cruel, and very efficient, yet she held high ideals concerning the rights of the people. Under the title of "Instruction," she issued a famous literary production in which she taught that religion should prompt us to do good to others; that all subjects should be equal in the sight of the law; that kings and queens were but the servants of the people; that laws should be framed to prevent crime rather than punish criminals, and many other doctrines, much in advance of the times.

She instituted many reforms in Russia and put the government on a basis never improved during the entire monarchy. Her analyses of political questions and conditions were the shrewdest of the day, and she was a match for Frederick the Great in characterizing her contemporaries with pithy phrases. She was rarely taken by surprise, for she seemed to be able to read and understand the motives of her friends and enemies almost as well as we do now in the light of more than a century of subsequent history. Catherine the Great was destined to cross the path of Maria Theresa many times, sometimes very much to the advantage of both, but at least once, greatly to Maria Theresa's injury as a historical character.

VII

At the time of Maria Theresa's accession, George II was on the throne of England, but his authority was much restricted by the British Parliament and ministers. He was a foreign king and seemed to be more interested in his Continental province of Hanover than in England. Both he and his father, George I, spent most of their time in Hanover, and neither of them could speak the English language without a marked German accent.

At that time the political horoscope of England indicated a certain definite policy, that of her king another which was not quite similar. England was ambitious to become mistress of the seas and develop into a great empire controlling North America and India, while Hanover was quite content to remain what she was, a little electorate of the Holy Roman Empire of the Germans.[28]

England's most formidable opponent in America was France. Thus far, England had only a narrow fringe of colonies along the shores of the Atlantic, although many of them held British grants of land extending westward to the Pacific. France also claimed vast territories in America, and by means of her missionaries had penetrated into the interior much farther than England. An attempt was made in the Treaty of Utrecht (1713), to settle their disputes concerning American dominions. Nova Scotia and Newfoundland were granted to England but the language of the treaty was so indefinite that new complications were added to the old.

Then followed an effort on the part of both claimants to establish fortifications, trading posts, and colonies in the valley of the Mississippi River. The French went west along the Great Lakes to the headwaters of the Mississippi and then followed the river all the way to the Gulf of Mexico, planting missions

---

[28] *Oesterreichischer Erbefolge-Krieg*, I, 984-985.

to convert the Indians to Catholicism, establishing trading posts, and building fortifications, until they had thrown a complete barrier across the future expansion of the British colonies. England was soon retaliating by attempts to establish trading posts along the Ohio River. Everything pointed to a severe struggle between the French and English over territory in the valley of the Mississippi.

North America was then a tremendous distance from the Danube but disputes over the New World were already projected into European politics, and their shadows fell darkly across the throne in Vienna, although Maria Theresa had no more intention of claiming something in America than in the moon.

What England most earnestly desired was that France might be completely engaged on the Continent, so as to entirely divert her attention from America and India while the British were building these rich lands into their great Empire. The power which had thus far served England best in this respect was Austria, and England hoped Austria might continue to be useful in the same way.[29] So much was England interested in retaining Austria as a counterweight to France on the continent, that British aid to Maria Theresa was more than probable. England had a strong selfish motive in saving Austria from dissolution, a motive almost certain to energize capital and set an army in action toward the Continent. Maria Theresa probably understood this intuitively, although she did not formulate it into words. Later, Kaunitz stated it

---

[29] Bright, 12.

to her very exactly when he laid down his principle that self-interest alone was the actuating influence in all diplomacy.

Here we may observe that this doctrine of self-interest may be applied fairly, by taking and giving so as to be mutually beneficial, or unfairly, by seizing as much as possible and yielding as little as possible in return. Almost without exception the latter was the manner in which it was applied during the reign of Maria Theresa. At the beginning she did not realize that this was to be the policy of her contemporaries, but she soon learned it by experience; we might add that she learned it very thoroughly.

But England's foreign policy might be influenced by her foreign king's Continental possession. George II would probably insist upon defending Hanover, which the long-headed, far-sighted British considered as of much less importance than America and India. All Europe understood this and knew the British lion would squirm whenever its Hanoverian tail was pinched. By threatening Hanover, England might be forced to turn her attention to the Continent, and thus be placed in the same predicament as France.

And there was something else which was not to be forgotten. George II was an uncle of Frederick of Prussia, a consideration which, at that time, was not considered as in any way unfavorable to Maria Theresa, for the two young and inexperienced monarchs were slated, as all supposed, to be friends. In the event of a dispute between them, however, George II would probably favor Frederick, since the House of Hanover was known to be one in which blood was thicker than water.

Contemporaries of the Queen 99

No doubt Maria Theresa weighed all this in her mind and talked it over with her advisers. She probably counted upon the assistance of England to offset the enmity of France and the Elector of Bavaria.[30] She reckoned among her friends, England, Prussia and Russia and among her enemies, France and Bavaria, with Saxony waiting to drift with the wind. The German states, outside of Saxony and Bavaria, she regarded as likely to remain true to the Emperor of the Holy Roman Empire of the Germans, soon to be elected, and seems to have held unwarranted hopes that this honor would fall to her husband, Francis of Lorraine.

VIII

We have now introduced the most eminent political characters of the time of Maria Theresa, the gladiators destined to contend in war and diplomacy across the arena of Continental Europe from 1740 to 1780. They stood facing her from the east, the north and the west, but to the south was a character less renowned, who was in a position to annoy her all the time and even jeopardize her dominions almost as greatly as any we have mentioned. A man whose friendship must be constantly purchased and repurchased at his own price, is likely to make a nuisance of himself.[31]

Charles Emmanuel of Sardinia was located at the front door of the Hapsburgs' Italian provinces, and at the back door of the possessions of the Bourbons in France and Spain. Squeezed in thus between the two most powerful dynasties of Europe he mastered the art

---
[30] *Oesterreichischer Erbefolge-Krieg*, I, 994.
[31] Carlyle, III, 449; Bright, p.

of playing one against the other. He was capable and clever but through sheer necessity became dishonest, tricky and very resourceful. His services, most valuable because he was a skillful warrior, were always for sale to either house, and protection was available when he was threatened, for by turning his territory and strength to one, he offered a most convenient avenue of attack upon the other.[32]

Having been rebuffed by Charles VI in 1734, he secretly allied himself with the Bourbons of France, and bursting suddenly into northern Italy, seized nearly all of Austria's possessions in Lombardy. At that time, he so completely deceived Charles VI that he actually drew supplies from Austria to be used in the campaign against her. The front door to Austrian Lombardy was left open to him while he was secretly bringing in his French allies through the back door of France.

The diplomacy which Charles Emmanuel practiced was the same as that so effectively used by Metternich a little later, when he found himself placed between Napoleon on the one hand and Czar Alexander on the other. The plan was to keep on good terms with both rivals until it was evident that one was to dominate, then join the winner and come in for a share of the spoils at settlement. The game was a hazardous one, but if skillfully played, converted a position of weakness into one of strength.[33]

The King of Sardinia had a feeble claim to the Hapsburg crowns through the Bourbons of Spain, who had long ago intermarried with the House of Austria. Naturally he dug this up and polished it to be sold for

[32] *Oesterreichischer Erbefolge-Krieg*, I, 914 seq.
[33] *Ibid.*, 919 seq.; Bright, 26.

whatever it would bring from Maria Theresa. The fact that his wife, then dead, had been a sister to Francis of Lorraine was entirely disregarded. Charles VI had already settled this claim some years before by certain territorial grants and privileges to the King of Sardinia, but, since it was the fashion in Europe to resurrect settled claims for the purpose of extorting something from the helpless young Queen, Charles Emmanuel presented his along with the rest.

But what the King of Sardinia had uppermost in his mind was to sell his services to Maria Theresa in her contest with France, and the price he intended to demand was very high. He felt that he had something which she must have, for, if she refused his offer, he could join France under a promise of protection while he helped himself to another large slice of Austrian territory in northern Italy. Maria Theresa felt herself conscientiously bound to retain her inherited dominions, and hence found herself almost obliged to make some arrangement to secure the alliance of Charles Emmanuel of Sardinia.

IX

There is one more personage, a woman—this was a period of contentious women—rapping to be admitted to the list of eminent contemporaries of Maria Theresa. She is Elizabeth Farnese, better known as the Termagant of Spain. Elizabeth was married to Philip V and had two sons—all Europe was grateful that there were not more of them—Don Carlos and Don Philip, both of whom were excluded from any likelihood of inheriting the Spanish crown, because Philip had an elder son, Don Ferdinand, by an earlier marriage. The Termagant was watching with the eye of a hawk for possessions for her sons; usually her gaze was fixed upon Italy whence she came, for Italy was known to be the land of paradise for destitute princes.[34] She had been a sharp thorn in the side of Charles VI whom she continually annoyed in one way or another. Once she had coaxed him into an agreement to marry both his daughters to her sons, but, owing to strong objections from several sources, he had abandoned the scheme; he even denied having made it, apparently because he was ashamed of having yielded to the importunities of a woman. The Termagant wrenched both Naples and Sicily from Charles at the close of the War of the Polish Succession, and Don Carlos was now sitting comfortably on the throne at Palermo, but waiting and hoping that mother would find him something better.

Spain still claimed Tuscany, and Maria Theresa knew that the Termagant had her eye on that possession as well as on Parma and Guastalla for Don Philip. It was necessary for her to bear the Termagant of Spain constantly in mind.

Such were the contemporaries with whom the Queen was destined to compete. Had she known them then as we know them now she might have been discouraged, for perhaps never in the history of Europe were there so many capable and unprincipled monarchs in power as during the reign of Maria Theresa. The cards were dealt for a strong game, to be played without regard for rules or honor.

[34] Carlyle, III, 447.

VI

THE FIRST CONTEST

I

THE contest started with a stupendous surprise—one which completely upset all calculations.[1] One day in December, 1740, an important messenger was announced at the Hofburg. His name was Gotter, and his title Grand Marshal to Frederick II of Prussia, hence his appearance sent a breeze of excitement through the old palace. Frederick had used much care in the selection of this special ambassador, for he thought it very important that the message he was sending be presented in a manner likely to prompt a favorable response. Gotter had a fine physique, and being well groomed, thought himself very impressive, especially to the ladies. His voice was loud and boisterous, and his manner domineering; he had just such a voice and delivery as Frederick had heard his own father use so effectively in putting a quietus to insubordination, cavil and quibble in the royal household.

The young King, who was very proud of his own literary ability, had taken much time and pains in writing this message, which he felt sure Gotter could deliver in a manner quite irresistible to a young queen. But, upon arriving at the Hofburg, the Grand Marshal

[1] Bright, 10.

was much disappointed to be received by Francis of Lorraine, and find himself obliged to make the speech, so carefully rehearsed all the way from Berlin to Vienna with a woman in mind, to a man. On the spur of the moment it was impossible to change his attitude, so he clicked his heels and began:

"I come with safety for the House of Austria in one hand, and the imperial crown in the other. The troops of my Master are at the service of Her Majesty, and cannot fail to be acceptable at a time when she stands in such sore need, and can depend only on so considerable a prince as the King of Prussia and his allies, the maritime powers and Russia. As the King, my Master, from the situation of his dominions will be exposed to great danger from this alliance, it is hoped that, as an indemnification, the Queen of Hungary will not offer him less than the whole Duchy of Silesia. Nobody is firmer in his resolutions than the King of Prussia; he must and will enter Silesia; once entered, he must and will proceed; and, if not immediately secured by the cession of that province, his money and his troops will be offered to the Elector of Bavaria and King of Saxony."[2]

The explosion of a bomb in the Hofburg could hardly have created greater consternation than this speech. No one could believe that this grim Prussian, standing like a statue of Ares and speaking like a Roman god, was to be taken in any other manner than very seriously. Yet it all seemed so inconsistent with the reputation of Frederick, the young King who played the flute, wrote poetry, and abhorred war.

---

[2] Coxe, III, 232; *Oesterreichischer Erbefolge-Krieg*, I, 1056.

The First Contest

Francis of Lorraine, as best he could in his surprise, answered the boisterous Gotter by interposing objections and arguments, whereupon Gotter, who was nettled at being obliged to waste his eloquence on a contentious husband, answered stiffly, "I have no further business here and will instantly return to my Master."

"Are your Master's troops already actually in Silesia?" demanded Francis.

"They are."

At this point Francis seems to have excused himself to consult the Queen, who had not received the messenger in person because she was sensitive over her condition, being soon due for her fifth confinement.

Who can imagine the horror with which she listened to her husband repeating Gotter's message? So all the rumors which had filtered in from the north were true. She had heard that Frederick was assembling his troops for some unknown purpose, and had sent her efficient minister Botta to Berlin to penetrate Frederick's designs and report to her, but the wily King of Prussia had succeeded in pulling the wool over Botta's eyes by protestations of friendship and straight-faced lying, so that the expedition got away to Silesia without any definite warning, and with no demands or declaration of war having been served upon the Queen. She had heard just enough to lead her to believe Gotter was telling the truth when he said the Prussian troops were already in Silesia. She was angry, and immediately sent her husband back with a message of defiance.

Francis reported to Gotter: "Return to your Master and tell him that, while he has one soldier in Silesia, we will perish rather than enter into any discussion with him. But if he will refrain from entering, or if already entered, will return, we will treat with him at Berlin. Botta already has instructions, others will be sent him today, and the King of Prussia may be gratified without presuming to extort what is not in our power to grant. Not for the imperial crown, nor for the whole world will we yield an inch of our territory." [3]

Such a spirited reply had not been anticipated by Gotter. Also, he had plumed himself for the occasion "like a victorious knight returning after capturing Constantinople," [4] and was greatly disappointed that the young Queen had not appeared to honor him and admire his uniform. He intimated that if Her Gracious Majesty would receive him and put her wishes in the form of a request, he would endeavor to persuade the King of Prussia to be satisfied with a few villages in Silesia.

Francis conveyed this conciliatory message to the Queen who indignantly refused to receive in person any messenger from Frederick as long as there was a single Prussian soldier in Silesia. To this Francis added a pinch of pepper by telling Gotter that the King's father had felt honored when allowed to hand a wash bowl and towel to the Queen's father, and that Frederick would do well to remember who he was and improve his manners. That ended the interview.

Gotter departed very much crestfallen. He knew he would be scolded because he had failed to secure any concessions whatever from the Queen, who had not

---
[3] Arneth, I, 121.
[4] This expression was used by Robinson in a letter referring to Gotter on Dec. 21, 1740.

even deigned to receive him in person, compliment him upon his appearance, and pretend to be impressed by his carefully rehearsed speech.[5]

The King of Prussia, upon hearing Gotter's report, was indeed very much surprised and disappointed. So much so that he immediately sent the ambassador back with an offer to purchase Silesia; if the Queen would not sell all of it, he would be satisfied with a part. No doubt he was still more astonished and chagrined when Gotter returned a second time to report that the haughty Queen refused to discuss the subject, unless Frederick marched every one of his soldiers out of Silesia.[6]

Meanwhile Frederick, quite unopposed, was progressing rapidly in his occupation of Silesia, but his conscience pricked him most annoyingly. He knew he had no right to the rich territory of Silesia with its important metropolis of Breslau. There had been disputes in bygone days over the province, but Frederick's grandfather had traded all his claims to Silesia for other territories of Maria Theresa's grandfather, and for a money consideration which had been paid. Frederick's invasion was a matter of conquest pure and simple.[7]

But that was not the whole story of Frederick's unfairness; he had gone about the invasion in a most dishonest manner. He had lied to Botta and sent avowals of friendship to the new Queen in Vienna. The carefully prepared message delivered by Gotter was a bundle of falsehoods. He had referred to the maritime powers and Russia as being his allies, when, as a matter

[5] Arneth, I, 122; Guglia, I, 67.
[6] Arneth, I, 128–129.
[7] Coxe, III, 234; Guglia, I, 64.

of fact, he had no allies whatever. The intimation that he would offer his troops to the Elector of Bavaria and the King of Saxony was pure bluff, and his adroit proposal to support the Queen's husband in the election of an Emperor of the Holy Roman Empire of the Germans, in return for Silesia, was little else than attempted bribery. Also, he had shown himself to be either ignorant or unscrupulous when he set out to seize the territory of a friendly neighbor without the formality of demands or a declaration of war.[8]

But in spite of all this, we must acknowledge that Frederick's conduct was the fruit of clear statesmanship, and in complete harmony with the principle of self-interest in diplomacy. England or France might have done the same thing, but certainly with a little less display of brusqueness.[9]

When we search the literature and documents of the day for some explanation of Frederick's psychology, we soon discover that there was then a conflict in his mind between the brutal training of his father and the natural tender emotions of his childhood; the former prevailed, but not without a struggle. Once Frederick wrote to Maria Theresa, "My heart has no share in the mischief my hand is doing your court," and in the same letter he renewed his offer to purchase Silesia; then in a letter to Voltaire he wrote, "I would gladly exchange this occupation for another if it were not for the ghost called Glory, which appears so often. In truth it is a great folly, but a folly one cannot escape if one is once obsessed by it."

[8] Goldsmith, 105; Guglia, I, 60.
[9] Bright, 11.

Facilis descensus Averni! The decline in Frederick's morals having begun, progressed rapidly. By subjecting his better emotions to strong willful repressions, he succeeded in freeing himself of all outward indications of tenderness and consideration for the rights of others, and became the very image of his heartless father, except that the son was more capable and efficient.

To the proud Maria Theresa, Frederick's repeated messages came as nagging taunts, and she determined to meet him with force. She appealed for assistance to the powers that had guaranteed the Pragmatic Sanction. Such appeals, doubtless very much to her surprise, proved to be absolutely in vain; not one soldier, not a single florin, was offered her from any source. How vividly she must have recalled Prince Eugene's brusque remark to her father—which we beg pardon for quoting again— "Two hundred thousand soldiers are worth more than all the sanctions in the world!"

Czarina Elizabeth declined with scant apologies to lend the Queen any assistance; Augustus of Poland apologized freely, but went no further until later, when he joined her enemies; France twisted out of her obligations, but at the same time made overtures to Frederick and a closer pact with the Elector of Bavaria; England, from whom she expected much, replied courteously, but said that for the moment she was seriously embarrassed with domestic troubles, and advised the Queen to make peace with Frederick at any cost so as to be in a position to use all her strength against France. England was so anxious to have Austria free to assist in the coming struggle with France, that the British Ambassador was instructed to offer his services to her as a mediator with Frederick of Prussia.[10] All this illustrates most forcibly what we have already stated concerning the potency of self-interest in diplomacy. The various powers, which had so often lined their nests with feathers plucked from the breast of Charles VI, in return for their worthless ratifications of his pet Sanction, were blissfully undisturbed by the appeals of his daughter.

Maria Theresa found herself thrown completely upon her own resources. She appointed General Neipperg to organize and lead an expedition to expel the Prussians from Silesia. The General was a brave old warrior, much beloved by Prince Eugene, but in the senseless scandals following the loss of Belgrade during the closing years of the reign of Charles VI, he had been disgraced and thrown into prison. Maria Theresa freed him and gave him the command of this important expedition, an act of clemency for which he was most grateful. He set forth with a strong determination to reward her kind-hearted generosity. The expedition departed for the north during the last days of March, 1741, and came in contact with the Prussian army on the tenth of April.[11]

It is not the intention to introduce here detailed descriptions of battles, but there are one or two incidents connected with this one which are too interesting to be omitted. The Austrians were totally defeated at Mollwitz, but the credit does not belong to Frederick, who was in command of the Prussian cavalry. No sooner had the battle opened than his horsemen were scattered, and Frederick lost his head so completely that

[10] Coxe, III, 235.
[11] Arneth, I, 161

General Schwerin, who commanded the infantry, begged his King to ride off the field and leave the struggle to be finished by more experienced warriors. Frederick was only too glad to follow Schwerin's suggestion, and since his horse was the best in the cavalry, soon found himself far in advance of the other horsemen in a wild flight for safety. Turning in his saddle he shouted, "Farewell friends, I am better mounted than you are!" [12]

Frederick was found late that evening cowering in complete nervous distraction in an old mill, and lamenting the fate of his lost army, but, upon learning that the Prussians had won a great victory, he recovered his *sang-froid* and exclaimed, "Young warriors should learn by this not to lose all hope so soon!" What had saved the day for Frederick was the excellent discipline of the Prussian infantry, for which he had no one to thank but the father whose name he still professed to abhor.[18]

Had Frederick lost the Battle of Mollwitz he would have been ruined forever, and had he not been a king, he would have been ruined as it was, for he would have been laughed out of the army. But, since he was a king, reports of his cowardly conduct were hushed up so completely that they were not heard by the world until much later. Under the circumstances he was a made man, and being a truly great one, he subjected himself to a severe course of self-analysis, and determined to profit by his errors. He resolved to do better

---

[12] Carlyle, III, 418; Arneth, I, 165; Coxe, III, 238.
[18] Whitman, 231; Goldsmith, 109. Frederick was found at Löwen, fully ten miles from the battlefield.—*Oesterreichischer Erbefolge-Krieg*, II, 241.

the next time and impatiently longed for the opportunity to redeem himself from a disgrace which he felt none the less keenly because it was held in secret.[14]

Maria Theresa's army had met Frederick's and been hopelessly defeated. Little Prussia, a mere upstart, had crossed swords with one of the great established powers of Europe and come off the winner. Silesia was, at least for the time being, lost.

II

It would be difficult to exaggerate the horror with which Maria Theresa received the news of the defeat of her army at Mollwitz. Before Frederick of Prussia invaded Silesia she seemed to have a fair chance of success in holding the hereditary dominions together, and even after Frederick's intention to make war on her was known, her cause was not regarded as hopeless. In April, just before the Battle of Mollwitz, England bet one and a half million dollars on the Queen by appropriating that amount to aid her. We may be sure this was a token of faith in the breast of John Bull that she could weather the storm, and that Austria would continue as a counterweight to France.[15] But after the Prussians so completely defeated the Austrians, England believed the Queen's cause to be lost unless she made peace with Frederick, and the British Ambassadors in Vienna and Berlin were instructed to bend all their energies to have her make such a peace, at the cost of all Silesia if necessary. All her own advisers, with the single exception of Bartenstein, who

[14] Carlyle, III, 491.
[15] Sir Robert Walpole, *Memoirs*, I, 679.

was most unpopular at the court, also urged her to sue for peace; even her own husband, whose self-interest centered more in securing the support of Frederick at the coming election of an emperor than in maintaining the dominions of his wife, joined in the clamor for peace which must have driven Maria Theresa almost to distraction.

Under such urging to do something which she considered a violation of her oath to maintain the Pragmatic Sanction and hold undiminished the sacred realms of her father, she became very petulant and showed bad temper, especially toward Sir Thomas Robinson, the British Ambassador. Finally she yielded a trifle and offered Frederick terms so unfavorable that he instantly rejected them with a fine show of indignation over her "base attempt to make him untrue to his allies."

Quite the opposite state of affairs prevailed in the Prussian camp where, seemingly right out of the mists, representatives of many powers appeared to offer favorable alliances.[16] At first the King rejected all proffers because he wished the credit of bringing Austria to his own terms without assistance or obligations, but presently he heard that English, Hanoverian and Danish troops were appearing in the Austrian army, whereupon he began to take on alliances with alacrity. Very soon he had formed a secret treaty with France, and open pacts with Bavaria and Saxony.[17]

The news of such alliances leaked through to Vienna and the propaganda for peace at any price became almost irresistible to the young Queen. When we con-

[16] Carlyle, IV, 13–18.
[17] Arneth, I, 170.

sider the deplorable condition of her cause at this time, we cannot help feeling that perhaps her stubbornness sprang more from ignorance and the inability to really comprehend her position, than from any shrewd calculation of her chances of success. With France and Bavaria already in action against her, and Frederick's victorious army ready to move on Vienna, which was so mutinous that it was almost willing to open the gates of the city to the Elector of Bavaria, it certainly seemed that her only hope lay in making as favorable a peace as possible through the assistance of her best ally, England.

But Maria Theresa did not yield. Instead she turned to what every one regarded as a forlorn hope; she resolved to appeal to Hungary. The court at Vienna thought the Hungarians unlikely to come to the aid of the Queen because it was well known that they disliked the Austrians. Hungary had ratified the Pragmatic Sanction, but without much enthusiasm, and already there was a strong undercurrent of opposition to crowning the young Queen unless she made heavy concessions, which amounted almost to granting the kingdom a separate government. Actuated by fear, the Austrians had forbidden the Hungarians to bear arms, and were opposed to the recruiting of a large army in the lower country for any purpose. An appeal to Hungary would surely stimulate opposition to the Queen at home, and seemed extremely hazardous.[18]

But in obedience to a keen intuition, Maria Theresa had courted favor with the Hungarians from the very hour of her accession. While Charles VI lay on his bier

---

[18] Arneth, I, 286; Guglia, I, 97; *Oesterreichischer Erbefolge-Krieg*, I, 902 seq.

she had sent for the seventy-seven-year-old Hungarian patriot, John Palfy, and made him her representative in the lower kingdom.[19] Had she spent weeks in consulting her advisers in Vienna, she probably would have made a worse selection, for Palfy was not popular among the Viennese. He was a very striking character—one whose traits challenge our sympathy. He was a brave old veteran who had fought for years with Prince Eugene, by whom he was greatly loved. John Palfy was what the world of today would call a "good old sport." He liked good whiskey, had a sinner's weakness for beautiful women; could swear like a longshoreman, and sneered at the *Hofrats* of Vienna. He was passionately devoted to the races and was renowned for his ability to pick a winning horse from among those which were unpopular; having made his choice, he backed it to the limits of his purse and very often won. The Hungarians loved him and his influence among them was tremendous.

It is not hard for us to understand why Maria Theresa appealed so strongly to both the lighter and deeper emotions of John Palfy. She was young, beautiful, and plucky, and her condition was so very helpless; his fine sense of chivalry was touched. To Palfy's mind she was being misused by the Austrians for whom he held very little respect. That alone was enough to put the aged veteran into action. He resolved that as long as his wobbly old legs could go, and his valorous right arm could wield a sword, she should have a fair chance to make good.[20]

Palfy was also stirred by a deep sense of patriotism.

[19] Guglia, I, 100; Bright, 15.
[20] Guglia, I, 100 seq.; *Oesterreichischer Erbefolge-Krieg*, III, 4.

To his mind Hungary was forced to choose between the House of Austria and the Sultan of Turkey, and, while he understood the perfidies of the Hapsburgs, he regarded them as better masters than the sultans. He had seen thousands of his people, both men and women, carried away to slavery in the Orient, and he understood fully that Mohammedanism was contending with Christianity for the mastery of the valley of the Danube. Palfy and Prince Eugene had often discussed this subject over camp fires, and always ended with such conclusions. Also they had frequently mentioned the little Archduchess, whom the Prince loved with that strange, tender affection so characteristic of rough warriors. If Palfy had had no other reason for espousing the cause of the Queen he would have done it out of respect for his old comrade. With Palfy's approval, probably at his suggestion, Maria Theresa called a meeting of the Hungarian assembly to elect her Queen and arrange for her coronation.

The event was well timed for Maria Theresa; she had just recovered from the birth of her son, the future Joseph II, and was not yet incapacitated by the approach of another confinement. It afforded her just such an opportunity as she desired to appear before the chivalrous Hungarians. She was perhaps, dimly conscious of her ability to sway audiences—she had often done so when taking parts in amateur theatricals at the court of her father. Very likely she also relied upon her power to move men by the charm of her personality, her youth, her sex, and her aristocracy. She meant to use every influence at her command to rouse the enthusiasm and win the support of the spirited Hungarians who, as she knew, were not friendly to the

Austrians. One thing was very much in her favor; she was being coached by her old patron John Palfy.

At the very beginning of her voyage, Maria Theresa showed her intention of making a strong spectacular appeal to the Hungarians, even at the risk of offending the Austrians. She had the boat which was to take her down the Danube completely covered with the red, green, and white flags of Hungary, and the crew and servants wore uniforms of the same colors; even the hull of the boat was painted with the colors of Hungary. She could have done nothing more certain to assure her an enthusiastic reception.[21]

At Wolfstal, near the boundary, she was greeted by a delegation and notified that the assembly had elected her King of Hungary. After much debate, it had been decided that the official cry to be used in greeting her was to be "Long live our Mistress and King!" There was a touch of sarcasm in this *viva*, for it meant that the Hungarians were too proud to greet their ruler as Queen. She noticed this and it cut her deeply, but the only reference she made to it was that she would be a "mother as well as a father to Hungary."

But, when she made her formal appearance before the assembly, she found herself facing a strong current of opposition. The Hungarians meant to exact as much as possible from her before agreeing to crown her as their King. She stated her propositions, which were debated at length, and with a considerable display of feeling both for and against her. She found it necessary to yield much, but with great cleverness, managed to avoid granting the Hungarians a separate Privy Coun-

[21] Guglia, I, 100.

cil.[22] She acknowledged their right to bear arms without the consent of Austria, and conceded many privileges to the nobility in the way of exemption from taxation.[23] Still the assembly hesitated until the balance was tipped in her favor by a most peculiar incident.

In the midst of the discussion a protest was received from the Elector of Bavaria, warning the Hungarians against espousing the cause of the Queen who was, according to the Elector, only a pretender. The protest stirred up a strong wave of resentment. Assemblymen were soon saying to one another, "Who is the Elector of Bavaria, that he should be giving advice to Hungary? Let him attend to his own affairs and not meddle with ours. If this is a fair sample of the opposition to the Queen, we are for her; let us proceed with the coronation." Maria Theresa was to have her day of glory, which she knew just how to use to her own advantage.

On her coronation day in Pressburg, she held her destiny in the hollow of her hand. Had she, on that fateful day, shown the least haughtiness, or awkwardly struck the chord of Hungary's hate for Austria, her cause probably would have been lost. Had she been ugly, clumsy, badly dressed, or even exhibited bad horsemanship, her appeal to the chivalry of the sons of the ancient Mongolians would have been in vain. On the other hand, the occasion afforded her a wonderful opportunity to use all her charms to win a race peculiarly sensitive to the appeal of a beautiful, plucky young woman in distress. That day was to decide whether or not she was to become a great leader. No-

[22] *Ibid.*, 105.
[23] Arneth, I, 296.

body understood this better than John Palfy, who felt his heart rise into his throat as he tossed aside the weight of seventy-seven years and appeared to coach and encourage her, perhaps prompt her now and then with a friendly nod or gesture of approval.[24]

In the presence of the assembly she was clothed with the tattered mantle of St. Stephen, girded with his sword, and received his shield in her left hand and the emblem of Hungarian authority in her right; then the old crown of St. Stephen was placed on her head and she was proclaimed a "Holy Apostolic Majesty," while all present shouted, "Long live our Mistress and King!" Next a procession formed and conducted her to two of the churches of Pressburg for religious devotions. Following this, she was taken by carriage to the foot of the famous coronation hill, where Count Joseph Esterhazy held a black stallion, the finest one in his stables, as she mounted. That was a crucial moment for the young Queen, for she was the cynosure of many eyes likely to be very critical of her horsemanship—the Hungarians could never love a queen who rode badly. Maria Theresa, fortunately, had often ridden with her father and her husband in their hunts, and had been carefully trained in the riding school of the Hofburg; she felt no timidity in mounting before such a discriminating audience. Spurring her horse to a swift gallop, she beat her escorts to the summit, where, quite unassisted, she reined her steed, drew her sword and slashed to the four cardinal points in defiance of the world.[25] The Hungarians were captivated by the way their new Queen rode and the dexterity and en-

[24] Guglia, I, 108.
[25] *Ibid.*, 106; Arneth, I, 277 seq.

thusiasm she exhibited, and they were moved to tears when, upon dismounting, she approached John Palfy and extended her right hand, which he seized and kissed while they both wept. In this little drama Maria Theresa was not merely acting; she was expressing the deep gratitude she felt for her heroic old patron.

Fortunately we have the written accounts of one or two men who were eyewitnesses of these ceremonies. Sir Thomas Robinson, the British Ambassador, was present and wrote: "The Queen was all charm; she galloped up the coronation hill, and, with her drawn sword, defied the four corners of the world in a manner which indicated that she had no need to use her weapon to conquer all who saw her." [26] Wraxall in his *Memoirs* wrote: "The antiquated crown received new grace when placed upon her head, and the tattered robes of St. Stephen became her as well as her richest gown, decorated with diamonds and pearls. Her appearance of delicacy, due to her recent confinement, only increased the attractiveness of this beautiful princess, and, when she sat down to dine, she was seemingly more charming than when wearing her crown. The warm weather and the fatigue of the ceremony diffused an animated glow over her countenance, while her beautiful hair flowed in ringlets over her shoulders and bosom." [27]

Maria Theresa had won the complete admiration of the Hungarians, but that was not enough. She needed soldiers willing to march to fields of battle and lay

---

[26] Robinson to Lord Harrington, June 28, 1741.
[27] Wraxall, II, 299. Robinson was an eyewitness, but Wraxall was writing from hearsay. Wraxall was born in 1751, and his *Memoirs* were published in 1799.

The First Contest

down their lives, if necessary, in fighting the Prussians—something entirely different from tossing hats in the air and screaming, "Long live our Mistress and King!" Months passed and still the Hungarian volunteers were numbered in hundreds, while she needed them in thousands even tens of thousands.[28]

She resolved to appear again before the Hungarian assembly and appeal to the loyalty and chivalry of the country to save her crown and her house from complete ruin. This celebrated appearance occurred on the eleventh of September, 1741. She entered the hall of the assembly wearing the crown of St. Stephen, and bearing the scepter of Hungarian authority. Walking slowly and majestically to the throne, she scanned the faces of the assemblymen while the Chancellor made a formal speech of introduction. Then she arose and addressed the assembly in Latin, which we are told all understood.[29] What she said was afterward written out from memory by Count Kolder, who was present. His memorandum reads: "The disastrous situation confronting us has induced us to lay before our dear and faithful Hungarians the recent invasion of Austria, the danger now impending to this kingdom, and a proposal for a consideration of a remedy. The very existence of the Kingdom of Hungary, of our own person and children, and our crown, are at stake. Forsaken by all, we place our sole reliance in the fidelity and long-tried valor of the Hungarians. We exhort the states and orders to deliberate without delay on the extreme danger, and devise the most effective measures

---

[28] Arneth, I, 288-297.
[29] At that time the Latin language was in common use among the Hungarian noblemen.—See Coxe, III, 261

for the security of our person, of our children, and of our crown, and to carry them into immediate execution. In regard to ourselves, the state of Hungary shall experience our hearty coöperation in all things which may promote the pristine happiness of this ancient kingdom and the honor of its people." Such, we understand, was the substance, but not the full text of her speech.[30]

From the rather disconnected accounts of various contemporaries, we infer that this formal speech was but the beginning of a very spirited session during which the Queen was freely questioned, and even heckled by members who were not friendly to her cause, and that she held her ground, most valiantly defending herself and winning her enemies by cleverly answering them in their own tongue, one of the most difficult in the world for a foreigner to use. At times the meeting became almost a riot, and such sentences as "Devil take the Queen," and "The Queen had better apply to Satan than the Hungarians for help," were flung into her face. According to a widely accepted tradition, she finally roused the assembly to a frenzy of enthusiasm by weeping with the infant Joseph in her arms, and dramatically consigning the future King to the care and defense of the "brave Hungarians." This brought on a grand climax, in which the valiant warriors leaped to their chairs, clanked their swords and screamed, "We will die for our good Queen Maria Theresa!"

She apparently carried her point beyond her fondest expectations, for the assembly voted to put one hundred thousand soldiers in the field, while every noble-

[30] Arneth, I, 299; Guglia, I, 111; Coxe, III, 265.

man present promised to sit in his saddle and fight for his beloved Queen.[31]

This story of Maria Theresa before the assembly has become one of the celebrated legends of the Hungarians,[32] and no doubt her heroism on that occasion has been somewhat exaggerated, but we may safely say it was one of the very few instances in which a Hapsburg ruler ever met subjects face to face and carried a point by sheer personal magnetism. It at once stamped Maria Theresa as a great ruler and a great woman. The legend of Maria Theresa, with the infant Joseph in her arms, before the Hungarian diet, is still told to tourists by guides in Pressburg. A beautiful monument commemorating the event stood in that city until some vandals—the Hungarians say it was the jealous Czechs—destroyed it at the close of the World War.

There are many instances in history in which great leaders have paralyzed opposition by the power of their personalities. There is the one in which Marius disarmed his would-be executioner by glaring at him fiercely and saying in a deep voice, "Darest thou slay Caius Marius?" Mark Antony changed history by his oration over the body of Julius Cæsar. Patrick Henry did it in the assembly of Virginia. We might pile up innumerable similar examples, but none of them reflect more credit upon the performer than this one in which Maria Theresa stood before the Hungarian assembly

---

[31] Although the Hungarian assistance was the salvation of Maria Theresa, it did not amount to more than half of what was promised by the assembly.—See *Oesterreichischer Erbefolge-Krieg*, III, 27; Bright, 17–18; Guglia, I, 113.

[32] *Oesterreichischer Erbefolge-Krieg*, III, 18.

and harangued it in a foreign tongue into an enthusiasm which completely altered her destiny. We are told that every knight in the room swore he would become a living hero or a dead martyr for his Queen, and most of them kept their oaths.

It is pleasant to recall that Maria Theresa never forgot John Palfy for what he did for her on this occasion. On his next birthday he received a picture of the Queen framed with precious stones, and later, many similar remembrances from her.[33] Maria Theresa never forgot a friend and rarely forgave an enemy.

What the Queen had accomplished at Pressburg reacted most favorably upon her subjects up the river. They were surprised at her exhibition of power and felt a trifle jealous of the Hungarians. They still urged her to make peace with Frederick, but no longer thought of accepting the Elector of Bavaria to replace her on the throne of the Hapsburgs. The Austrians and Hungarians united in defense of their Queen to such a degree as had not been witnessed for a century.

News of what had happened in Pressburg also reached Frederick of Prussia and made him eager to abandon his allies by making a separate peace with the Queen, but it was only because of insistent urging on the part of England that she finally consented to sign the Treaty of Ober-Schnellendorf.[34] In this treaty she ceded Silesia to Prussia, but both she and Frederick understood that she was not yielding it permanently.[35] She felt that she must have time to concentrate her forces for a drive against the French and Bavarians,

---

[33] Khevenhüller-Metsch, I, 237-238.
[34] *Oesterreichischer Erbefolge-Krieg*, III, 20.
[35] Coxe, III, 267-268.

who were almost to the walls of Vienna, and Frederick desired an opportunity to fortify Silesia and rid himself of entangling alliances. The Treaty of Ober-Schnellendorf was but a strategic maneuver on the part of both contestants, and a most treacherous one toward his allies on the part of Frederick of Prussia.[36]

III

While Maria Theresa was spellbinding the Hungarians, the French and Bavarians completely overran upper Austria as far down the Danube as Linz, only two or three days' march from Vienna. Had they advanced upon the capital from the west while Frederick drove down from the north, Vienna might have fallen, and the victorious invaders could have dictated a peace to Maria Theresa from the Hofburg—a peace in which she would have been fortunate to retain even the crown of Hungary. But the Queen, with her deep faith in the protection of Providence, probably believed the same beneficent Hand that feeds the hungry sparrows and tempers the wind to the shorn lamb sowed discord among her enemies and saved her from destruction.[37]

A lack of unity among the invaders was foreordained by their diverging self-interests. Frederick's sole purpose was to extend his dominions; at that time he was thinking only of the retention of Silesia. France sought to humble her traditional enemy, Austria; the Elector of Bavaria was especially interested in the imperial crown, and wished to conquer Bohemia because he

[36] Guglia, I, 119–125; Bright, 19.
[37] Carlyle, IV, 92; Arneth, I, 318 seq.

thought that would enable him to intimidate the electors. In the conquest of Bohemia both France and Bavaria saw a common means of accomplishing what was uppermost in their minds; so they turned aside from Vienna and made the capture of Prague their goal.[38]

Frederick then saw the French and Bavarians advancing in his direction and became alarmed lest they might forget to stop at Prague, in which case they would ultimately arrive at Breslau or thereabout, thus endangering the metropolis of his newly-acquired Silesia. Although they were supposed to be his allies, he had no desire to have them too near his dominions. He feared they might begin dreaming the dreams of the ancient Romans and Macedonians and decide to conquer all Europe, including the Frederick who was already hoping that he might eventually be called "Great."

He realized that what he had in mind to do would very naturally provoke such an idea among the French and Bavarians, for he was at that very time in the act of abandoning his alliance with them by making a separate peace with Austria. He decided to pursue his own game, but, like a sly fox, to conceal his tracks carefully; hence he wished the Peace of Ober-Schnellendorf kept secret—at least until the Hungarians got into action to oppose his allies, who at any moment might change to enemies. Such a plan necessitated a conspiracy with Maria Theresa, and strange to say she fell in with the scheme; they put their heads together, and with the aid of England undertook to deceive all

[38] Guglia, I, 117.

The First Contest

Europe.[39] The queen was to carry out active maneuvers on Frederick's front, while he was to stage a bogus siege of Neisse. The result of this conspiracy was that Frederick hauled cannon into position and bombarded the town for four days, knocking into ruins about half the buildings and killing many citizens. As a gesture of deception this was surely vigorous.[40] Frederick also corrupted the British Ambassador who arranged the treaty, to such an extent that he gave out a written statement saying that the peace negotiations had been without result.

During this year Seckendorf, whom Maria Theresa had freed from an imprisonment imposed by her father, turned traitor and went over to the Bavarians to become their supreme commander. This abandonment of the Queen's cause was not due to any ill will on the part of Seckendorf; it was merely an attempt to get off a sinking ship in good time. The fact that he was placed in command of the Bavarian army shows how lightly the crime of treason was regarded in that year, when every power of Europe was striving to outdo its neighbors in crooked dealing.[41]

The Peace of Ober-Schnellendorf was a life-saver to Maria Theresa, for it removed her most efficient enemy and enabled her to concentrate upon a drive against the French and Bavarians. By splicing the remnants Neipperg had brought back from Mollwitz, two regiments from the garrison of Vienna, which was no

---

[39] Arneth, I, 334; Guglia, I, 224-225; *Oesterreichischer Erbefolge-Krieg*, II, 518.

[40] Carlyle, IV, 78-82; Arneth, I, 334; *Oesterreichischer Erbefolge-Krieg*, II, 534. The garrison at Neisse was ignorant of the fact that the siege was a ruse, and gave Frederick a stiff fight.

[41] Carlyle, IV, 360.

longer threatened, and the new recruits from Hungary, she organized an army of sixty thousand men, and placed it under the command of her husband who pleaded for an opportunity to redeem himself from the disgrace of Belgrade. But the hero of the campaign was destined to be Ludwig Andreas Khevenhüller, a veteran who had served under Prince Eugene. In the War of the Polish Succession Khevenhüller had won the reputation of being the best cavalry commander in the Austrian army, and he was still in the prime of life at fifty-eight. During the approach of the French and Bavarians, he had been repairing the dilapidated bastions of Vienna to resist the overwhelming foes coming from the west. Had the enemy actually reached the walls of the city, Khevenhüller would have shown them something reminiscent of the days of Niklas Salm and Bürgermeister Liebenberg.[42]

The garrison at Prague was still holding out, and Francis of Lorraine marched to its relief, but owing to his lack of energy, arrived one day late; Prague fell, and the first part of Cardinal Fleury's plot was brought to a successful conclusion.[43] Maria Theresa's husband had once more proved himself to be a poor warrior, so she replaced him by his brother, Prince Charles—at the same time letting Francis down softly by saying that she could not live without the immediate presence of her dear husband. Prince Charles—we should say General Traun who was with him—made a plan of campaign which was entirely different from what the enemy expected. To hold the invaders from

---
[42] *Ibid.*, 103; Guglia, I, 130 seq.
[43] Arneth, I, 340 seq.; Coxe, III, 270.

returning he took a strong position between Prague and Bavaria, while Khevenhüller, with a small force from Vienna, advanced to regain upper Austria, and if possible, conquer Bavaria. The plan was a good one and Khevenhüller carried out his part of it with great skill and energy; in a little while the Austrians had reconquered all their own territory and nearly all the dominions of the Elector of Bavaria, whose single-track mind was completely occupied with the idea of obtaining the imperial crown, even at the cost of his realm. He won the election through the intimidation of the electors by the French army, but the very day that he was crowned Emperor of the Germans the Austrians entered the capital of Bavaria. Some humorist of the day struck off a medal, bearing on one side a picture of Francis of Lorraine with the inscription, *"Aut Cæsar aut nihil"* (Either Emperor or nothing), and on the other side a likeness of the new Emperor with the inscription *"Et Cæsar et nihil"* (Both Cæsar and nothing).[44] Charles Albert had reached his goal only to find it one of the emptiest of empty honors, while the plans formed at Versailles had fallen down entirely.

This was one of the most successful campaigns ever carried out by the Austrian army, and since Prince Charles had been in supreme command, Maria Theresa seems to have given him the credit and formed the opinion that he was a great general; the opinion was erroneous and eventually cost her a great deal. The success of the campaign was the fruit of the combined

[44] Whitman, 234; Bright, 19.

efforts of the best two commanders in her service, Khevenhüller and Traun, both of whom were modest enough to remain in the background.[45]

The triumph of the Austrians immediately scared Frederick of Prussia so badly that he broke his secret Treaty of Ober-Schnellendorf, putting the blame—like Adam of old—upon the Queen by saying that she had violated the pledge of secrecy. Frederick, as usual, played the part of a lone wolf and did not join France and Bavaria, but made a hurried trip to Dresden where he induced the King of Saxony, who would rather have been excused, to forsake his amenities and serve under Prussia in attacking Maria Theresa on the north. Frederick was apparently convinced that the stubborn Queen would be completely overwhelmed by the weight of so many antagonists. Prince Charles immediately set out to meet the combined forces of the Prussians and Saxons, and fought the bloody Battle of Chotusitz, in which the Austrians were defeated.[46] In this battle Frederick led his army and completely redeemed himself from the secret disgrace which had worried him ever since the Battle of Mollwitz. But the King of Saxony soon had enough of war, and in the words of Frederick, "disgracefully abandoned his ally" to return to his soft life at Dresden. Frederick, again alarmed, sought and obtained another peace from Maria Theresa, with a second quitclaim deed to Silesia.[47]

---

[45] *Oesterreichischer Erbefolge-Krieg*, III, 257, IV, 679 seq.; Coxe, III, 271.
[46] Arneth, II, 51.
[47] Arneth, II, 76 seq.; Carlyle, IV, 166 seq.; Bright, 21. This was known as the Treaty of Breslau.

From this time forward the Queen's army met with uninterrupted success, and England became much more pronounced in her alliance. Walpole, who had always set the brakes when Parliament was about to offer money and soldiers to Austria, was driven from power and succeeded by Carteret, who openly avowed his willingness to place the immense resources of the British Empire behind the plucky Queen whom he conceived likely to become a little more than a counterweight to France. In fact, England was beginning to believe that, with the addition of British might, Maria Theresa could conquer the whole Continent. The British press was calling her the "Joan of Arc of the Danube," and chanting her beauty, cleverness, and virtue in harmonious refrains. England was proudly claiming the honor of having discovered her, brought her out, made her, and saying how old England "jolly well" meant to stand by her.[48]

Maria Theresa now felt that she could afford to swallow her pride and pay, or at least agree to pay, the price demanded by the shifty King of Sardinia, who as we have said, was always for sale to the highest bidder. This price was a portion of Lombardy and the Marquisate of Finale. The King became her ally and undertook to defend her Italian border against a raid which was being planned by France and Spain for the purpose of diverting her attention from Prague. The affairs of the Queen certainly looked beautiful when viewed from the Hofburg. Thus we see that merely because a young Queen in Vienna insisted upon holding what every ruler of Europe had agreed—by ratifica-

---

[48] Coxe, III, 259, 276–277.

tions of the Pragmatic Sanction—belonged to her, the dear people, who were more concerned about what they were to have for dinner than about the realms of kings and queens, found themselves fighting a world war comparable to the one which followed the murder of an Austrian Archduke in 1914.

The French army under Belleisle was soon shut into Prague, facing winter without provisions, and confronted with the necessity of arranging terms of surrender. Cardinal Fleury then made overtures for peace with Austria by writing a most contrite letter to Königseg, who commanded the army before the beleaguered city. In this letter the dear old Cardinal actually begged for peace, and based his plea upon grounds that were largely personal. He exculpated himself and placed the blame for the whole plot to dismember Austria upon Marshal Belleisle who, as the Cardinal claimed, had undermined the Chancellor's influence at the corrupt court of Louis XV. Königseg immediately sent this letter to the Queen.[49]

This was the first time Maria Theresa ever received an important appeal for mercy, and she quickly revealed the fondness for revenge which was to become one of the marked traits of her character. The letter, which must have cost the eighty-nine-year-old Cardinal much pride and perhaps not a few tears, was immediately published to the world by the Queen. He then wrote another, protesting over such a breach of diplomatic confidence; it likewise was published, but neither letter was answered.

Marshal Belleisle offered to capitulate if allowed to

---

[49] Arneth, II, 108; Bright, 21. For the full text of this very humble letter, see *Oesterreichischer Erbefolge-Krieg*, V, 611.

return to France with his arms and baggage. When this proposal reached Vienna it created a lively discussion in the court, one in which the Queen found herself on one side and everybody else, including her husband, on the other. Her court thought it wise to accept the offer because of the difficulty in maintaining a siege during the winter, and the distress necessarily imposed upon the inhabitants of Prague who were citizens of the Austrian Monarchy,[50] but the Queen indignantly and vehemently refused to listen to any terms for Belleisle except unconditional surrender. In order to quell all discussion she called her court together, and without asking anybody's opinion, made a defiant statement well worth quoting:

"I will grant no capitulation to the French army. I desire no proposition nor project from the Cardinal; let him address himself to my allies. I am astonished that he should make any advances; he, who by money and promises, incited all the German princes to crush me. I have acted with too much condescension toward the court of France. Compelled by actual necessity, I debased my royal dignity by writing to the Cardinal in terms which would have softened the most obdurate rocks; he insolently rejected my entreaties, and the only answer I obtained was that His Most Christian Majesty had contracted obligations which he could not violate. I can prove by documents in my possession, that the French endeavored to start sedition in the very heart of my dominions; that they sought to put aside the fundamental laws of the Empire and set fire to the four corners of Germany; and I will transmit these

[50] Coxe, III, 281.

proofs to posterity as a warning to the Empire against France." [51] This was the same Maria Theresa who stood with the infant Joseph in her arms weeping so helplessly before the Hungarian assembly less than two years before. What rendered the spirited statement a trifle amusing was that all suspected it was aimed at her husband as much as at Cardinal Fleury.

Marshal Belleisle, instead of surrendering as he should have done had he cared a whit for the lives of common soldiers, slipped out of Prague on the sixteenth of December, and with tremendous sacrifice of life and untold suffering on the part of his army, made his way to Eger. Pelzel says, "The roads were dreadful to behold; they were littered with corpses; heaps of one and two hundred men, each with their officers, stiffened in the frost or dead from fatigue." [52] Carlyle in his "Frederick the Great" says, "There have been three expeditions or retreats of this kind which were very cold: that of the Swedes under the great Elector (not to mention that of Karl XII's army out of Norway after poor Karl got shot); that of Napoleon from Moscow; and this one of Belleisle, which was the only one brilliantly conducted, and not ending in rout and annihilation." [53]

Marshal Belleisle, who set forth so auspiciously and enthusiastically with forty thousand men selected from the flower of his nation's manhood, to give law to the Germans and rob an inexperienced young queen of her inherited dominions, came back on a stretcher, with eight thousand sick and exhausted men ready to totter

[51] Arneth, II, 110; Bright, 22.
[52] Pelzel, 881, quoted by Coxe, III, 286; Khevenhüller-Metsch, I, 113.
[53] Carlyle, IV, 221 seq.

into their graves. At first the French people rather avoided him because he smelled too strongly of fresh blood, but presently he was received at Versailles and wined and dined by a dissolute king and his mistress, and in the end became a hero and left a name and fame still venerated by the French nation. But at what a price this glory was bought! Like most such reputations in history, the cost was never named, because none ever knew it except those whose tongues were silenced in death.

When Marshal Belleisle quit Prague, he left a guard of six thousand to protect the sick and wounded. Chevert, who was in command, was immediately summoned by Prince Charles to surrender. The reckless Chevert answered: "Tell the Prince that if he will not grant me the honors of war, I will set fire to the four corners of Prague and find my grave in its ashes!" A desire to save the capital of Bohemia caused the Austrians to allow the French to depart unmolested, and this remnant of Belleisle's army left in much more comfort and safety than the main body.[54] Thus the whole French army, like a big fish, slipped off the Queen's line and flopped back into the water just as she was about to drop it into her basket. Sir Thomas Robinson said the Queen's mental agony over this unexpected turn of events was pitiable to witness. She was so provoked by the inefficiency of her commanders that she vowed only the fact that she was perpetually disabled by confinements prevented her from taking command of her army in person.[55]

[54] Coxe, III, 286; Arneth, II, 138.
[55] Carlyle, IV, 226.

IV

We may put it down as a rule to which there are but few exceptions, that all the great characters of history have been princes of propaganda. The pharaohs set the pace when they carved records of their mighty deeds all over the temples and tombs of ancient Egypt; Alexander followed their example when he traced his ancestry to Amen-Re in the Temple of Luxor; Cæsar wrote his own bombastic story of how he conquered the Gauls; and we might add that Napoleon was one of the best advertisers of them all. This ponderous introduction is perhaps more than sufficient for what we are now about to tell. Maria Theresa was not unlike our "Teddy" Roosevelt when it came to exciting enthusiasm by exhibiting herself in public. Her faith in the divine right of kings and queens was no less exalted than that of the other Hapsburgs, but unlike most of them, she improved every favorable opportunity to sweep her subjects off their feet in frenzied adoration, by joining them in the celebration of victories.

In spite of her disappointment at the escape of the French army, she dried her tears and appeared in person for a grand jubilee over the recovery of Prague. She went to the capital and had herself crowned Queen of Bohemia with wildest acclaim. In the coronation fêtes she drove four horses in one of the Roman chariot races, and saw to it that her sister Maria Anna did likewise. We may easily imagine the applause with which such a reckless, dramatic act of daring was received. All the wild scenes enacted on the coronation hill at Pressburg were repeated in Prague. The Bohemians screamed themselves hoarse crying, "Long live our noble Queen, Maria Theresa! We will die for Her Exalted Majesty, the Queen!"[56]

The recovery of Bohemia was a milepost in the reign of Maria Theresa. For the first time since her accession she was recognized as ruler in the three most important of her hereditary dominions, Hungary, Austria, and Bohemia; and instead of Silesia she was in possession of Bavaria, which more than balanced the territory lost. She was favored with powerful allies, such as England, Sardinia, and Saxony, and on most friendly terms with Czarina Elizabeth of Russia. She had humbled her archenemies of France, Cardinal Fleury and Marshal Belleisle, while the Elector of Bavaria, now almost a pauper with his imperial crown, was groveling at her feet and begging for mercy. She had accomplished all this in less than three years. Maria Theresa had every reason to be satisfied, but she was not, for she had not yet wiped out her grudge against Frederick of Prussia whose name led all the rest in her bad book.[57]

V

During the early part of the summer of 1743 Maria Theresa was riding the crest of a wave of triumph. She was no longer fighting to defend the Pragmatic Sanction and save herself from complete destruction, but flushed with victory, assumed the mental attitude of a conqueror, and like so many other great characters, does not command our admiration in success to the same degree that she does in adversity. She immedi-

[56] Coxe, III, 287.
[57] *Oesterreichischer Erbefolge-Krieg*, V, 274.

ately began dreaming of conquests; she would annex Bavaria, recover the lost Province of Lorraine for her husband, and in the end regain Silesia and dismember the domains of the King of Prussia.[58]

It is not difficult to trace the psychological steps by which she very naturally arrived at such determinations. In dispossessing the Emperor, formerly Elector of Bavaria, she was merely paying back in kind what he had plotted to do when he united with France for the purpose of dismembering her dominions and depriving her house of the imperial crown. To punish him for the latter offense, which he had actually brought to completion, she planned to depose him and substitute her husband as Emperor. Then she could not resist the temptation to win back Lorraine, which had been extorted from her husband as the price of her hand in marriage. She knew this sacrifice had lingered most unpleasantly in her consort's mind; the day she restored their ancient heritage to the Lorraines would be one of the happiest she had ever experienced. As for Frederick, she longed to see him on his knees begging for mercy from the woman he had wronged. In Maria Theresa's mind she was no longer fighting in defense; she was in quest of retribution, conquest and revenge.

While all these schemes were most natural, under the circumstances they were not very wise, because her hopes of executing them were based upon false assumptions concerning her allies and enemies. She had not yet learned the lesson, later so forcibly called to her attention by Kaunitz, that self-interest is at the bottom of all diplomatic undertakings. She did not realize

---

[58] Bright, 27.

that England cared little or nothing for her plans, but was interested solely in keeping her strong so that she might serve as a check to the French; that the King of Sardinia was looking out for himself alone; and that Frederick would never sit quietly in Berlin while his enemy in Vienna sealed his fate. Maria Theresa was a better psychologist in adversity than in triumph.[59]

The Queen's hopes were greatly buoyed by the death of the ninety-year-old Cardinal Fleury—on the thirtieth of January, 1743—and still more exalted by the decision of Louis XV, whom she knew to be a weak ruler, to be his own chancellor in imitation of his great predecessor, Louis XIV.[60] She foresaw that the French government would be in the hands of various ministers who were not likely to act in harmony. Cardinal Tencin, a licentious prelate, was to be Minister of State; Argenson, who knew more about law than arms, became Minister of War; Orry, who was parsimonious in all expenditures except those which gratified the lust of his king, was to be Controller; and Maurepas, famous only for his wit and pleasing manners, was named Minister of the Marine. It was a weak government as Maria Theresa knew, very much to her own satisfaction.[61]

The attitude of England at this time seemed most favorable. At the request of George II, Parliament voted another subsidy of three hundred thousand pounds to Austria, and two hundred thousand to Austria's ally, the King of Sardinia. Russia had formed an alliance with England, and the Netherlands joined in

[59] *Oesterreichischer Erbefolge-Krieg*, V, 274-275.
[60] Guglia, I, 197.
[61] Coxe, III, 289.

the coalition against France with more vigor than before.[62]

The plan of campaign for the summer was for the Austrians, under Prince Charles, to march west and unite with the British advancing from Hanover. After the union, Charles was to turn to the conquest of Alsace and Lorraine. For some months the British had kept an army in Hanover, but it had been there merely to guard the province against the French, who had now gone toward Prague under Maillebois in a fruitless attempt to relieve Belleisle. The British were apparently free and set out to unite with the Austrians, but in this enterprise they were soon opposed by a hastily assembled force of the French, who managed to cut their communications and imperil the whole British army. Finally they were hemmed in but extricated themselves in the renowned Battle of Dettingen—celebrated principally because King George was present and escaped being captured. Although the claim of victory on the part of the British rested upon the fact that they managed to get out of a bad predicament, the battle was celebrated in both Vienna and London as a great triumph.[63] In reality it was a defeat in that it meant a failure of England's part of the campaign, and a retreat in which the sick and wounded were abandoned to the mercy of the enemy.

Prince Charles, in command of the Queen's army, set out with great vigor and was soon at the Rhine in his advance upon Alsace, but on the way he halted to visit King George at Hanau, and confer on the plan

---

[62] Arneth, I, 201; Robinson to Carteret, July 3, 1743.
[63] Carlyle, IV, 226 seq.; Arneth, II, 259; Bright, 23; *Oesterreichischer Erbefolge-Krieg*, V, 277.

The First Contest

of campaign. At this conference the King revealed that he was worried over something which was at that very moment, the source of keen pleasure and fond hope to Maria Theresa—the sad condition of Emperor Charles VII. It soon became apparent that the Emperor had been fingering at the heartstrings of King George, and had found one attached to very tender emotions because it was also linked to a strong self-interest.[64]

Emperor Charles VII, stripped of his dominion of Bavaria and completely helpless at Frankfort, had appealed to King George to mediate between him and Maria Theresa, and in this appeal was strongly backed by Frederick of Prussia. George seemed to think something should be done to relieve the distress of the poor Emperor, who in spite of all his mistakes, was entitled to fair consideration as a monarchial being. Frederick thought so too, and also felt that order should be restored in the Holy Roman Empire of the Germans, and the imperial office returned to its original dignity and prestige.[65] What lay back of these openly expressed sentiments was something entirely different. King George wished to remove Bavaria from the list of Maria Theresa's enemies so that she could devote her full strength—and the subsidies received from England —against France; Frederick desired to prevent any advancement of Austria through her annexation of Bavaria, since such an addition to the Queen's power would surely result in another attempt to recover Silesia.

King George listened very sympathetically to the pleas of the Emperor, and presently they united in a

[64] Arneth, II, 262 seq.
[65] Coxe, III, 295.

treaty. Charles VII renounced all claims to the dominions of the Hapsburgs—we forget whether this was the third or fourth time he had done this—and received George's promise to support a demand upon Maria Theresa for a restoration of Bavaria to the Emperor; also England was to grant the Emperor a nice subsidy. King George apparently believed the Queen would be so delighted at the renunciation of the Emperor's claim that she would gladly return all the winnings from her victories over Bavaria. Some historians intimate that he even expected her to be grateful for his brotherly act in securing this renunciation for her at such a low cost; George thought the psychology of Charles VI over his Pragmatic Sanction still pervaded the court of Vienna.[66]

But the King very soon discovered his mistake. Maria Theresa was indignant that he had taken upon himself the task of attending to something which she regarded as her own business, and in doing so, almost knocked to staves her carefully constructed plans to avenge herself upon the Emperor, and at the same time secure a compensation for the loss of Silesia by annexing Bavaria. Here we see the very beginning of an estrangement between Austria and England, one which was destined to grow until it revolutionized the politics of Europe—perhaps we might say of the world. The misunderstanding destroyed the unity of the allies to such an extent that the entire summer passed without any effective movement against the French.

Without expressing any opinion as to the merits of

---

[66] Carlyle, IV, 365; Guglia, I, 191.

The First Contest 143

this controversy, we might again call attention to the fact that it grew out of the difference between the self-interests of England and Austria. England was on the Continent with money and soldiers for the sole purpose of gaining an ascendancy over France; Austria was in the war to defend the rights of her Queen, and recover Silesia or secure some compensation for its loss; each looked at diplomacy through a colored glass.

This year's campaign in Italy was also disappointing to the Queen. Her mind was so completely centered on the affairs of the north that she rather neglected the King of Sardinia whose head was full of schemes which did not coincide with hers. Not being well supported, he became offended at the Queen and threatened to unite with France and Spain in opposition to Austria and England. This brought a prompt response from King George who again took it upon himself to play big brother to the Queen. He framed an alliance of England, Sardinia, and Austria, and provided the King of Sardinia with another subsidy. In this treaty King George unfortunately undertook to secure certain cessions of territory to Sardinia, evidently supposing the Queen would be glad to grant them in return for the continuation of such a valuable alliance.[67]

Maria Theresa again felt degraded and had no hesitancy in saying so. She thought of herself as a conqueror who was able to negotiate her own treaties in her own way. All that kept her from breaking with England entirely was her sore need of the British subsidies, without which she could hardly continue the war. England laid down the money and was thereby enabled

[67] Arneth, II, 279.

to lay down the law; the Queen swallowed her pride and accepted the terms arranged for her. They were known as the Treaty of Worms.[68]

During the reign of Maria Theresa subsidies of this character were very common, and not regarded as in any way dishonorable. Almost every power in Europe gave or received assistance in this manner. Later, Austria received a similar subsidy from France; Prussia received one from England and once gave such aid to Russia; at another time Austria was even subsidized by Turkey, while the American colonies received large sums from France during the Revolution.

The Treaty of Worms contained a secret clause introduced especially to conciliate the Queen; George II probably wished many times afterward that it had been omitted. The signatories agreed to do their best to expel the Bourbons from Italy, and in the division of spoils, Maria Theresa was to receive Naples and Sicily. From this time forward, the Queen was continually nagging King George because she thought he was making no effort to carry out this clause—something he probably never had any intention of straining himself to accomplish, and preferred very much to forget.

The summer of 1743, which had opened so auspiciously for the Queen, ended without anything of importance—from her standpoint—having been achieved except the generation of a feeling of suspicion toward her best ally. Her sweet hope of avenging herself upon Emperor Charles VII and annexing Bavaria, had almost turned to vinegar, and she had made no progress

---

[68] Guglia, I, 201; Bright, 24.

toward her other goals, which were the recovery of Silesia and Lorraine.

VI

The winter of 1743–44 saw much internal strife and turmoil in England. A party strongly opposed to rendering further assistance to Maria Theresa arose under the Pelhams, and it was with great difficulty that George II and Carteret prevented the British from completely abandoning the Continental war. The people had grown weary of pouring out blood and treasure in what was beginning to be regarded as a sentimental attachment, and insisted that John Bull get over his affair with the Queen of Sheba of the Danube, and go about his business like a mature man of reason and judgment. Also, many thought England should forget the King's petty dominion of Hanover—which was not worth what it was costing—and strive only to become mistress of the seas and to build India and North America into the British Empire.

But during the winter and early spring this opposition was completely squelched by a most unexpected event. We have already mentioned how all the nations of Europe were taking lessons from the wolf of Berlin. Wolf-diplomacy was the fashion, and one of its marked characteristics was the abolishment of all preliminaries before beginning hostilities in war. A wolf never sends a lamb notice of his intention to feast upon its carcass the following night. War in those days was usually fought for plunder, and giving notice often defeated the very purpose for which war was made. The idea was to strike quickly, hard, and unexpectedly; to seize and then defend what was acquired. For a nation to sound an alarm by preliminary notes and declarations was just as silly as for a burglar to ring the doorbell before breaking into a house. The shining example of the merits of the new system was Frederick's conquest of Silesia. He was soon to furnish another by an up-to-date seizure of Bohemia.

In February of 1744, France, without giving any warning, sent a formidable squadron across the channel with troops to invade England. Her intention seemed to be to steal up behind John Bull while he was gazing at promised lands beyond the water, seize and disarm him, then either plunder—or possibly annex—the British Isles, according to the new method recently discovered in Berlin. The fleet appeared off the Isle of Wight and was on the point of attempting to disembark an army when a tempest arose and drove the French ships back to the coast of France. At almost the same time, the French fleet which had been lying in the harbor of Toulon, sailed into the Mediterranean and fought an indecisive battle with the British. It was true that the landing of a French army would probably have been interrupted by British warships concealed in the harbor, but the people of England lost confidence in their navy and many declared that only an act of God had saved the country, which was so torn with internal strife as to be almost helpless before a foreign invasion.[69] A wave of terror, somewhat comparable to that of a flock of sheep when a hound leaps at the fence of a corral, swept across England.

This outbreak of hostilities was followed by a dec-

---

[69] Lord Horatio Walpole, *Memoirs*, II, 67–68.

The First Contest

laration of war on the part of France, so England and France suddenly found themselves contending in dead earnest over the dominion of the world. It was an issue of such vast importance as to convert the Queen's contention into a mere episode; they had actually taken little Maria Theresa's war away from her through "main force and awkwardness." In the light of this new condition, Continental affairs appeared entirely different to the people of England. France was out to conquer the earth because Austria had been too weak to hold her in check; there was no longer any argument over the advisability of strengthening the Queen; it had been all too forcibly demonstrated. It was not a matter of sentiment, after all, but a matter of life or death to England.[70]

Nor was this the end of the demonstration. Soon a French army of one hundred thousand men assembled in Flanders and began sweeping through the Low Countries toward Hanover, very much as the Germans swept in the opposite direction at the beginning of the World War. In Marshal Saxe, a foreigner, the French had found a commander who moved with the speed of a Napoleon. Since all this country was immensely valuable to England commercially she could hardly rest supinely while France annexed it.

At the same time, Prince Charles burst into Alsace, and began a rapid conquest of Alsace and Lorraine for Maria Theresa. Both France and Austria seemed on the verge of helping themselves to what they desired, while England stood on the side as an amazed spectator. The British troops had been largely withdrawn

---

[70] *Oesterreichischer Erbefolge-Krieg*, VI, 289 seq.

to England to take care of internal disturbances. The French were apparently more intent upon a conquest of the Low Countries than a defense of Lorraine, but presently they were able to detach a strong force which, under the command of the King, set out to meet the Austrians in Alsace and Lorraine.

Then came another big surprise, one which might have been anticipated, but apparently was not. Frederick of Prussia, partly because he dared not allow Maria Theresa to become too strong, and partly because he also saw a rich land of promise near at hand, began another war on Austria and set out to seize Bohemia. Almost before the Queen realized he was at war, he had reached and captured Prague, which had been left with an insufficient garrison.[71] While Frederick's invasion seemed very precipitate, it had in reality been carefully and secretly prepared. He had come to an understanding with Bavaria and probably with France. The Bavarians were also to advance in the direction of Prague and together they were to sever the army under Prince Charles from Austria. Then, with the assistance of France, the Prince's army was to be ground as if between two millstones. What would be the final outcome of this well-laid plan Frederick had probably not fully determined, but he foresaw the conquest of Bohemia for himself and that was all that interested him.[72]

Fortunately for Maria Theresa several delays occurred. The Bavarians were not as active and enthusiastic as the Prussians. They were more concerned in driving the Austrians out of their own territory, and when

---

[71] Carlyle, IV, 342; Coxe, III, 304.
[72] Carlyle, IV, 339; Guglia, I, 224-225.

this was accomplished, winter arrived and cooled their ardor. The French army advancing to meet Prince Charles was delayed by an illness of the King, and the Prince crossed the Rhine ere Louis, nursed by a mistress and a queen, was restored to health.[73] When the King recovered it was late in the season, and recalling the recent wintry experience of Marshal Belleisle, Louis abandoned the pursuit of the Austrians. This time Prince Charles had General Traun, a most resourceful Hungarian commander, with him, and before long the Austrians managed to get behind Frederick and pinch off his communications with Prussia and Silesia. For a while he subsisted fairly well by foraging from the country about Prague, but Maria Theresa had gone to Pressburg on another mission of spellbinding, and soon secured the assistance of Hungarian "rough-riders" who cleaned up Frederick's outposts and left him without food.

Maria Theresa's second appeal to Hungary was most interesting and picturesque. She again availed herself of the services of her good friend John Palfy who raised her standards and soon enlisted seventy-four thousand men. Forty-four thousand immediately went to the field, and thirty thousand were held in reserve. In spite of his gout, the white-haired octogenarian succeeded in electrifying all Hungary with enthusiasm for the Queen who as a girl, had been commended to his care by his old comrade, Prince Eugene of Savoy.

---

[73] The mistress was Madame Châteauroux. During this illness, Louis XV, believing himself about to die, repented of his sins, dismissed his mistress and sent for his Queen. But, upon recovering, promptly returned to his evil ways.

In token of her appreciation Maria Theresa sent Palfy her favorite horse, a sword with a gold hilt set with diamonds, and a costly ring. With these valuable presents was a letter which read: "Father Palfy, I send you this horse, worthy of being mounted by none but the most zealous of my faithful subjects; receive at the same time this sword to defend me against my enemies; and take this ring as a mark of my affection for you." [74]

In speaking of this event a contemporary said: "The amazing unanimity of a people, so divided among themselves as the Hungarians, especially in point of religion, could only have been effected by the address of Maria Theresa, who seemed to be capable of making every man, with whom she came into contact, a hero. The wildest enthusiasm in favor of this captivating princess spread from the aged Palfy to the meanest vassal of the kingdom." [75]

Frederick was soon compelled to abandon Prague and retreat in the direction of Silesia, losing much of his army by exposure and capture on the way. His campaign had frozen out and he considered himself fortunate to escape complete destruction. While the credit for this defeat of Frederick has usually been given to Prince Charles, those best informed on the military affairs of the time say it really belonged to Traun, and the promptness with which Maria Theresa succeeded in securing help from Hungary.[76]

The year 1744 brought a great calamity in the death of Field Marshal Khevenhüller, who had proved himself to be the most capable commander in the Austrian

---

[74] Arneth, II, 411; Tindal, Chap. XXI, 76, quoted by Coxe, III, 305.
[75] Coxe, III, 305.
[76] Carlyle, IV, 366 seq.

army. When he was taken ill the Queen immediately went to visit him, a mark of affectionate condescension none of her predecessors would have deigned to show. He died in January.

In selecting his successor, Maria Theresa defied the traditions of her house by passing over the names of several high-born aspirants and naming a man of real merit, Count Traun, a Hungarian, though she did not have the courage to place him over her brother-in-law, Prince Charles.[77] When Traun accompanied the Prince the army was usually successful. When the Prince was alone in command it almost always met with disaster.

During this year Maria Theresa again failed completely to realize her hope of restoring the Province of Lorraine, and nothing was accomplished in her behalf in Italy, but she was by no means downhearted, for she had humbled Frederick of Prussia. That was more than enough to balance all her disappointments.

VII

On January twentieth, 1745, Emperor Charles VII, formerly Elector of Bavaria, sinking beneath his heavy load of humiliation and misfortune, died in Munich. Few Emperors of the Holy Roman Empire of the Germans had such a disappointing career. Having been made Emperor through the intrigues of Cardinal Fleury, he had found France a very heartless master.[78] In spite of his high office most of his time was spent in a miserable exile, completely abandoned by the power from which he expected protection. On his death-

[77] Arneth, II, 352.
[78] Ibid., III, 4.

bed he warned his son, Maximilian Joseph, to make peace with the House of Austria, and never permit any power to induce him to aspire to the imperial crown.[79]

The death of Charles immediately started a wild scramble for the imperial crown. Although Louis XV was not an elector, his court was soon busy with intrigues to prevent the election of Maria Theresa's husband, who was sure to be a candidate. The French exhorted Maximilian Joseph to disregard his father's dying admonitions, revive the claims of his house to the dominions of the Hapsburgs, and become a candidate for Emperor, but Maximilian was unmoved. The King of Saxony was also solicited, but having recently formed an alliance with Austria, he refused to enter the race.[80] Frederick of Prussia aspired to the office, but knew the other electors were too jealous of his recent successes to permit him to secure such an additional advantage. The choice simmered down to Maria Theresa's husband, but, while his election was comparatively certain, there was a disposition everywhere to extort something from the Queen before agreeing to give him votes.[81]

England was in favor of Francis, but much worried over the entrance of Frederick into another war with Maria Theresa—a war which had so completely consumed her power as to render her useless as a check

---

[79] Carlyle, IV, 403; Bright, 35 seq.; Robinson to Harrington, Jan. 20, 1745.

Maximilian Joseph was then but eighteen years old, but this did not prevent France and Prussia from urging him to enter the race for the imperial crown.

[80] Arneth, III, 30.

[81] *Oesterreichischer Erbefolge-Krieg*, VI, 166 seq.

The First Contest 153

to France. England now needed Austrian assistance very badly, but was tired of putting good hard pounds into what she considered a misappropriation of funds; she wanted every shilling's worth of fight she bought used on Louis XV, and not on the King's nephew Frederick. The obvious course for England to pursue was to put an end to the war between Austria and Prussia. With this object in view Sir Thomas Robinson, the British Ambassador in Vienna, arrived one morning at the Hofburg and made the following speech:[82]

"England has this year supplied Austria with one million seventy-eight thousand seven hundred and fifty-three pounds, not to mention the subsidies expected by the Electors of Cologne and Bavaria. The English nation is not in condition, in a war like the present, to maintain such essential financial superiority, and, by endeavoring to provide for so many services, will fail in all; the strength of the enemy must therefore be reduced; and, as France cannot be detached from Prussia, Prussia must be detached from France. This return the English nation expects for all it has done for the House of Austria. What is to be done must be done immediately, and at once, while France is hesitating over the subsidies demanded by the King of Prussia, which, if once granted, will fix him irrevocably." Sir Thomas Robinson then demanded that the Queen immediately make peace with Prussia by ceding whatever was necessary to secure it.[83]

Maria Theresa remonstrated against such harsh demands and a very spirited conversation occurred. She expressed her eagerness for another blow at Frederick.

[82] Coxe, III, 323.
[83] Carlyle, IV, 479.

"Let me but have until October," she pleaded. "If I knew I must make peace with him tomorrow, I would fight him this evening." Sir Thomas was compelled to abandon all hope of securing her consent to make peace immediately with Prussia.[84]

Maria Theresa might have anticipated what was to happen very promptly, but apparently she did not. She was still diplomatically unsophisticated, and thought England was imbued with some sort of friendship, such as occasionally exists between old-fashioned individuals. She was very quickly enlightened. George II, excusing himself on the ground of domestic disturbances, united with Frederick of Prussia in the Treaty of Hanover, in which the kings mutually guaranteed their existing territories, which meant of course, that England had underwritten Frederick's right to Silesia.[85] George II knew very well that this would be a severe shock to his ally, Maria Theresa, but he believed she would submit to it without much complaint if the blow were softened by securing the election of her husband as Emperor of the Germans. For this reason he had pledged Frederick to support Francis, which practically insured his election, since Maria Theresa had already secured the support of the young Elector of Bavaria by the Treaty of Füssen, in which the Elector relinquished all claim to the possessions of the House of Hapsburg, and in return for the Queen's protection, became her active ally against France.

Frederick, sure that the Queen would ratify the Treaty of Hanover, spread the report that the war was over, suspended hostilities, and began negotiating with

[84] Arneth, III, 89; Robinson to Lord Harrington, Aug. 3, 1745.
[85] Coxe, III, 326; Arneth, III, 92.

The First Contest

Prince Charles for an armistice. King George had agreed to use his good offices to secure this ratification, and since Frederick and Maria Theresa were just then fighting over nothing but Silesia—Frederick having abandoned for the present the idea of annexing Bohemia—the treaty transferred England to Frederick's side, and he thought this meant a cessation of the subsidies without which the Queen would be unable to continue the contest.

But Maria Theresa received the news of this treaty with much resentment and a spirited display of indignation toward England. She had regarded George II as her best ally, but suddenly the witch of Potsdam dropped a magician's scarf over her friend's countenance, and when it was withdrawn, lo, there stood an enemy! She never recovered from the shock of that startling revelation. Like a young woman when she first discovers that her *fiancé* is untrue, the Queen was crushed for a while. After that came defiance, and in the end, hate and enmity.[86]

Augustus of Saxony, who had been the Queen's enemy in the beginning of the war, was seized with fear—completely justified by later events—that Frederick would annex a part or all of Saxony if relieved of the opposition of Austria, so he also pretended to be indignant and did everything possible to stir the Queen's wrath.

Maria Theresa sent word to Prince Charles to disregard all overtures for peace and immediately engage the Prussians in battle. Frederick, believing the war was over, had allowed his army to become much re-

[86] Bright, 40–45. At this time Maria Theresa made overtures to France for a separate peace.—See Arneth, III, 190 seq.

duced and felt unable to meet the Austrians, who outnumbered the Prussians two to one, in an open battle. He prepared to retreat to Silesia while Prince Charles endeavored to head him off and compel an action, quite confident that the Prussian fox had at last put his foot into a trap.

Very much to the Prince's surprise, Frederick suddenly turned and attacked the Austrians with great fury. In this celebrated Battle of Sohr, Frederick outgeneraled Prince Charles and defeated him with fearful slaughter, thus snatching victory from the very arms of disaster. At the close of the battle, Frederick said, "Since the Austrians did not beat me this time, they can never beat me." [87]

The manner in which Frederick escaped, when she thought him as good as caught, was most disappointing to Maria Theresa. It was a sad reminder of the way Belleisle had slipped out of Prague in 1741, and again brought home to her the painful truth that her commanders were inefficient. She had been nursing the fond hope that her brother-in-law, Prince Charles, was an able general—another Prince Eugene—and the disillusionment greatly depressed her.

But Maria Theresa was a woman who always made the best of her circumstances and surroundings. She now saw an opportunity to secure the election of her husband to the imperial crown—something which ap-

---

[87] Bright, 42; Arneth, III, 114 seq.

Prince Charles blamed this defeat upon his soldiers, who, as he alleged in a letter to his brother Francis of Lorraine, refused to stand before the fire of the Prussians. Maria Theresa was inclined to relieve Prince Charles of his command, but yielded to the pleadings of her husband in behalf of his brother.

pealed to her very strongly, partly because she wished to bestow a great honor upon her consort, and partly because it meant a vindication of her house which under her reign, for the first time in centuries, had not held the office of emperor. All the intrigues of France failed to induce the Elector of Bavaria or the King of Saxony to become candidates, and Frederick was excluded by his promise to England under the Treaty of Hanover. No other candidate appeared, so Francis was elected without opposition on the thirteenth of September, and crowned on the fourth of October. The Queen went to Frankfort for the coronation, but would not consent to be crowned Empress because she knew her presence in the ceremonies would divert attention from her husband, and she very generously wished Francis to have one day of glory not eclipsed by his wife. When he returned from his coronation she ran to meet him, leading the crowd in crying, "Long live Emperor Francis I!" [88]

From this date Francis outranked his wife in title, although she was often called Empress-queen. In reality, he was only an emperor *en parade*, while his wife dominated all his official actions.

Maria Theresa, still at war with Frederick, formed the bold design of joining the Saxons in a drive on Berlin, but just as she was about to set forth on this enterprise Frederick compelled her to abandon it by suddenly invading Saxony and triumphantly capturing Dresden. The King of Saxony then pleaded pitifully for her to make peace with Prussia under some terms which would deliver him from his conqueror. Moved

[88] Arneth, III, 106; Carlyle, V, 14 seq.

by the distress of her ally rather than by her own difficulties, the plucky Queen accepted the mediation of England and signed the Treaty of Dresden, which restored his lost kingdom to Augustus of Saxony, but again confirmed the cession of Silesia to Frederick.[89]

This ended the campaign of 1745, in which Maria Theresa had had her cup thrice filled with bitter disappointments: first, by the conduct of England; second, by her failure to recover Silesia; and third, by the unsatisfactory termination of her campaign in Italy. Her only triumph of the year was the election of her husband to the imperial crown.

George II had succeeded in his purpose of making peace between Prussia and Austria in order that the latter might be free to oppose France, Frederick had renewed his grip upon Silesia, and Augustus of Saxony had been delivered from the sharp claws of Frederick of Prussia, but none of them had given such a fine exhibition of pluck and courage as had been displayed by Maria Theresa. She immediately began preparing for the next year's campaign with undiminished vigor. She had temporarily abandoned her fight to recover Silesia because she had been moved by pity for Augustus of Saxony, a pity he scarcely deserved.

During the summer of 1745, the English colonists in America came into the war with most astonishing results by capturing Louisburg, the key to all Canada because it controlled the mouth of the St. Lawrence River.[90] Of such vast importance was this conquest to

---

[89] Arneth, III, 165.

[90] This expedition was fitted out in New England and commanded by Sir William Pepperell. Louisburg surrendered on the 16th of June after a prolonged siege.

The First Contest 159

England that it offset in advance all the territory the French were destined to win in the Netherlands by their brilliant campaign of the next year. The French were fully aware of the importance of Louisburg, for, with the English colonists holding the Atlantic coast from Nova Scotia to Virginia, France was completely severed from the great empire she had dreamed of possessing in the New World. During the remainder of the war the dominating motive of the French was to recover the cherished road to their colonies in North America.

At this point it is interesting to pause and notice how far the war, which had lasted five years and involved three continents, had drifted from its original moorings. Saxony and Bavaria, Maria Theresa's most active opponents at the beginning, were now fighting at her side; Frederick of Prussia had been in and out of the contest three times; the King of Sardinia had once almost gone over to the other side for higher pay; and France and England, who at first were nothing more than auxiliaries, had now become the principals.[91] It was preëminently a war among monarchs in which the common people were sacrificed like pawns in a game of chess, and it supplied one of the best arguments against the monarchial form of government to be found in all history. No king or queen had been wounded in battle or deprived of food and shelter on account of the vast destruction of property, but thousands of helpless subjects had been pressed into armies and lost their lives fighting for something which meant little or nothing to them.

[91] Bright, 52.

VIII

William Coxe in his *History of the House of Austria* says: "The rapid progress of the Prussian arms against Saxony was ultimately a fortunate circumstance for the House of Austria; as it overcame the obstinacy of Maria Theresa, and reduced her to the necessity of concluding peace with the enemy against whom she had in vain sacrificed her best troops, and who clogged all her operations for the security of her distant dominions."[92] To this we might add that a peace with Prussia was no less fortunate for Maria Theresa than for George II. In the spring of 1746, England found it necessary to withdraw nearly all her troops from the Continent to quell a rebellion in Scotland. This left the Queen to contend almost unaided with the French, who had become enemies of the English rather than the Austrians. At that time she might have sent back some of the admonitions so often received from England, which read: "Cease quarreling with your neighbors, so you may be strong to oppose France."

Had England been able at this period to do her share in the war against France, the rapid progress of the French army through Louvain, Mons, Charleroi, Antwerp, and Namur—names destined to be heard so often in the great World War—might have been checked.[93] As it was, Prince Charles was quite helpless before the conquering French under Marshal Saxe.

Maria Theresa had not foreseen this withdrawal of English soldiers, and had dispatched a large part of her troops to coöperate with the King of Sardinia

[92] Coxe, III, 232.
[93] *Oesterreichischer Erbefolge-Krieg*, VI, 343 seq.

(whom she had been obliged to neglect during the war with Prussia), in recovering her lost possessions in Italy. In this undertaking she was very successful, partly on account of the preponderance of her troops, but to a large degree because of an unforeseen event in distant Spain. Philip V died in July, 1746, thus removing Elizabeth Farnese from her domineering position in Spain. His son and successor, Ferdinand VI, was married to Barbara, a princess of Portugal, who was friendly with England, and a relative of Maria Theresa. Queen Barbara was destined to rule the royal house of Spain and soon ordered the Spanish troops out of Italy. In a short time Maria Theresa was in possession of all her former Italian provinces, but as usual under such circumstances, she coveted something more. Since she had not been able to recover Silesia she conceived the idea of compensating herself by the conquest of Naples and Sicily, out of which the Bourbons had swindled her father.

So absorbed was the Queen in her own interests that she seemed to forget how they conflicted with those of the King of Sardinia, who did not wish to have her capture Naples, and feared her ascendency in Italy might leave no room for his own expansion. The two armies failed to coöperate and the whole enterprise ended in a jangle of discordant movements, in which the Queen eventually lost Genoa through an insurrection. But at the end of the summer she still held all she had claimed in Italy at the time of her accession.[94]

Although France, at this period was desirous of making peace, Maria Theresa was still full of enthusiasm

---

[94] Bright, 48-50.

and eager to continue the war.[95] She had recently formed a very important alliance with Elizabeth of Russia, in which the Czarina had agreed to dispatch thirty thousand soldiers to the assistance of the Austrians in the Netherlands.[96] It was a long way from Russia to the Netherlands, but both these courageous women believed the distance could be covered by Russian troops in time to get them into the contest, provided the Queen could sustain the courage of the King of France who seemed on the verge of quitting. The Russian troops never reached their destination, but the fact that they were on the way was an important factor in the peace negotiations.

From this time forward, both the French and English fought with the peace conference constantly in mind; the French striving to secure a little more territory in the Netherlands, so as to be sure to have enough to make England willing to yield back her winnings, which were insignificant aside from Louisburg and Cape Breton; and the English struggling to prevent the French from getting more than they might be willing to exchange for what they had lost, which likewise simmered down to the same strategic point at the mouth of the St. Lawrence River. In the space of seven years, the central issue over which the long-drawn-out war was being waged had travelled very far—so far that on the Continent the original meaning of the war had been almost forgotten.

At about this time some humorist penned the following verse:

[95] *Ibid.*, 55. Bright thinks Maria Theresa was, in reality, eager for peace, and her pretended desire to continue the war largely bluff.
[96] Arneth, III, 138.

"For what have the gentry these long years been fighting?
For what have our statesmen been treating and writing?
For what have our thousands been killed, would you know?
Why, to make it as 'twas only five years ago."

IX

In their secret conferences the French and English soon discovered that the principal difficulty in framing a satisfactory peace was to find an accommodation for Don Philip, the son of Elizabeth Farnese, and a means of compensating Maria Theresa for the loss of Silesia; in other words, a scheme for quieting the two stormy female petrels. The former might be accomplished by taking the duchies of Parma, Piacenza, and Guastalla from Austria, but this only rendered the latter requirement all the more difficult to meet. Count Kaunitz, who very ably represented Maria Theresa, refused to listen to the loss of the Italian duchies unless at the same time, Naples or Silesia were bestowed upon his country as a compensation.[97] In order to bring the Queen to terms, Sir Thomas Robinson was instructed to interview her and threaten her with the loss of the Austrian Netherlands if she refused to yield, but in the midst of his speech she broke in with an indignant harangue: "You, Sir, who had such a large share in depriving me of Silesia; you, who contributed more than any other person in procuring from me additional cessions for the King of Sardinia; do you still think to persuade me? No! I am neither a child nor a fool! If you will have an instant peace, make it. I can negotiate for myself. Why am I always to be excluded from transacting

[97] Coxe, III, 352; Arneth, III, 366 seq.

my own business? Good God! how I have been misused by your court!"[98]

Sir Thomas Robinson then began reading a passage from a letter of the Duke of Newcastle: "An establishment for Don Philip, which, in the opinion of the King of England, cannot be more moderate, or liable to less inconvenience, than by yielding the Duchies of Parma and Piacenza, to revert to the present possessor should Don Philip succeed to the Kingdoms of Naples and Sicily in consequence of the accession of Don Carlos to the crown of Spain—"

At this point, the Queen made a significant gesture and exclaimed, "No, no! I would rather lose my head!" With this, she closed the interview.[99]

It was evident that the Queen had more fight in her blood; far too much fight to suit George II and Louis XV, who had had quite enough. The other belligerents went right ahead with negotiations for peace, resisted at every step by Maria Theresa, who declared she preferred to make her own treaties in her own way. Kaunitz, who represented her, several times asked to be relieved of his post, but she insisted that he remain at the conference to throw as many obstacles as possible into the wheels of progress.[100] There can be but little doubt that this display of stubbornness on the part of the Queen won much better terms than would otherwise have been accorded her, for all recognized that there would be no peace if Maria Theresa re-

---

[98] Bright, 42 and 59.
[99] Robinson to the Duke of Newcastle, May 1, 1748, quoted by Coxe, III, 353.
[100] Bright, 56, seq.

mained at war. Conditions must be such as she could be induced or compelled to accept.

At length the definite treaty was framed and signed at Aix-la-Chapelle by France, England, Holland, and Spain, in the order named, but the Empress-queen did not sign it until more than a month later, on the seventeenth of November, 1748. The treaty took the name of Aix-la-Chapelle, and its provisions were substantially as follows:

All conquests in Europe and America to be returned to the original owners; Parma, Piacenza, and Guastalla to be given to Don Philip, but eventually to revert to Austria; Modena and Genoa to retain what they had at the beginning of the war; cessions to the King of Sardinia to be made according to the Treaty of Worms; the House of Hanover to be confirmed in its right to the throne of England; Maria Theresa's husband to be recognized as Emperor of the Germans; and the Pragmatic Sanction to be ratified. As a mark of the distance to which this war had migrated we might note that Madras, on the east coast of India, which had been taken by the French, was returned to England; also that France recovered the mouth of the St. Lawrence River.[101]

Maria Theresa was very much dissatisfied with this treaty, and when the British Ambassador asked for an audience to congratulate her, she replied that condolences would be more in order, and begged him to spare her all conversations upon a subject which was to her highly disagreeable. But a little analysis of the

[101] Coxe, 357 seq.; Arneth, III, 385 seq.

terms reveals that she should have been more than satisfied. The results of her loud wails and vigorous display of wrath only prove that, in the affairs of this earth, those who are in a position to make their cries of protestation heard in high places, and do so most vigorously, usually receive great favors.

She had lost nothing but the relatively insignificant duchies of Parma, Piacenza, and Guastalla, for she had already three times signed away her rights to Silesia, and probably entertained no hope of recovering it in this final treaty to which Frederick of Prussia was not in reality a party. But before signing, she registered her protest over the loss of Silesia, and indicated her intention of not holding herself bound by the provisions of the treaty concerning that province. She had secured the recognition of all the leading nations of Europe as heir to the dominions of the Hapsburgs, and their acknowledgment of her husband as Emperor of the Germans. But that was by no means all; she had consolidated her inherited dominions into a fighting unit and done much to weld them into a real nation; also she had won the respect—we might almost say fear—of the greatest powers of the world.

England has sometimes claimed the credit for saving Maria Theresa, especially at the beginning of the Wars of Accession, but this claim is without very much merit.[102] The old files of the British newspapers show that the English people were moved to great sympathy for the Queen who seemed to be so helpless and so harshly treated by her covetous neighbors, but the real

---

[102] "It has been customary to speak of the chivalrous conduct of England in affording aid to the oppressed Queen. Such a vaunt is futile."—Bright, 23.

source of much of this feeling was probably hatred for France. The subsidies do not prove that the sympathy of the English people for the Queen was shared by their government. In September, 1741, the darkest period of the war for Maria Theresa, King George issued a declaration of neutrality because he feared Frederick might invade Hanover;[103] we may say that every pound of subsidy received from England sprang from selfish motives.[104] England feared the advancement of France which might result from a destruction of Austria.

On the other hand, Maria Theresa's loud wails and vigorous protestations do not prove that she was being imposed upon by England. The British government at times certainly attempted to intimidate and coerce the Queen by threatening to withhold subsidies, and arranging treaties behind her back for the purpose of overcoming her obstinacy, but in the end she usually turned the tables, and to a greater degree intimidated England; this is one of the best tokens of her cleverness. England's subsidies were neither loans nor gifts; they were, for the most part, the price paid for definitely stipulated assistance to England in opposing France. Early in the war, the arrangement brought more immediate benefit to Maria Theresa than to England, but after France declared war on England, the matter was reversed.

In the final balance Maria Theresa usually came out the winner. If Sir Thomas Robinson tried to bluff her by threats of withholding the subsidies, she met him by interposing that she could not supply the stipulated

[103] Sir Robert Walpole, *Memoirs*, I, 685.
[104] Coxe, III, 250; Arneth, V, pp seq.

troops without the subsidies. In fact she almost invariably fell short of the specified assistance but nearly always collected the subsidies in full. Her flares of ill temper toward the British Ambassador may be looked upon somewhat in the same light as the tears she spilled before the Hungarian assembly. Her motives in both instances were genuine, but there was always a definitely planned purpose beneath her outbursts.

Like most of the great characters of history, Maria Theresa had very high ambitions, supreme courage, and endless perseverance, but was never satisfied with her accomplishments. She was dissatisfied with the Treaty of Aix-la-Chapelle because she was not awarded Silesia or any territory which might be regarded as a compensation for its loss. But she had no more intention of abandoning her struggle to recover Silesia than of abdicating. She had sworn to hold the inherited dominions of her house intact, and there was no better method of assuring another war in Europe than by leaving this unfulfilled oath rankling in her breast.

To Maria Theresa herself belongs almost the sole credit of accomplishing what she did in this long, bitter struggle. None of her generals were better than second rate warriors, and at times she was much handicapped by permitting her incompetent husband to attempt to redeem himself from his military disgraces. Her loyalty to her family prompted her to place her brother-in-law, Prince Charles, in the supreme command which could have been exercised with much more credit by others. This was much to her disadvantage, since her enemies were commanded by exceptionably capable warriors, such as Frederick of Prussia, Marshal Belleisle, and Marshal Saxe. The truth is that Maria

The First Contest

Theresa won the Wars of Accession in spite of the fact that her armies were usually defeated. Her advisers, with the single exception of the unpopular Bartenstein, were all old and incompetent, and she was obliged to form her own diplomatic policies and plan her own campaigns.

In speaking of her ministers of this period, she said later, "Providence, by death, at last relieved me of counsellors too prejudiced to give useful advice, but too respectable to be dismissed." A chronicler of the times wrote: "At the beginning of her reign, Maria Theresa was without any army, without money, without credit, without experience or knowledge, and even without counsel, for her prime minister always gave his first attention to how the matter under consideration would affect himself." [105]

Finally, we might add that during the eight years of her Wars of Accession, Maria Theresa had seven babies and buried three children. More will be said of this in another chapter.

[105] Arneth, IV, 7.

VII

REFORMS IN THE MONARCHY

ALTHOUGH Maria Theresa manifested an eagerness to continue the war, and would undoubtedly have done so had she not been deserted by her allies, there is much evidence to prove that she secretly desired peace and was willing to make whatever sacrifice was necessary to secure it. She was disgusted with the whole organization in which she personally, was the only active and enthusiastic unit. She was tired of being reminded of subsidies by the British Ambassador, and offended at the manner in which England had ignored her in forming treaties dealing with her rights. She probably longed for the day when she might break with England entirely, very much in the way a debtor frequently longs for the time when he can settle with a tormenting creditor, look him squarely in the face, and tell him to go about his own business.

She was also chagrined because Prussia, a mere upstart, hitherto considered as of no great military importance, had degraded her army, and three times brought her to yield in writing, one of her richest possessions. Prussia had a population of a little more than three millions, while her monarchy had at least five times that number; yet Prussia was able to put five soldiers in the field every time she recruited seven. Her sagacious mind quickly discerned that Prussia was far

Reforms in the Monarchy 171

more efficient in war than Austria, and she began searching for reasons. It was easy to see that none of her commanders had equaled Frederick in ability, and this brought her to realize that she had not used good judgment in her choice of generals. No doubt she blushed with secret shame when she recalled the ignominious failures of her husband. Regardless of all domestic consequences, she resolved to keep him out of the army. She was also beginning to fear that she had placed too much confidence in her brother-in-law, Prince Charles of Lorraine. She had done this largely to please her husband, and for the same reason had too often trusted General Neipperg because of his friendship for Francis; war was a stern business in which favoring the family was most perilous.

She was disgusted with her ministers who were all out of date, and still imagined themselves in the middle ages. They had no national spirit but were always thinking of themselves and their narrow circle of constituents, rather than the welfare of the whole nation.[1] She also realized, as never before, the lack of unity among her dominions. She could not fail to be impressed with the fact that the monarchy was but a loose bundle of principalities and kingdoms, each jealous of its own rights and unwilling to make sacrifices for the others, except as it was urged on by her own personal magnetism. She was tired of going to the leaders of her distant provinces with petitions in her hands, exhausting her powers of argument and persuasion, and even pleading for the protection of her family and crown, in order to rouse their drowsy patriotism. Each prov-

[1] Bright, 65-66.

ince was in the habit of bickering and bargaining with her annually over provisions for the army; she had always had to yield something to obtain what she should have had upon request. In this manner her predecessors had surrendered far too much to the nobility and the clergy, and she herself had yielded authority which was essential to efficiency in war.

With Frederick it was entirely different in reality, if not in theory. Prussia was completely awed by the army which had been raised to such high efficiency by Frederick's father. When Frederick needed provisions he took them. He had substituted impressment for conscription; he had even surrounded churches and seized young men for military service; if any one objected, which was seldom, he disappeared. Prussia was a most striking example of the tremendous power of an absolute monarchy with a most capable monarch—no other form of government could compare with it in efficiency. Maria Theresa was shrewd enough to discern this, and knew that she must strengthen the central authority of her monarchy if it was to survive against such an enemy.

Incidentally we may note that the most liberal governments of today exercise powers which would have been called tyrannical in the days of Maria Theresa. The idea that men could be taken by force from their homes, put into an army and killed in battle, without their own consent, was still regarded as preposterous—in fact, little short of legalized murder. The Queen of Hungary dared not go so far as to levy a general tax for the support of a national army; an income tax, such as that now levied by most nations during peace, would not have been tolerated for one moment by the Hungarians, not even in time of war.

Reforms in the Monarchy 173

The masses of the Austrian Monarchy were but little better than slaves; they were held in ignorance by the nobility and the clergy, had almost no rights as tenants, and lived in poverty and degradation, but they could not be conscripted. The nobility and the clergy were more tyrannical than the imperial house occupying the highest political position in the nation. The landed estates and the church governed the masses, were exempt from taxation, owned most of the property, and ran the government. The monarch often found himself making common cause with the people against the infringements of the clergy and nobility. The weakness of such a government was beautifully illustrated during the Wars of Accession.[2]

Since Maria Theresa realized all this she wished for a period of peace, not because she was willing to abandon the hope of regaining her beloved Silesia, but to enable her to reorganize her monarchy, find better ministers and commanders, and possibly secure less exacting allies; then she meant to renew her attempt to square her account with Frederick of Prussia. But we must also give her credit for having uppermost in mind a desire to improve the general condition of the masses. She knew that a well-fed and enlightened population was sure to be more efficient in war; she planned to take some of the burden of taxation from the shoulders of the common people and place it upon the backs of the clergy and nobility; she meant to institute schools, hospitals, and almshouses, and give the lowly subjects something worth defending. She would endeavor to build a real nation out of the discordant realms of the

[2] *Ibid.*, 68.

monarchy. She had a beautiful name for this idea; she called it *Benevolent Monarchism*, by which she meant a strong central government devoted to the welfare of its subjects and worthy of their loyal support.

She voiced her sentiments in this regard in the following words: "I consider it unnecessary to yield more to the church which is already so well established, because it does not need more power, and does not use what it has for the benefit of the people. No cloister keeps within the limits of its rightful domain, and many of them shelter idlers who demand more and more that belongs to the state. Also too much has been given to the nobility which has extended its power so far that it is more feared and respected than the monarch. The nobility has continually strengthened its position at the expense of the crown and the people. If I wish support for my army of defense, I must appeal to the ministers of the various realms; certainly no land can be efficiently defended under such conditions. Nevertheless, the monarch, who is but the servant of the nobility, is held responsible for the defense of the nation.

"Each minister insists upon using all the money raised in his realm for its own benefit, very much as if the other divisions of the monarchy were foreign lands and not ruled by the same Queen. The ministers are so divided into contesting units that they think only of themselves and not of the commonwealth. The monarch is regarded as an outsider who is entitled to little or no consideration. Thus the nation as a whole is often greatly imperiled." [3]

[3] Arneth, IV, 3-4.

Then she goes on to tell of the inefficiency of her ministers, who were always seeking positions for the members of their families and their friends, without much regard to capability. "My ministers led me deeper and deeper into a labyrinth, until I almost lost confidence in myself, and, if God had not come to my relief by removing some of them through death, I should have been completely lost."

It was just after the Treaty of Breslau, in 1742, that Maria Theresa first had her attention called to Frederick Wilhelm Haugwitz who had occupied a prominent office in Silesia, but who remained true to her when his country was conquered by Frederick of Prussia.[4] He had fled to Vienna, where he was forced to subsist upon the charity of a friend, rather than change his allegiance to the Prussian king. This was enough to win the favor of the Queen, who appointed him to be president of the small portion of Silesia remaining to her. There he made himself conspicuous by his ability in organizing the finances of his little province. He was very peculiar in appearance; one writer says, "He impressed me as being either a fool or a great man, I was not sure which."

Haugwitz had the audacity to send the Queen a letter, in which he warned her that should Frederick be left undisturbed for three or four years, he would not be satisfied with Silesia but would also attempt the conquest of Bohemia. In two years this prophecy came true, and Maria Theresa was very much impressed with the shrewdness of his forecast. She attempted to draw him out farther, whereupon he reminded her that

---

[4] Guglia, II, 2 seq.; Arneth, IV, 10 seq.

Silesia had been lost because she had too small an army in that dominion when Frederick attacked it. Most of her strength was in Hungary and could not be brought into action until it was too late. The same thing had occurred in Bohemia, proving that she required a national army which could be hurried to any land for defense, and be reinforced promptly by troops under the immediate control of the monarch. She must have an army and the means of supplying it without the delay involved in appealing to the provinces. Such an army could only be supported by a national tax from which the nobility and clergy must not be exempt.

It was not difficult for Haugwitz to win the Queen to this idea, and she asked him to submit a plan in writing.[5] He responded with a scheme for collecting a tax of fourteen million guldens, which he thought would support an army of one hundred and eight thousand men constantly in the field and under the immediate command of the Queen. This was without the participation of Hungary, which probably would not consent to the plan on account of the difficulty of obtaining the ratification of its diet.

The proposed scheme would free the provinces of furnishing material in kind for the use of the army, since supplies would be paid for in money derived from the tax, and would further compensate them by greater security against foreign invasions. Its justness, advisability and expediency are so apparent to us that opposition to it seems almost absurd, but it was received with great indignation by the clergy and nobility, because it abolished their long-established right to

---

[5] Guglia, II, 5; Arneth, IV, 13.

Reforms in the Monarchy 177

exemption from taxation. In their minds the common people were created to serve in the army and pay taxes; otherwise they were not needed. Of course an enlightened nation would not tolerate such a brutal institution as slavery, still existing in uncivilized countries, but the masses could not expect the burden of supporting the government, which afforded them protection and employment, to be lifted from them and put upon the men who fed them. To place a heavy tax upon rents was allowable, but not on the property which belonged to the proud nobility and clergy. The privileged classes prepared to defend their treasured rights against infringements from the crown.

They found a most capable leader in Count Frederick Harrach,[6] who was chancellor of Bohemia and acting as land marshal of Austria below the Enns, during the absence of his brother, Count Ferdinand Harrach, then serving as governor of Lombardy. Frederick Harrach was a member of the ministry in Vienna, and married to a daughter of Prince Liechtenstein. He had served as special representative of the Queen in the conference which formed the peace treaty of Dresden, was very wealthy, and in every way a most formidable opponent of the Queen's plan.

Count Harrach contended that the scheme of Haugwitz placed too much power in the hands of the monarch, and was able to find many faults with the manner in which the taxes were to be applied.[7] But he made the mistake of offering a substitute plan, providing for the granting of all the crown had asked by the estates, but to be determined annually by the provinces and raised

---
[6] Bright, 70 seq.; Arneth, IV, 15.
[7] Arneth, IV, 23.

by indirect taxes upon the necessities of life, thus shifting the increased burden upon the masses. It was very easy for the Queen to stir up the population against this scheme, and the common people were not dumb. Even the estates drew back from the plan of their leader, fearing it might result in a popular uprising.

Thus the battle was drawn between the Queen and the people on one side, and the clergy and nobility on the other. In the midst of the struggle the Queen sent Count Haugwitz to Bohemia and Moravia to secure ratifications of her plan by the councils of those realms, and very much to her delight, he returned with the ratifications of both provinces.[8] Encouraged by this success, she became bolder and began exerting all the power at her command to subdue Count Harrach. Once in discussing the subject with him, he became so vehement that she rebuked him by reminding him of the fact that he was addressing a sovereign, and would do well to be more respectful. Realizing that she was backed by the people, she removed Harrach from his post in the ministry and completely degraded him. Shortly after this he died of smallpox, but many thought his death was due to the manner in which he had been humiliated by his monarch.[9] In waging this campaign Maria Theresa was considered a despot by the clergy and nobility, but gained popularity among the lower classes who looked upon her as the champion of their rights. She understood very well that the people were irresistible, especially when aroused in support of a just cause, and she was determined to assert the right of the government to tax the rich as well

[8] Guglia, II, 5 seq.
[9] Arneth, IV, 24.

Reforms in the Monarchy 179

as the poor, for in her sagacity she conceived the very existence of the monarchy to be at stake in this contention. In the end she triumphed and the Haugwitz plan was adopted by all the provinces except Hungary and the distant possessions.

It is difficult to exaggerate the importance of the Queen's victory in this contest. She did exactly what Louis XV neglected to do in France, and what Louis XVI tried later and failed to accomplish. By her clear statesmanship and dauntless courage she obviated the destruction of the monarchy, or at least a bloody revolution, which otherwise could hardly have been delayed longer in Austria than in France.

Having carried her point in regard to taxation, Maria Theresa soon extended her reforms into other fields. She established military schools for the training of officers, introduced camps for maneuvers, and equipped the army with uniforms, arms and ammunition. She endeavored to take advantage of all Frederick had taught Europe concerning military organization, and very soon had a national army far more efficient than any Austria had known since the days of Prince Eugene.[10]

Presently she concentrated the ministries of Bohemia and Austria into one office known as the *Directorium*, withdrew the department of justice from it, and established crown courts in the various provinces. To these courts the people were able to come for justice against the impositions of the nobility and clergy, in this way being reminded that the highest authority of the land rested with the crown and not with the

---

[10] Coxe, III, 361; Arneth, IV, 91 *seq.*

master of the estate upon which they resided, or the parish priest. From the provincial courts appeals could be taken to the high court of justice in Vienna; even the common people discovered that they had rights which were guarded by their Queen.[11]

The establishment of a uniform system of courts necessitated a codification of the laws of the monarchy, which had thus far been without uniformity or system. To meet this need the Queen appointed a committee of jurists which labored for several years upon the task of systematizing the criminal and civil procedures of the monarchy.[12] Until the time of Maria Theresa there had been no such a thing as justice in the monarchy; people were punished or liberated according to the whims of local authorities.[13]

The next measure that engaged the Queen's attention was education, which had been entrusted almost entirely to the church. She expelled the Jesuits from the university and made it a state school. High schools were founded throughout her realms, and a system of common schools, under the control of the state, established as far as possible.[14] A vast system of roads was built from taxes, collected from property regardless of whether it belonged to the nobility or the clergy.

Gerhard van Swieten, a Dutch physician whom she had summoned to be her personal medical attendant, was placed in charge of the medical department of the university and became the founder of the celebrated

---

[11] Arneth, IV, 30.
[12] This was not finished until near the end of the Queen's reign.
[13] Guglia, II, 32 seq.; Steed, 99.
[14] Arneth, IV, 111.

Reforms in the Monarchy 181

medical school of Vienna.[15] The eminence of that city as a medical center dates from the reign of Maria Theresa.

The reforms of Maria Theresa were so far-reaching that we may declare she converted the loose-jointed monarchy into a real nation, even going so far as an attempt to establish the German language throughout the provinces of Austria and Bohemia. Such reforms were accompanied by a tremendous increase of central power. This form of monarchial authority afterward developed into a most cumbersome bureaucracy which, under Francis Joseph, became so unwieldy as to completely defeat the purpose for which it was originally created. The system of national taxation also became oppressive under later rulers, but the blame for all this can hardly be laid upon Maria Theresa. Any system of government thus far devised, can easily be converted by unscrupulous politicians into a means of oppression.

Maria Theresa was very desirous of extending her system of taxation to the wealthy province of Hungary, which shared in all the benefits of security provided by the national army, without contributing its just portion for support. It was for this purpose that she called a meeting of the Hungarian diet in 1751, and appeared before it in person to urge the adoption of her system. She remembered the success of her appeal in 1741, and was confident that she could again sway the assembly to her cause in 1751. But this time she was sadly disappointed. The gallant Hungarian

---

[15] *Ibid.,* 117.

noblemen had clanked their swords and swore to die for their beautiful Queen, but no display of sentiments could induce them to agree to pay taxes for her; they saw no romance whatever in a tax levy. She asked for one hundred and twenty thousand guldens—much less in proportion to their wealth than the other provinces were paying—but after bargaining with the assembly for weeks, was compelled to be satisfied with seventy thousand.[16]

Since Hungary held herself aloof, other provinces sought to establish tariff laws against her, but this was unfortunate, for it drove the Hungarians to seek markets for their produce in Italy, and widened the breach between Austria and her rich neighbor. It also raised the price of commodities that were produced in Hungary and thus punished the very people it was intended to benefit. This unsuccessful attempt to bring Hungary to terms largely neutralized the good will which had grown out of the Wars of Accession.

For various reasons Maria Theresa was also unable to bring her provinces in Italy and the Netherlands under her general system of taxation, and did not attempt to do so at the risk of too much opposition. She was always willing, if not content, to do what she could and excuse herself for what she could not do, on the ground of expediency. Had she realized the probability of failure in accomplishing the purpose for which she called the Hungarian assembly in 1751, she would never have called it, no matter how much she felt that her demands were just. Her reforms were all promulgated with great caution, and she never grew impet-

---

[16] Bright, 75; Guglia, II, 12 seq.; Arneth, IV, 180–219.

uous in bringing them into effect until she saw she was certain to win; then she stopped at nothing, no matter how despotic it might appear to others. Her conduct in this respect contrasted strangely with the rash behavior of her son Joseph, who had all her courage, but lacked her wonderful discretion.

VIII

THE CHANGE IN ALLIANCE

AT the close of the Wars of Accession, Maria Theresa was in a bad humor toward England, and probably for that reason, began a flirtation with France, England's rival and also the traditional enemy of the House of Austria. This *rapprochement*, which could hardly have been intended seriously in the first place on account of the century-old feud between the Hapsburgs and Bourbons, ripened into an alliance which completely estranged Austria and England. All the details of how and why this occurred will probably never be known, for the whole affair was conducted with secrecy and willful attempts to deceive. To review the documents relating to this change of alliance would involve searching the records of half a dozen capitals, in some of which the archives have been open to the public only since the World War. Probably such a search would still leave us in doubt over several points, for the documents would not reveal the heartaches, jealousies and bad temper of the Queen, out of which sprang the rejection of an old ally for an attachment to a new. Regardless of its origin, this new alignment completely changed the whole aspect of European politics for a quarter of a century; and a very striking sequence was the birth of an infant nation in the western hemisphere—a nation destined to become one of the most powerful the world has ever seen.[1]

The man whose name was most intimately associated with the formation of this new alliance was Wenzel Anton Count Kaunitz, a very clever diplomat, and a most peculiar character in many respects. Kaunitz played such an important rôle in the life of Maria Theresa that it is well worth while to sketch briefly his biography. He was born in Vienna in 1711, and was one of the younger of somewhere from sixteen to twenty children—the Viennese are so prolific that they sometimes lose track of the exact number of their offspring.[2] His father, Maximilian Ulrich Count Kaunitz, at first intended his son for the church, but owing to the deaths of earlier sons, altered his mind and educated Wenzel to be a diplomat. Deeply affected by the loss of so many of her children, young Wenzel's mother petted him until she completely spoiled him. The result of such tender, well-meant solicitude on her part was that all his life he was afraid of the faintest draft of fresh air, demanded the most carefully prepared delicacies for his stomach, and spent hours each day in primping and removing tiny specks from his clothing.

He studied in the universities of Vienna, Leipzig and Leyden, after which he travelled in the Netherlands, England, France and Italy, making as close observations as possible of the courts of London, Versailles,

---

[1] Had Austria remained the active ally of England, France would have been so completely engaged on the Continent that she would not have been able to send aid to the American Colonies, and the Revolution would probably have ended in a failure. Hence this new alliance made possible the independence of the United States of America.

[2] Bermann, 652

and Turin. Upon returning to Vienna, he married the daughter of Count Starhemberg, who was the son of the renowned defender of Vienna during the siege of Kara Mustapha in 1683, and naturally well connected in high political circles of the court of Charles VI. Of Kaunitz's wife we know very little except that she died early. He never married again, and all through his eventful career led the life of a bachelor—in fact, several well-informed Viennese have told me that Kaunitz was never married.

At the accession of Maria Theresa he was prominent enough to be enumerated among the Queen's counsellors, and was soon named as ambassador to Francis of Lorraine's province of Tuscany. From there he was promoted to Rome, and a little later to the important post of Turin, which was then the capital of Sardinia. Upon reading his first report from Turin Chancellor Ulfeld exclaimed, "Here is a man who will become chancellor!"[3] But Ulfeld surely did not foresee that he was speaking of his own successor. Shortly after this Kaunitz became acting governor of the Netherlands, where he was a helpless witness of the triumphant advance of the French against the futile resistance of the English and Austrians. This spectacle probably convinced him of the advantages to be derived from an alliance with the French rather than the British. Next he was named as the Queen's representative to the peace conference at Aix-la-Chapelle, where his mind was further affected by the rude inconsideration given the Queen by the British. The result of these ob-

[3] *Ibid.*, 653.

servations was that he resolved to use all the adroitness and enticing address, for which he afterward became so famous, to bring about a reconciliation between Austria and France, if necessary, even at the cost of alliance with England.[4]

A little later he obtained the Queen's ear and began winning her to his ideas, although opposed by all her other ministers and even by her husband. There is no doubt that Kaunitz had a strong personal appeal for Maria Theresa, but she soon saw that he was not merely a "carpet diplomat"; he had a strange way of presenting a subject so that there appeared to be nothing to say in opposition to his views. It was not long before he won a most unusual influence over the Queen. From this influence she never escaped and through it the clever minister wrought no less than three miracles; he formed an alliance between Austria and France in spite of their traditional enmity, which had endured almost unbroken for three centuries, he ousted the Jesuits from all their strongly fortified positions in the Austrian government, and he virtually dictated the marriages of several of Maria Theresa's children. The extent to which he actually accomplished these tasks may be regarded as somewhat problematic, for the Queen was in a most receptive mood toward many of the important measures which seemed to originate with Kaunitz, but we may safely assert that the deciding factor in most of them was surely her favorite minister. It was Kaunitz who put her rather hazy ideas into definite, concrete form, and framed the political

---
[4] Arneth, IV, 272.

policies which she adopted to meet the changed conditions confronting her after the close of her Wars of Accession.

The central figure in all the Queen's policies at that time was Frederick of Prussia who was looked upon very much as Napoleon was a little later. Frederick was without conscience, without principle, and apparently unlimited in strength. Kaunitz stated, and the Queen agreed with him, that Prussia, and not France, was the real enemy of Austria, and any policy which could afford protection against the "Ogre of the North" was advisable.[5] They knew Prussia had great influence over England, partly because their kings were related, and partly because the King of England knew Prussia could easily invade Hanover. The fact that King George had guaranteed the integrity of Frederick's territory was enough to indicate that England would never unite with Austria in a war against Prussia. The Queen's greatest desire was security in the possession of her inherited dominions, with a restoration of Silesia, and it was not unmixed with a longing for vengeance upon the King of Prussia; this desire could never be gratified through an alliance with England. On the other hand, France might easily be led into a quarrel with Prussia, because Frederick had played "fast and loose" with the French during the last war, with no regard whatever for their welfare and wishes. Kaunitz thought he might present this to Louis XV and Madame Pompadour in such a manner that they would be led to seek revenge upon the King of Prussia.[6]

Very soon the Queen dispatched Kaunitz to Paris as

[5] *Ibid.*, IV, 275-276.
[6] Coxe, III, 373; Bright, 62 seq.

her Ambassador. There he scanned the field and formed his plan of action. He gave little attention to the dissolute society of the court of Versailles, but in every possible manner sought to win favor with Louis XV and his powerful mistress. Once he was reproached for holding himself aloof from French society, whereupon he replied, "I am in Paris for only two purposes, the service of the Queen—that I am performing to her satisfaction—and my own pleasure; with the two persons in whom I am interested, I am on the most intimate terms." Doubtless he spoke the truth, for he was making costly presents to the Madame, and appealing to her vanity by forwarding to her intimate messages from the Queen. Maria Theresa later denied that she had ever written letters or made presents to Madame Pompadour, but this was only technically true; she did both through the good offices of her Ambassadors, especially through Kaunitz' successor, Starhemberg.[7]

When Francis I heard that his proud wife had been writing letters to Madame Pompadour, he banged his fist on the table, rose in anger, and left the Queen's presence, but she paid little or no attention to this angry outburst, and went right on with what she considered her own business. The low-born mistress of

[7] Arneth, IV, 334 seq. Arneth gives an itemized statement of the cost of a lacquer *écritoire* presented to Madame Pompadour by Maria Thesera. The total was 77,288 livres.—Arneth, V, note 661.

While Maria Theresa seems to have been ashamed of having made friendly overtures to Madame Pompadour, she had no just reason for feeling so. Madame Pompadour was at that time the real ruler of France, the only one with whom diplomatic affairs could be successfully conducted, and morally she was in no way inferior to Louis XV, Czarina Elizabeth, and many others with whom the Queen was obliged to deal. What really galled her was that she felt that she was degrading herself by becoming intimate with a parvenue.

Louis XV was greatly flattered by the attention she was receiving from one whom she considered the greatest sovereign in all Europe, and employed all her power to promote the Queen's enterprise. The alliance would have been effected immediately but for the fact that a western wind brought scent of it to the keen-nosed Frederick of Prussia, who succeeded in thwarting it by pressure brought to bear upon the Madame through the agency of some of his spies who were influential at the court of Versailles.

Kaunitz, his plans frustrated, made a showing of having abandoned the attempt, and pretended to use his influence with the Queen to form some sort of an alliance with Prussia. This was probably for the purpose of pulling wool over the eyes of Frederick, and it seems to have succeeded temporarily. Kaunitz knew very well that the Queen would form a union with the devil as quickly as with Frederick of Prussia.

Having carefully prepared the ground and sown the seed for an alliance between France and Austria, Kaunitz returned to Vienna and was immediately appointed Chancellor.[8] This part of the plot cost the Queen very much, for it involved a displacement of Ulfeld whom she liked, although she had little confidence in his ability. She soothed the old diplomat by paying off all his long-standing debts, and naming him to the very honorable but less powerful post of *Obersthofmeister*. This was rather easy, but much more difficult was the disposal, at Kaunitz' demand, of Bartenstein who held the office of Referendary and had been of the greatest service to the Queen ever

---

[8] Bright, 94 seq.; Arneth, IV, 343.

since her accession.[9] She eased Bartenstein down as softly as possible by giving him a membership in the Secret Council, thus making him an aristocrat and fulfilling a hope he had long cherished, although by birth he was not of the "elect."

From that time forward Kaunitz was the Queen's right hand, and entrusted with the execution of nearly all her important policies of state. She valued his opinion much more than that of her son Joseph, even after the latter was her co-regent and Emperor of the Romans, and she always listened to her Chancellor in preference to her husband who was strongly opposed to the whole scheme of an alliance with France.

Several events occurred to boost the Minister's project of *rapprochement* with France. England showed no consideration for the Queen's rights in the Netherlands, and the result was an exchange of several sharp notes between Kaunitz and the British Minister. One note in particular, from Kaunitz, seemed well calculated to cause a break between the two powers, but the final fillip was given to Kaunitz' scheme by the formation of a new pact between Prussia and England in 1756.[10] Frederick felt toward France very much as Austria felt toward England; he regarded the French as inconsiderate of his rights and prestige. "France thinks I should make war and peace according to her orders," he said. Since he cared nothing for old friends or new enemies, except as they promoted his own interests, he did not hesitate to make a new treaty with England, and let France do as she pleased concerning an alliance with Austria. Then Madame Pompadour

[9] *Ibid.*, IV, 345.
[10] Coxe, III, 375 seq.

and the Queen of Austria fell into one another's arms and made an offensive and defensive alliance.[11]

In doing this Maria Theresa seems to have cherished the hope that she could retain her alliance with Great Britain. Her plot was to encircle Frederick with enemies on the continent very much as she had been surrounded at her accession. She had already formed an alliance with Elizabeth of Russia, so that Frederick beheld to the west, Madame Pompadour, to the south, Maria Theresa, and to the east, Czarina Elizabeth; all enemies, and the most formidable petticoat triumvirate ever organized in Europe; we might add that one of their principal motives in living was to oppose the greatest upstart King of his day, Frederick of Prussia.

While Kaunitz and Maria Theresa knew that England was disposed to be friendly toward Frederick, they could not see how England's self-interest would prompt her to mix very heavily in a war on the Continent. England was interested mostly in sea power and the preservation of her rights in the New World and India. Of course England had Hanover to protect, but none of the three enemies of Prussia had any designs upon Hanover; it could remain where it was and just as it was, without any inconvenience to the triumvirate.

Before passing from this phase of European diplo-

---

[11] *Ibid.*, 383; Bright, 107 seq.

Concerning this treaty of alliance, Kaunitz wrote Madame Pompadour: "All that has been concluded between the courts of France and Austria is entirely due to your zeal and sagacity. I am sensible of it, and I would be denying myself a pleasure were I not to assure you of my feelings." This letter continues at considerable length in the same strain.—Arneth, IV, note 553.

The Change in Alliance 193

macy it is interesting to turn for a moment and view at closer range the personality of this remarkable minister who had acquired such an ascendancy with the most headstrong queen the Continent had seen up to that period. Kaunitz' habits contrasted strangely with those of Maria Theresa. He usually lay in bed until noon, and most of his state papers were dictated from his pillow. He could never endure fresh air, and rode in a hermetically sealed coach. Since the Queen always had her windows wide open, even in winter, this became a serious matter during their conferences, and in the end, she formed the habit of closing all windows upon the approach of the Minister, something she did not condescend to do for her own husband. When she heard Kaunitz coming she screamed to her attendants, "He's coming! he's coming!" and immediately the windows went shut, very much to the amusement of all present, including the Queen.[12]

Kaunitz was a baby about his food, and refused to attend banquets and feasts unless permitted to have his own servants bring his food from home. When in the presence of the Queen his hands were always busy, usually sharpening his pencil or brushing flecks from his trousers or coat. He wore a French peruke and used French perfumery; the Queen once remarked that she liked to smell Kaunitz. When he came to his writing desk, he fumed and scolded if the servants had not arranged his pencils, pens and rulers exactly parallel.[13] All this amused the Queen who had a delightful sense of humor, but she overlooked his idiosyncrasies because she valued his intellect and diplomatic skill, and above all,

[12] Bermann, 659–663.
[13] *Ibid.*, 661.

his absolute incorruptibility. There may have been a faint shadow of romance over the relations of Kaunitz and Maria Theresa, but it was only such as any sensible German *Frau* might legitimately feel toward a pernickety old bachelor. She admired him principally because he was exceptionably competent and trustworthy; he said what he thought very politely and respectfully to her and kept his lips sealed to all others. He was the first really reliable, agreeable, and competent minister she had ever had, and she felt completely upset whenever he spoke of resigning.

Probably not one move had been made by Maria Theresa without the full knowledge of Frederick of Prussia [14] whose spies infested every court of Europe. He began massing troops on the Austrian front, apparently for the purpose of meeting an invasion from that quarter, whereupon the Queen moved her army toward Prussia. Pretending to be greatly surprised by such hostile maneuvers on the part of a friendly power, Frederick sent a special messenger to the Queen to ask what she meant by sending troops in his direction. To this messenger she replied: "The critical state of affairs has led me to think such measures necessary for my own safety and the defense of my allies. They have no object beyond this, and are intended to injure no one." Frederick was not satisfied by such an evasive answer and sent the envoy back with a note saying: "I must know whether we are at peace or war; of that the Queen is the arbiter. I cannot, however, put up with an oracular answer. If such is returned, the Queen is responsible for the consequences." This message was

---

[14] Bright, 118 seq.

The Change in Alliance

turned over to Kaunitz to answer, and he sent Frederick a long document in which he expressed great indignation over the curt and insolent notes directed to a friendly power; this was followed by several pages of meaningless ambiguities. Kaunitz considered this a very suitable answer to Frederick who was manifestly playing with the Queen while securing reliable information from spies.[15]

Some see in the conduct of Maria Theresa at this time the result of associating with such a clever and deceitful adviser as Kaunitz. She was indeed, not quite the same high-minded and straightforward woman who answered Frederick's notes in December, 1740, but she was surely honorable enough to transact business with Frederick of Prussia who was doubtless only amusing himself with questions to draw her out. As to her conduct with France and England, we may easily justify her on the ground that evasions and deceptions were the order of the day in diplomacy, and no country was dealing squarely with its neighbors.[16] Every nation on the Continent was playing fox or wolf and it was no time or place for a ruler to take the part of a dove.

[15] Goldsmith, 158 and 161.
[16] Bright, an English author, who is usually very fair toward Maria Theresa, seems to think she was justified in breaking with England, but strongly condemns her for the manner in which she formed her alliance with France.

IX

THE SECOND CONTEST

I

DESPITE the limitations of her sex, lack of training, and want of experience, Maria Theresa succeeded in encircling her archenemy with the strongest ring of opponents that ever encompassed any ruler of modern times. Technically Frederick's position was even more hopeless than hers had been at the time of her accession, for his single ally, England, was already engaged in an evenly matched tussle with France over world dominion. Frederick could expect little help from England aside from subsidies and difficulties, such as the Queen had experienced in the previous war, in accounting for the manner in which he spent them. He had hoped that his sister Ulrike, who was married, not too happily, to the King of Sweden, might bring Scandinavia to his aid, but this hope proved to be vain; Sweden eventually joined the coalition against him and brought little Denmark with her, leaving Holland—very clever Holland—standing smugly aside under the cover of a declaration of neutrality.[1]

If Frederick studied census reports, he must have shuddered, for it was a hard problem in arithmetic to compute the enormous preponderance of his oppo-

[1] Coxe, III, 398.

nents in population, territory, and wealth. The Queen's dominions alone held four or five times as many people as Prussia; Czarina Elizabeth, his despised neighbor, had about as many subjects as the Queen; the German states, nearly all yellow with envy of Prussia, had twice his population, and were likely to rally to the standards of the Emperor who happened to be Maria Theresa's husband; Augustus of Saxony and Poland—soft, fat, pleasure-loving Augustus—who above all, wished to be left in peace to enjoy his green diamond, his art galleries, and his operas, ruled nearly five times as many people as Frederick, when Poland was counted in, and was, according to the reports of well paid Prussian spies, in secret collusion with the Queen. France, although facing England and grimly engaged, might kick back like a mule at any moment. Such was the situation, or very soon to be the situation, in August, 1756.[2]

In a sense, Frederick had no one but himself to blame for being thus ostracized and distrusted by his neighbors, for he had broken treaties and alliances most shamefully, especially with France, and he had raided the Queen's dominions like a highway robber. Such were his political offenses, and they were serious enough. But he was also guilty of many personal indignities toward several of his most influential contemporaries who happened to be very proud and haughty women. During the interval between his Silesian Wars and the Seven Years' War, he maintained at Potsdam, merely for his own amusement, a little court of loud-mouthed scoffers, such as Voltaire, Al-

[2] Coxe, III, 400.

garotti, Maupertuis and Argens, who indulged in all sorts of racy, offensive jests at the expense of several prominent women of the times.

The Potsdam "School for Slander" discussed the intimate affairs of Madame Pompadour, a woman so lowborn according to the opinion of Potsdam that she really never should have been born at all; it chuckled over how Czarina Elizabeth loved her fleshpots, drank too much toddy, and wore dirty dresses; and it chortled at the very mention of Maria Theresa's senile *Hofrats*, her renowned "College of Chastity," and the wild escapades of her gay husband. The Potsdam jokes were too good to be kept from the world, and were tattled all over Europe to vex their victims who soon longed to give the "scurrilous upstart" King of Prussia a good dose of feminine vengeance. Frederick had much sport in jesting about women in those days, but it was not a mark of good statesmanship to allow the ringleader of the "petticoats" to consolidate all Europe against him in such a perilous manner; few jests in history cost so many lives or had such a great international influence as those of Frederick the Great.[3]

But we are not justified in asserting that Maria

[3] Frederick called Maria Theresa "Empress Petticoat I" and Madame Pompadour, "Queen Petticoat II." According to his nomenclature, "Queen Petticoat I" was Madame Châteauroux, a previous mistress to Louis XV. He named his pet dog, which lay in one of his armchairs during the day and shared his cot at night, "Madame Pompadour." What he said of Czarina Elizabeth is unprintable these days. Voltaire wrote that when he arrived in Potsdam, he presented Madame Pompadour's respects to Frederick, who sneeringly remarked: "I don't know the woman. This is not a court in which shepherdesses and swains shine; nevertheless, I will write the Madame that Mars welcomes the compliments of Venus." He kept his word by writing her a stinging bit of poetry. See Letter of Voltaire to Madame Denis, Aug. 11, 1750.

The Second Contest

Theresa was actuated entirely by a desire for vengeance. An unbiased study of her conduct at this time convinces us that she was thinking more of self-protection than of the destruction of Frederick. He had raided her possessions when she was helpless, without the customary diplomatic formalities and with no just cause whatever; he never offered any excuse except to say that he was prompted by a desire to win fame and power. If such were his principles, would he not seize Bohemia at the first opportunity; might he not covet Hungary, and in the end deprive her of all her inherited dominions? Self-preservation compelled her to enclose him with alliances capable of holding him in restraint, and the same legitimate purpose would be served by weakening him, or better still by destroying him.

Any of the highly civilized nations of today, such as France or the United States, would endeavor to accomplish exactly what was in the mind of Maria Theresa if placed under similar circumstances, and would deny the charge of plotting vengeance. Her motives were first of all self-defense; second, the recovery of Silesia which she still regarded as rightfully hers; third, the destruction of Frederick of Prussia whom she considered a menace to her very existence. The last is the only one of her motives we can condemn, and it was no worse than the raging sentiment to depose the Emperor of Germany which ran riot throughout France, England and the United States during the trying days of the World War; no more ignoble than the manner in which Germany and Austria were stripped to impotency at Versailles.

The Seven Years' War was not Maria Theresa's

war in the same sense as her Wars of Accession in which she was the central figure at the beginning. We have seen how the Wars of Accession gradually spread from family disputes over rights of accession in the House of Hapsburg until an issue of world dominion was contested by France and England. The Seven Years' War was precisely the opposite; it began with the same great issue between France and England, and the quarrel was taken up by Frederick and the coalition formed by Maria Theresa against him. It was a double-headed monster with two separate and distinct purposes. Frederick and Maria Theresa were not interested in what was uppermost in the minds of the French and English.

The continental part of this great struggle was Frederick's war; he began it in the hope of conquest, as is shown by his invasion of Saxony and Bohemia, but he soon found himself engaged in a bitter fight for his very existence. If he won, he doubtless meant to annex both Saxony and Bohemia; if results were indecisive, he expected to retain Silesia; if he lost, he would be lucky to escape with empty hands and a head on his shoulders. His previous successes had made him egotistic and set him dreaming of becoming a Cæsar or an Alexander. Frederick hated mediocrity and was willing to take desperate chances because the prize was so alluring. For the lives of his subjects he cared little or nothing, except that he must make every soldier killed contribute as much as possible to a final victory.

Maria Theresa also welcomed the war, because she felt so very certain of winning it. If she won as she hoped to win, she would recover Silesia and partition Prussia, thus paying Frederick back in kind for what he had done during her previous wars; if her success was only partial, she would probably have to be satisfied with regaining Silesia; if results were indecisive, she could continue as at the beginning; if she lost, which hardly seemed possible with such powerful allies, she would lose Bohemia and become a second-rate power.[4] The war was not likely to add much to the glory she had already achieved in her first plucky fight —for existence—against such overwhelming foes, nor could her motives prompt such wonderful deeds of heroism as she performed in those first wars.

Europe had spent twenty-two years of the first half of the eighteenth century in wars over the disputes of monarchs, having little interest to the people whose blood was being spilled like water; it was now beginning another contest destined to last seven years and be more bloody than any of the previous ones. In the Seven Years' War the casualties in several battles mounted to one-third of both armies, but the final results were little more than the creation of two or three military heroes; we might almost say that the sole fruit of this bitter struggle was one very celebrated historical character, Frederick the Great. Perhaps never was glory bought at a higher price.

To recite the details of the campaigns and battles of the long Seven Years' War would be a thankless and useless task in this little story of the life of Maria Theresa, for they neither added much to nor subtracted much from her character as a woman and ruler. But charges of war-guilt can hardly be brought against her fairly in this connection; it was Frederick

[4] Carlyle, V, 274.

and not she who first pulled the trigger, and it was he who always stood in the limelight, received the applause, walked away with the glory, and won renown.[5] We shall tell the story of the beginning of the war, and perhaps the first campaign, in order to bring out some interesting features of the Queen's life.

II

Maria Theresa had hardly finished setting the trap to catch Frederick if he misbehaved, before he sprung it, and as usual, with a big surprise. On the twenty-eight of August, 1756, he set his army in motion, and marched, not as all expected into Bohemia to make war on Maria Theresa, but into Saxony, almost the only peaceably disposed country on his boundary.[6] By the ninth of September he had captured Dresden and sent Augustus scurrying away to the fortifications of Pirna in the direction of Bohemia. One could never guess what Frederick was about to do, but usually his reasons were most apparent shortly after he acted. He knew there was wealth in Dresden, and being short of money, decided to take it. He helped himself to Augustus' thalers, and seizing the porcelain works at Meissen, proceeded to sell the stock on hand and put the proceeds into his pocket. It was an easy, clever move for a man like Frederick, who was untrammeled by the ordinary usages of polite robbery through diplomacy, declarations of war, and formal invasions.

But there were several other reasons why Frederick violated the neutrality of Saxony. The kingdom lay

[5] Goldsmith, 159–160.
[6] Carlyle, V, 318.

between him and Bohemia and he did not wish to be bothered by going around it during a war with Austria. Again, he was sure he could easily overpower Saxony, probably without a serious battle, and hoped to impress most of the Saxon army into his service. To carry out the latter design, he promptly besieged Pirna and summoned Augustus to surrender and disband his army.[7]

Such a high-handed procedure toward Augustus, who had become somewhat of a favorite with the Queen during recent years, kindled her ire to a white heat. Also, it was only too apparent that this was but the first step in making war upon Austria. The next step would probably be taken without the formality of a declaration. A few meaningless notes passed between the two monarchs; then Maria Theresa dispatched an army under the very capable General Browne to rescue the Saxon martyrs. The result was the first battle of the war at Lobositz.[8] While the battle was indecisive, and was even celebrated as a victory in Vienna, its results were very much to Frederick's advantage. Browne was forced to retreat toward Prague while the helpless Saxons surrendered and both soldiers and officers were, as far as practicable, impressed into Frederick's service. Augustus was permitted to withdraw to his other kingdom of Poland, and Frederick settled himself comfortably in Dresden, to spend the winter in tormenting the Queen of Saxony who remained to keep a watchful eye on the affairs of her absent husband. The Queen was Maria Theresa's cousin and the two women were on very good terms at that time.

[7] *Ibid.*, 325 seq.
[8] *Ibid.*, 341 seq.; Bright, 123; Arneth V, 1.

Probably Frederick liked to have the cousin about so he could tease her; he was peculiar in that respect.

The invasion of Saxony was regarded in those days very much as the invasion of Belgium was viewed at the beginning of the World War, and Maria Theresa did not fail to make the utmost possible of such an "atrocity" by directing the attention of the supposedly civilized world, especially the Catholic world, to the heathen methods of the "Brigand from Berlin." Her continual harping on this chord finally got under the thick skin of the King of Prussia, because it was bringing down upon him the wrath of the German states, some of which he had hoped to keep out of the combination against him. To justify himself, he added another atrocity by seizing the Queen of Saxony—very roughly, according to reports—and compelling her to yield the secret correspondence of her husband. From such documents Frederick secured, or at least pretended to have secured, proofs that Augustus was in a plot to partition Prussia, and was to receive his portion of the melon when it was sliced and distributed. Naturally Frederick published such documents to counterbalance the propaganda coming principally from the court of Vienna.[9]

But in spite of all that Frederick published, his rough, undiplomatic methods enabled Maria Theresa to strengthen the league against him by confirming her alliances and adding a new one with Sweden, which had been sitting "on the fence" in indecision.[10] A disinterested observer probably would have regarded the price

[9] Carlyle, V, 323 seq.
[10] Arneth, V, 157.

the King was likely to pay for his ruthlessness as rather high, and such proved to be the case in the end, but headstrong Frederick did not bother with such considerations; he wanted to be a big king or no king at all; he loved to gamble with high stakes.[11]

Early the following spring, 1757, Frederick was in motion, advancing by three columns into Bohemia; he was off before the Queen and her allies had settled upon a plan of campaign, or even fully decided that war was unavoidable. It was usually unnecessary for Frederick's enemies to plan campaigns; when able, he always attended to that for them. He knew that France was preparing to send a huge army over through Hanover, where it might be halted temporarily by an insufficient force of the British; Russia might come rolling, he hoped very slowly, in from the east; and Sweden would possibly drift down from the north like a large iceberg, but all this did not cause him to hesitate, or quail for a moment over the tremendous slaughter he was calling down upon his people. He conceived the very first task to be the one nearest at hand, which was to attend to the Austrians under the command of Prince Charles of Lorraine whom he found special delight in beating, partly because the Prince was a double brother-in-law to Maria Theresa.

Prince Charles had taken a very strong position on a hill commanding the city of Prague, where he awaited the arrival of the Prussians. The Austrians also had another army under Daun, which had been recruited in Moravia and was now moving to join Prince

[11] Goldsmith, 156.

Charles. Having beaten Daun to Prague by only a few days, Frederick felt obliged to attack immediately, lest he find himself pinched between two foes. He reconnoitered the Austrian position, which appeared impregnable except at one point where there seemed to be an easy approach across a level, green meadow. Schwerin, his best general, advised Frederick to allow his men to rest a day because they were so exhausted from forced marches, but the King brusquely disregarded the counsel of his general. The next morning the attack was made across the supposedly green, level meadow, which proved to be a snare and delusion. It was not a meadow but a chain of drained fish ponds in which grass was standing waist high—a quagmire where the poor soldiers sank to their thighs and the horses to their bellies. This was but one of the many instances in which the lack of care, and the failure to do proper scouting, cost the King's army thousands of lives.[12]

Men and horses wallowed in the bog, doing their best to advance with wagons of artillery, while the Austrians from above slaughtered them with grapeshot. Time and again Frederick sent men into the morass only to have them murdered. It was a severe test to the discipline of the Prussian soldiers, for a command to charge was nothing less than a death sentence, but the well-trained infantry and cavalry of the King did not falter until it was apparent that the army was rapidly committing suicide; then Schwerin remonstrated with the King, only to be reprimanded and charged with cowardice. This was too much for brave old Schwerin; wrapping the Prussian flag about his

---

[12] Carlyle, V, 395 seq.; Goldsmith, 170; Coxe, III, 402.

body he cried, "Come on, brave men, follow me!" Then he rode into the quagmire and was riddled with grapeshot.[13]

The death of their beloved leader so enraged the Prussians that they plowed through the bog and stormed up the hill, routing their foes and turning their own cannon against them. The Austrian infantrymen were thrown into a panic. Browne, their cherished commander, had been carried from the field with one leg shot away, and Prince Charles could not control the men. Screaming in terror they fled down the hill and through the gates of the city with Charles raging and swearing at them all the way. Inside the walls he succeeded in rallying them for one more charge, but they soon turned and fled past him like scared rabbits into the refuge of the fortifications. There was nothing for Charles to do but get as many of his frightened soldiers as possible inside the city walls and then close the gates to keep out the Prussians, who were at the heels of their conquered enemy.

Such was the famous Battle of Prague in which Schwerin and Browne won everlasting glory, surpassed only by that of Frederick of Prussia. But the price of this glory was very high. Frederick gave his own loss at eighteen thousand, most of whom were killed, and the Austrian loss was twenty-four thousand, made up largely of prisoners who failed to beat the Prussians to the shelter of the city. Many tears were shed for Schwerin, the brave old veteran who had been Frederick's "father" in war, and who saved the King's crown for him at Mollwitz after His Majesty had left the

---

[13] Arneth, V, 177; Wraxall, I, 162; Carlyle, V, 409–410. Carlyle gives a very dramatic description of Schwerin's death.

field as fast as a good horse could carry him. To the Austrians the loss of Browne—brave, tubercular, Irish Browne, for whom the soldiers fought for the honor of giving their coats to make a bed on the frozen ground—was irreparable. It was Browne who had enabled Prince Charles to play commander and come off with a fair showing as a general; Browne did the fighting, and Prince Charles took the credit. The two distinguished slain generals got exactly what they were fighting for—adventure, monuments, and a few paragraphs in books of history. But what about the thousands of brave men who fought and died unhonored, only to be buried in long trenches and forgotten—we suspect the carp cleaned up the bodies left in the fish ponds. What did they win in that bloody Battle of Prague? How little their lives meant to Frederick of Prussia and Maria Theresa.

Frederick and his Prussian braves immediately settled down to besiege Prague, where there were forty-six thousand Austrian soldiers and one hundred thousand noncombatants, all of whom were blasted with red-hot cannon balls for a month. One fourth of the buildings of the city were wrecked or burned, and thousands died of injuries, sickness, and starvation, in that month of horrors during which the King of Prussia was vainly endeavoring to break down the resistance of the stubborn city.

The news of the battle at Prague was received with consternation in Vienna, but serious as this reverse was, it did not faze the courage of the Queen. She succeeded in smuggling a message into the beleaguered city, saying, "I am greatly concerned that so many of my generals and so much of my army remain besieged in

Prague, but I predict a favorable termination of the siege. I cannot impress too strongly upon your minds that my army will incur an everlasting disgrace should it not effect what the French, in the last war, performed with far inferior numbers. The army under General Daun is being strengthened daily, and will soon be able to raise the siege. The French are approaching with diligence. The Swedes are also coming, and in a little while, with the aid of Providence, affairs will be much more favorable for us." [14] This message inspired and encouraged Prague to continue its resistance, but we cannot help wondering what Prince Charles thought of the suggestions it contained for his guidance. True, he had a much larger force than Marshal Belleisle had when he made his famous escape, but the city was now guarded by a Frederick of Prussia and not a Francis of Lorraine, a fact which amounted to the difference between impossibility and possibility. Charles knew that if he ever opened the gates of Prague, he would soon be saluting Frederick as a prisoner.

Frederick fully realized the menace of the approaching army under Daun, a rising young Bohemian commander whose ability was as yet unknown. As a measure of precaution the King sent Bevern with an army of twenty thousand, to halt him, but Bevern found himself facing an army of sixty thousand, and not having the impetuosity of his master, allowed himself to be slowly driven back toward Prague. The King now saw that he was likely, after all, to be attacked by Daun on the rear and Prince Charles on the front,

[14] Coxe, III, 404.

and decided to lead a part of the besieging army to join Bevern and dispose of Daun. This new army must be conquered quickly or the whole Prussian campaign might end in a fiasco.

It was in such a humor that Frederick and Bevern came upon Daun who had selected a most formidable position at Kolin. There he was, standing like a sphinx on a well chosen hill, apparently with no intention of attacking Frederick's very much inferior force. Daun seemed to regard war as a very comfortable and deliberate occupation. He could afford to wait, for Frederick had been compelled to take his cannon away from Prague, and Daun knew the allies were rolling in from all sides of Prussia. "Very well," thought Frederick, "if he won't attack, I will." Nothing but fish ponds had any terror for Frederick who was beginning to believe his army invincible. He began flinging charges at Daun at two o'clock in the afternoon of the eighteenth of June. It was one of the longest days of the year, so long that by the time darkness came Frederick's army was almost completely ruined. In vain he sought some weak spot in the defenses of Daun's position; every clump of trees, every rock, and every crevice of the hill concealed nests of death to the attackers. Remembering his experience at Prague, Frederick continued sending column after column to its doom. Finally he led a charge himself, but after advancing a short distance one of his generals called, "Majesty, you and I cannot win this battle alone!" Frederick turned round to discover that half the men he had been leading had fled. He then called Bevern and ordered a retreat "to and across the Elbe, a good fifteen miles away." There he meant to assemble his Prussian conquerors and count them, before attempting anything more. When he finished his enumeration, he found that he had lost nearly half his army; most of his artillery was also gone, presumably into the hands of the cautious Daun.[15]

But Daun did not attempt to follow and complete the ruin of his antagonist; he paused to spend some weeks in digging up the terrain of the whole neighborhood for entrenchments, and felling forests to construct an abatis, just as if he feared Frederick might return at any moment and lunge once more at an impregnable foe in a second attempt to commit suicide with his army. Thus Frederick was given the time he so very much needed to reorganize his army, bring in new recruits, and gather new artillery.

The siege of Prague was immediately raised amid a medley of *Te Deums*, cries of victory, fireworks and illuminations, and Prince Charles went to take command of Daun's army. When the news reached Vienna joy reigned supreme, especially in the heart of Maria Theresa who felt that she had passed a new milestone in her path to power. She was reaping the harvest of her arduous labors in reorganizing the army and the nation into a fighting unit. For the first time the Austrians had defeated the Prussians under the command of the King—in fact, it was the first time her army had ever met Frederick's and gotten away without a ter-

---

[15] Carlyle, V, 447–463; Goldsmith, 171; Coxe, III, 407; Arneth, V, 197 seq.

Frederick took the result of this battle very much to heart. He is said to have broken into tears, crying, "This is our Pultowa! My Hussars all are lost!" Shortly afterward he wrote to Voltaire, "You, who are only a spectator of this bloody tragedy, can well afford to hiss the drama we are playing."

rible beating. Let *Te Deums* be sung in all the churches, let the city be illuminated, let cannon boom on the walls, and the people march in triumphant parades. Austria was safe! The Prussians were not invincible! The King's army had fled in disorder, a veritable rout, under the King's personal command! She was recompensed, vindicated, avenged! Daun should have a letter of thanks written in her own hand, and every one of his soldiers should have an extra month's pay as a present from the Queen. She would show her brave men that she was not lacking in appreciation.[16] But that was not enough. The shouts of triumph would die away into silence, the soldiers would spend their bonuses and forget about it, and Daun's letter was not sufficient recognition of his glorious victory. The attainment of this goal, the fulfillment of her fondest hope, the answer to her prayers, must be commemorated in a manner never to be forgotten. She would found a military order; let it be called the Order of Maria Theresa, and let Daun be the first member and the first chief of the society. Only men who rendered great service in the army should be admitted to membership; its proud emblems should be worn in parades, and, after a hero's death, be regarded as the most cherished possession of descendants. What the Queen willed came to pass; the Order of Maria Theresa was instituted with the Queen sitting on the throne, and the occasion honored by paintings on broad canvases. From that day its membership was coveted by every Austrian warrior. Thus the eighteenth day of June, the day Daun de-

[16] Carlyle, V, 463 seq.

feated Frederick at Kolin, became a red-letter day in the Austrian calendar.[17]

But the story of the year's campaign is only half told. The next we hear of Frederick he had marched far away into Saxony and defeated the French at Rossbach; in the words of Carlyle, "sent the Frenchmen, much in rags, much in disorder, in terror, and here and there almost in despair—winging their way, like clouds of bedraggled poultry caught by a mastiff in corn, across the Weser, across the Ems, finally across the Rhine, every feather of them—their long-drawn cackle, of the shrieky type, filling all nature in those months, and the mastiff still following." [18]

Then by the fourth of December, the mastiff—I think it would be better to call him a fox—was back sniffing at the tracks of the Queen's victorious army, now under the command of Prince Charles. On the fifth of December the fox bit the Queen's army, and bit it very hard at Leuthen. Prince Charles had what seemed to be an impregnable position on a hill, plenty of artillery, and much cavalry. Frederick feinted on the Prince's right, drawing all the artillery and cavalry down the slope on that side; then, using a trick copied from an old Greek warrior, charged the Prince's left, throwing the Austrians into confusion and routing them with tremendous slaughter.[19] The reports of this battle filled the Queen with terror; ten thousand Austrians left on the field, three thousand of them slain,

---

[17] Guglia, II, 154; Arneth, V, 199.
[18] Carlyle, VI, 24.
[19] It is claimed that Frederick derived this maneuver from Epaminondas who used it at the Battle of Leuctra.

twelve thousand taken prisoners—twenty-two thousand Austrian soldiers, one hundred and sixteen cannon, and the longed-for conquest of Silesia, vanished in the smoke of a day's battle! Her grief was intensified when she learned that Frederick had lost, all told, less than one third as many soldiers and no artillery. Thus the winter set in on a scene of ruin for the Queen, and triumph for her foe.[20]

But to every war there is always a political background shifting in sympathy with the success or failure of the contending armies. The three stable factors in that bleak winter of 1757–58, proved to be the three women of the female triumvirate, Maria Theresa, Madame Pompadour, and Czarina Elizabeth. The French minister was for giving up. In a letter to Vienna he said: "I see that in ten or twelve days, Austria has lost three fourths of her troops and officers, and Russia is selling her artillery horses for a hundred sous apiece. Is it possible that the Czarina, in her weakness, can counteract the plans of the British minister and the vast bribes of England? There is the Empress without an army, and the French ill-disciplined and without a general, hemmed in between the Prussians and Hanoverians. If the Austrian court will let us negotiate, or negotiate for us, we may get ourselves honorably out of this difficulty." This letter was most disheartening to the Queen but she soon recovered her courage. In a little while the minister retracted this gloomy note and Louis XV wrote her a cheerful letter in his own hand, all of which reflected the influence of Madame Pompadour.[21] Maria Theresa was not sorry then that she had

[20] Carlyle, VI, 50 seq.
[21] Arneth, V, 272 seq.

The Second Contest   215

made presents and written letters to the Madame, and Kaunitz, who was doing his best to calk the seams of his leaky ship of alliance, was thankful that Madame was where she was and what she was.[22] We may also be sure the Queen offered daily prayers for the Czarina who was reported to be on the verge of passing out with the dropsy.

In this one campaign in 1757, we have an epitome of the whole Seven Years' War, the campaigns and battles of which are too numerous to be told here in detail. It was a long series of victories and defeats following one another in an apparently endless procession, teaching the Queen valuable lessons and testing her courage to the limit. She very quickly discerned that she must dispose of her brother-in-law Prince Charles, before he wrecked the monarchy with his incompetence. Removing him from the supreme command probably cost her many tears, for fidelity to her family was a weakness with the Queen; but she did it, sending him back to his soft berth as Governor of the Netherlands, where he could hang his sword and medals on the walls of his palace, drink good whiskey, and dream of the bygone days when he was considered one of the greatest generals of Europe. We shall hear no more of him, except that he may come in for an occasional mention in connection with the affairs of the family.

The natural choice for his successor was Daun, the hero of Kolin, and the first name on the membership

---

[22] Upon hearing that the French Minister had written to Vienna urging peace, Madame Pompadour was very indignant. She immediately wrote Kaunitz: "I hate Frederick worse than ever. Let us put forth every effort to crush the Attila of the north; when that is accomplished, you will see me as content as I am now mortified."

list of the Order of Maria Theresa. The appointment was made without delay. It was a great pleasure for the Queen to make Daun Field Marshal, for he was married to a daughter of the much-loved Countess Fuchs, her teacher. The winter was spent in recruiting new troops for the army which had been so shattered by Frederick's last victory.

III

During the winter there was a strong undercurrent of criticism directed against Daun, because he had failed to follow up his victory and destroy the remnant of Frederick's army, which had so quickly recuperated and wrought havoc upon the French, and later upon the Austrians. His enemies called him a dawdler and his friends took up the term of opprobrium and converted it into one of honor; he was a new Fabius the Dawdler who would worry this modern Prussian Hannibal to death by dawdling.

In the spring Daun further imitated the tactics of his Roman prototype by avoiding battle with Frederick, and following him at a safe distance until the Prussians were before the walls of Olmütz, dangerously near to Vienna. Then there was consternation in the Austrian capital and the following conversation is said to have occurred.

Said a minister, "Majesty, shall we not flee for our lives?"

"No," replied the Queen, "we shall remain here until the enemy is at the gates of the city!"

"And then what shall we do, Your Majesty?"

"Flee until we come to the last town in Hungary."

"Then what, Your Majesty?"

"Then," replied the Queen, "I will send the King of Prussia an invitation to meet me alone with pistols, powder and bullets to settle our quarrel." [23]

At this stage Gideon Loudon, a Scotch soldier of fortune, entered the play as a star performer by destroying a train of Frederick's provisions with a slaughter of the convoy, compelling the Prussian King to retreat. In this adventure of Loudon's there was one ghastly incident. In the Prussian convoy were seven hundred young recruits, "mere boys," who had never tasted battle, and all but thirty-five of them were left cold in death on the road—war meant something to those boys, and something to their mothers too.[24]

Loudon's victory brought joy to the Queen, but in its wake came trailing much trouble and annoyance. The enemies of Daun set up a clamor to have Loudon placed in supreme command, and the Queen was seriously embarrassed. Loudon had entered the Queen's army in 1744, after having offered his services to the King of Prussia who refused them because he said he did not like Loudon's face. Then he came to Vienna and was immediately accepted. He was of Scotch parentage, but had been born in Russia where he grew up in the army. He was exactly suited to the command of the Croat rough-riders, who were known as Pandours, and they were soon in love with him. He and his Pandours swooped down upon detached groups of the Prussians, did them to death and then disappeared like wolves in a forest. They were very reckless, but swift

---

[23] This dialogue is based upon a letter of Maria Theresa to her daughter Maria Christina, May 10, 1758.

[24] Carlyle, VI, 104 seq.; Coxe, III, 411.

and certain. Loudon was a rough character, but unusually capable; the Queen became very fond of him.

Then there was another soldier of fortune in the service of the Queen; he was an Irishman, named Lacy, who was a skillful tactician and did much to improve the discipline of the army. Loudon and Lacy presented strange contrasts. Loudon was awkward and ill at ease in the Queen's presence, but she did her best to make him comfortable, never tolerating a smile from her courtiers over his ungainly appearance. Lacy was a veritable lion about the Queen's court; he could affect all the punctilious formalities of the *Hof* with a real Irish swagger, meet the *Hofrats* on equal terms, and beat them at their own game of kissing hands, bowing, and pawing the air in the presence of the high-born. Lacy was of noble parentage, so that he naturally "chummed" with Daun and his followers.

It took all the Queen's diplomatic tact to keep peace between the two military factions, and her position became all the more intolerable as Loudon forged to the front and Daun continued dawdling. Eventually she was involuntarily forced to conclude that Loudon was the best commander in her army, and may have been a trifle sorry that she had committed herself so strongly to Daun by written letters, by conferring upon him the highest honor in her new military order, and in many other ways. She tried to remedy the mistake by placing Loudon in command of a separate army and making him independent of Daun, but the climax of her difficulties in this respect was reached when, in the Battle of Liegnitz, Loudon fought the whole Prussian army alone and was defeated, while Daun and Lacy were within easy reach but did not come to his assistance.

Daun claimed he did not know Loudon was engaged, had not heard the cannonading or seen the smoke, but many refused to believe it and there were charges and countercharges in the ministry at Vienna. Maria Theresa had the troublesome part of a peacemaker, defending both generals and doing her best to bring about the order and harmony that were so very much needed.[25]

Daun's conduct as a general was very peculiar. He won as many battles from Frederick as Frederick did from him, but he never had the power to follow his victories to completion, always allowing the King time to recuperate from his defeats. We are told that Washington considered Frederick a great general, Napoleon said he was, and Thomas Carlyle wrote eight volumes to prove it, but when we read the history of the Seven Years' War, we sometimes wonder if his greatness was not largely due to his good fortune in being opposed by weak commanders.

As might have been expected, the French were scarcely a factor in the continental end of the Seven Years' War. They were fully engaged in their contest with England for world power, and were continually losing. In 1758, the English camel again got its head into Canada by the capture of Louisburg and Cape Breton; the next year in came the shoulders with Wolfe's defeat of Montcalm at Quebec. France had plenty to do without assisting the Queen against Frederick,[26] and as a result Maria Theresa looked more

---

[25] After the Battle of Liegnitz, Maria Theresa was so annoyed that she spoke of abdicating, but soon recovered her courage.—Arneth, VI, 242–247.
[26] Carlyle, VI, 119.

and more in the direction of St. Petersburg, from which came a large army. There were many difficulties and disputes between the commanders of the Russians and the Austrians, but they managed to get along well enough to bring Frederick several times to despair; once or twice he even contemplated suicide. Several times his head seemed to be sliced off even with his shoulders, but like the *Lernæan* Hydra, he grew a new one, always a little better than the old.

But Frederick's semi-magical power could not last indefinitely against such tremendous physical odds; that it lasted as long as it did was amazing. The autumn of 1761 found him at the end of his resources and reduced to helplessness. Much of his territory was in the possession of his enemies who stood facing him from every quarter. He had made a wonderful fight but manifestly a losing one in the end, which was near at hand.[27]

At this stage something of the greatest importance occurred in St. Petersburg. Czarina Elizabeth died on the fifth of January, 1762. In that little sentence, we read the salvation of Frederick and the failure of Maria Theresa in the Seven Years' War. Elizabeth's successor was her nephew Peter, often called "Silly Peter," who had always worshipped Frederick from afar; he had even been accused of doing spy service at the court of Russia for the King of Prussia. No sooner had Peter taken the oath of office than he ordered the whole Russian army to quit the Queen's service and join Frederick. With a servility most unbecoming a great monarch, Peter sought and received a commis-

[27] Arneth, VI, 252.

sion in the Prussian army. The change in Russia was echoed by a similar one in Sweden, which had accomplished little for the Queen, but was likely to become very much of a factor in the hands of the near-by Frederick.

Such a sweeping shift in alliances almost completely overwhelmed Maria Theresa, who had thought herself on the verge of realizing her fond dream of recovering Silesia. The many castles she had built in imagination fell as if shattered by a thunderbolt.[28] On the other hand Frederick, who had been sulking in a slough of despondency, refusing to speak to his friends, and so completely dejected that he no longer took the pains to wash himself and comb his hair, suddenly bounded to life and appeared joyfully before his army and friends.[29] His army was now equal to that of Maria Theresa, and the Russian commanders were in possession of all the secret plans of the Austrians. He immediately undertook to contest the possession of Silesia which had fallen into the hands of the Queen.

Events moved very rapidly that year. In a few months Peter's wife, Catherine, had started a rebellion, overthrown the government and taken the throne. Peter was sent to prison and presently murdered—according to gossip, at the request of the wife Frederick had given him some years before. Catherine was German but hated Frederick; she ordered her army to quit his service. Her first motive was to get her soldiers away from Frederick because she feared he would incite them to a counter-revolution and restore Peter. Then,

---
[28] Coxe, III, 473–474.
[29] *Ibid.*, VI, 285. "*Morte la bestia,*" wrote Frederick in exultation upon hearing of the death of Elizabeth

after she had made herself doubly secure by placing the army beyond Frederick's influence and making a restoration of his puppet impossible, she heard Frederick had made some pleasant remarks about her—said that she was beautiful, clever, and the like—so she refused to allow her soldiers to return to the service of Maria Theresa.[30]

Frederick, confounded by the new order from Catherine, which he said was "sufficient to overthrow all the projects of man," managed to bribe the Russian commander to pretend for a few days that he had not received Catherine's order.[31] During those days Frederick defeated and almost destroyed a detachment of the Austrian army which Daun did not attempt to rescue, because, believing himself facing the combined strength of the Russians and Prussians, he was afraid to weaken his force by sending relief. This defeat of the Austrians, due entirely to Frederick's foxy bribery and deceit, was of the greatest significance, for it enabled the Prussians to reconquer almost all of Silesia and retain it until the peace conference, where actual possession was easily converted into ownership, just as in the earlier Silesian wars.[32]

With the Russians out of the contest neither side was able to conquer the other, and the seven-year-long bloody struggle terminated in a drawn game. The war materials of both contestants, such as young men, courage, and resources in cash and credit, had been completely consumed by seven years of conflagration. Frederick was no longer receiving subsidies from Eng-

---

[30] Arneth, VI, 331; Coxe, III, 475–476.
[31] Goldsmith, 181.
[32] Arneth, VI, 336 seq.

The Second Contest 223

land—he had gotten from that source not less than thirteen million dollars. He had melted and coined most of the silver of the churches and palaces of his kingdom, and reduced the purchasing power of his money by mixing copper with the silver. He had exhausted the capital of all his banks, and pawned everything possible from his private estate. He had impressed every available young man of his kingdom into the army, and they were for the most part dead or disabled. According to his own statement, he retained his honor, but it was so badly tarnished that none of his neighbors could recognize its value.

Maria Theresa had also reached the end of the resources at her command, although her dominions had not been stripped to the same degree of barrenness then existing in Prussia. As early as 1758 she had pawned her jewels; in 1760 there had been a public subscription and her officials had been urged to bring their silver to the mint. France had long ago discontinued the promised subsidies. Many young men still remained in her dominions, but she could not reach them by conscription, and did not dare to resort to impressment as Frederick had done in Prussia. She had even dismissed men from the army because she could not find means to equip and feed them.[33] Peace had become an actual necessity to both Austria and Prussia.

Under such conditions the Treaty of Hubertsburg was formed. The terms may be summed up in one sentence, "Let everything be as it was in the beginning." [34]

---

[33] Gotthold Dorschel, 109.
[34] The war between England and France terminated with the Treaty of Paris in February, 1763. By this treaty France lost Canada permanently to England.

But everything could not be as it was in the beginning. No treaty could bring back the youth of Europe out of hundreds of thousands of graves, or remove the pangs of sorrow from the hearts of millions of bereaved women and children. A generation must pass before that blight could be lifted from Prussia and Austria.

Most histories convey the impression that Maria Theresa lost, and Frederick won, the Seven Years' War. If we assume that Maria Theresa deliberately planned and started the war for the purpose of regaining Silesia and partitioning Prussia, we cannot avoid such a conclusion. But the assumption is not warranted because it is not supported by facts. In the formation of alliances, the Queen had uppermost in her mind the protection of her dominions from raids, such as Frederick had made, and she believed would make again at the first favorable opportunity. That she was right was proved by the manner in which he seized Saxony and virtually annexed it by appropriating its resources and impressing its army into his service, and the idea is further supported by his haste to invade Bohemia with the evident intention of using it in the same manner. Frederick's conduct in 1756 and the early part of 1757 signified that he meant to take and keep both Saxony and Bohemia. He was bent upon conquest, not defense.

If the Queen's primary object was to make her dominions secure against Prussia she certainly succeeded, for Prussia was cured of all attempts to seize Austrian territory for a hundred years. Frederick's habits in this respect were very much improved, and he became a fairly decent neighbor, at least toward Maria Theresa.

Maria Theresa's conduct in continuing her alliance with France has been much criticized, but it was not bad diplomacy. France had not been of much service to the Queen in this war, but nothing had occurred which seemed to her as false as the manner in which England had bartered away Silesia to Frederick in the Treaty of Hanover. Austria required a strong ally in Europe, and under the circumstances, it appeared to be good statesmanship to continue the alliance with France, rather than switch back to a power which she believed had betrayed her.

A little more than twenty-two years had passed since Maria Theresa's accession, and fourteen of them had been spent in most discouraging wars. She was sick and tired of blood and plunder and hoped her land would remain at peace for the rest of her life. She wished to devote herself to reforms, education, the arts, music, and the affairs of her family; all of which she had been compelled to neglect during the wars for the preservation of her dominions. She ceased to hope for the recovery of Silesia, and spoke of its conquest as a "chimera"; she thought compensation for its loss might be obtained through the marriages of her children, or through diplomacy, but never at the cost of a war.[35]

The Seven Years' War made an old woman of Maria Theresa; the truth of this statement is verified by a study of her pictures. In 1757 she was forty, but in spite of having borne sixteen children, she appeared

---

[35] "I, who have suffered so much grief on account of this war, am resolved to live at peace hereafter. I love my family and my people too much to sacrifice them in another war."—Letter of Maria Theresa to Field Marshal Lacy, Nov. 27, 1770.

"It is better to be a second class power with peace and a happy people, than a first class power and always at war."—Letter to Lacy, Aug. 6, 1778.

young. In 1763 she was old, unmistakably old, if we may judge from her portraits. Her feeling of age is also proved by the fact that in two short years she made her son co-regent, and would gladly have resigned all the duties of state to his care but for the fact that she feared his rashness.

X

THE QUEEN AS A WOMAN

I

THERE was nothing mysterious about the genius of Maria Theresa. She had a large, well-shaped head filled with excellent brains and supported by an exceptionally strong body, which she lashed to the limit of endurance in hard work. Her eminent position was held largely through relentless toil backed by unusual physical strength and rare mental talent. The same might be said of Napoleon and many other renowned characters of history. Genius demands much, but nothing more insistently than hard work.

At the beginning of her reign, Maria Theresa sought to make the most of her time by dividing all her waking hours into definite periods for various duties. She was so much in earnest about this that she summoned Count Silva-Tarouca to her aid and asked him to serve as her monitor, private adviser, and confidential critic; with his assistance she made out a written daily program.[1] She was to rise at eight o'clock and devote her first half hour to prayer and coffee. The next half hour was to be spent in hearing her physician's report concerning the children, after which she was to apply herself to public business until noon. Then came an

---
[1] Silva-Tarouca, 26–30; Arneth, II, 194.

hour for lunch, to be followed by finishing whatever tasks had been left uncompleted during the forenoon. After that, she might spend the time with her family until four, when she was to begin receiving and consulting her ministers, and continue till six. The interval from six to eight was to be her own to use in any manner she saw fit; then came dinner which must be over in time to retire at ten.

But she soon found herself unable to abide by this schedule, on account of the endless interruptions from unforeseen events. How she actually used her time is discussed, among other interesting topics, by Count Podewils who came to her court as Prussian Ambassador at the end of the Wars of Accession. Frederick of Prussia seems to have been very curious concerning the personal affairs of the Queen, and had his Ambassador write many details in regard to them.

In one of his letters the Count wrote: "Her gait is free, her bearing majestic, her figure large, her face round and full, and her voice clear and pleasant. Her countenance is beautiful, and her hair is blond with a slight tinge of red. Her eyes are very large, lively and mild, and their deep blue most striking. She has a regular nose, not hooked, and not blunt. She has very white teeth, and they are most charming when she laughs. Although her mouth is large, it is rather pretty; her neck and chest are well modeled, and her hands are exquisite. In spite of her grief and anxiety, her expression is fresh, and her skin very clear although she gives it but little attention. Her demeanor is sprightly and happy, and her greeting always warm and pleasant; there is no denying that Maria Theresa is a most charming and delightful woman." We imagine Frederick read all this with keen interest, for she was the woman he might have married had there not been trouble over religion.

In the same letter Podewils continues: "She loves pleasure, but never allows it to interfere in the least with her work. Formerly she danced most passionately, and was very fond of attending masked balls, but now she dances very rarely and attends but few balls. She also sang and played the spinet, but seldom does either any more. Her principal diversions are long walks and rides into the country. You know she was compelled to learn to ride well in order to please the Hungarians at her coronation in Pressburg; it was a matter of politics then, but now it is merely a means of health and pleasure. She rides here and there, and everywhere, stopping now and then for a cup of coffee or a light lunch with her friends, often at the *Richterhaus* in Lainz, the *Jammerpepi* in Baden, or the *Peperl* in the Prater. Also she walks, sometimes for three or four hours at a time, into the country, but seldom goes hunting and then only to please her husband."

From this paragraph one gets the idea that Maria Theresa led a rather happy, care-free life, but the impression is corrected by still another part of Podewils' gossipy letter which reads: "The Queen leads a very regular life. In the winter she rises at six, but in the summer at four, or never later than five, and works the whole forenoon at reading dispatches, signing documents, and attending meetings of her ministers. She lunches at one, after which she rests, but generally not longer than a half hour. Very often she eats alone to save time. In both summer and winter she frequently takes her meals in solitude, and after them hurries for short walks; during all the time thus spent she is constantly glancing at important papers and dispatches. From seven to half past eight in the evening, she amuses herself; then eats a light supper—often only a bowl of broth—takes another short walk and goes to bed."

Another paragraph of this lengthy letter reads: "She never bothers about her health, but relies entirely upon her vigorous body for strength and endurance. She is warm-blooded, and, even in the middle of winter, often sits by an open window; as a rule the windows of her apartment are wide open very much to the discomfort and annoyance of her associates. Her physician scolds her dreadfully about this, but she only laughs at him. Sometimes only a few hours before the birth of a child, the Queen may be seen in the opera, and the people scarcely hear that she has been confined before she is racing through the streets in her carriage, or sitting at her desk at work."

Podewils wrote further: "I have told you something of the state of her mind; she is most unusually ambitious, and hopes to make the House of Austria more renowned than it has ever been. She has, as you well know, a terrible hatred for France, with which nation it is most difficult for her to keep on good terms, but she controls this passion except when she thinks it to her advantage to display it. She detests Your Majesty, but acknowledges your ability. She cannot forget the loss of Silesia, nor her grief over the soldiers she lost in wars with you." [2]

In the early part of her reign Maria Theresa had

---

[2] Podewils to Frederick II, quoted by Bermann, 523–527.

no confidence in her ministers, and delegated no important responsibilities to them without her careful supervision. Usually upon rising she found her desk piled high with important state papers, but before she retired every one of them had been carefully read, and if possible, disposed of, often through long nerve-racking conferences with her advisers. In addition to this, especially during the latter part of her life, she wrote voluminous letters to her children and friends, only portions of which have been preserved. Being troubled with insomnia more and more as she grew older, she often propped herself up in bed and wrote for hours. Many of her letters are dated at two and three o'clock in the morning.

As a girl and young woman Maria Theresa spent much time on her toilet, but became careless under the stress of important work. On rising she passed a stormy half hour with her maid, who considered her position little better than that of a royal slave. The Queen wished to appear well, but wanted to be made pretty in a very short time. She took the most pains with her hair because Francis often admired it and she was anxious to retain his affection, which had an annoying habit of wandering into forbidden paths seeking other ladies with soft, silky locks. She desired to be *chic* in the presence of her *Franzerl*, but above all, felt that she must get to work.

During the Wars of Accession, she never attended balls except in celebrations of victories, when she led the crowd in wild jubilation, scattering flowers among her officers and fraternizing with her generals in a manner which would have made her ancestors shudder with horror. But no sooner were the festivities over than she was back at her desk with apparently renewed vigor and vim.[3]

There seemed to be no limit to her endurance, even under exertions that would have sent an ordinary woman to bed with doctors and nurses dancing attendance on all sides. She was very temperate in eating and drinking and often found herself bored to distraction at the state banquets, where her guests gorged themselves with a dozen varieties of rich meat and lapped up liters of heavy wine, while she minced at her fruits and sipped lemonade, all the while wishing the performance were over so that she might get to bed, rise early in the morning, and return to her labor.

The few hours Maria Theresa spent with her children were not devoted to hugging and kissing, but usually to settling their noisy wrangles and disputes, putting them in their proper places from the standpoint of behavior, and trying to bring some semblance of order out of the bedlam which ten husky youngsters always make for a busy mother. Probably she was often glad to get away from them, but all the governesses and her physician had orders to call her instantly in the event of an accident or illness in her little regiment of offspring.

It is surely no exaggeration to say that Maria Theresa was one of the busiest monarchs the world has ever seen, and that she went about her duties with a vim and alacrity scarcely surpassed in history. Her reservoir of strength was immense, but it drained in so many directions that we may regard her endurance

[3] Extracted from Podewils to Frederick II, quoted by Bermann, 523–527.

as marvelous. In strange contrast to her busy life sat her arch enemy in Potsdam, smug and selfish, lording it over his little bigoted court of male *literati*, quarreling with Voltaire, sneering at Maria Theresa, Madame Pompadour, and Czarina Elizabeth, and writing second-grade poetry. But in spite of all the Queen's impediments she reeled off more hard work than the King of Prussia ever did in an equal length of time.

II

Maria Theresa had a delightful sense of humor, but so completely encased in a hard shell of piety that it was only occasionally revealed; almost never was she humorous when a question of morals or religion was involved. Nearly all the other Hapsburgs were also very pious, but almost without exception, their moral conduct was such as to render them hypocritical, and they all lacked the saving grace bestowed by Maria Theresa's fine sense of humor. Very likely the Queen was indebted to her husband for much of her appreciation of mirth, for Francis was a gay man of the world and always saw the funny side of the serious events of life. We shall relate three anecdotes of the Queen's humor, the first being one in which her husband played a leading rôle.

One delightful day in the autumn of 1742, Maria Theresa and her husband went for one of their long walks into the country among the vineyards. The day was warm and the Queen presently became very thirsty, but her husband could find no water, so he gallantly scaled the stone wall into a vineyard and brought her a bunch of ripe, juicy grapes. It was very jolly sitting in the shade of the wall and eating the delicious fruit—until the keeper of the vineyard arrived and demanded, "Who gave you permission to pick grapes in this vineyard?"

"Nobody," replied Francis.

"What is your name?"

To this question Francis, prompted by his sense of humor, gave a false answer and added rather defiantly, "Now what is about to happen?"

"What is about to happen," replied the keeper, "is that you are fined five guldens," and they saw a hard calloused hand stretched for the money.

Francis searched his pockets and was distressed to discover that he had no money with him. Inquiry brought the information that the Queen was also destitute of five guldens. At this stage Francis wished to confess their identity, but the Queen accounted it a point of policy to stick to the lie to which they had committed themselves. She did not wish it repeated about the beer halls of Vienna that the Queen and her husband had confessed themselves guilty of both thieving and lying; she thought the little incident might be brought to some better termination than that.

"We will send you the five guldens tomorrow," said Francis.

"N-a-h, that don't go," drawled the keeper. "If you can't pay, you shall spend twenty-four hours in jail."

No sooner was the sentence pronounced than its execution began. The keeper marched them off to a near-by building, which proved to be one in which bacon was being smoked, and locked them in, saying as he left, "I'll bring you bread and water; you need nothing more."

So the royal pair found themselves sitting on a dirt floor in a dismal smoky room, where they might repent of their sins at leisure. By the time the keeper arrived with the bread and water their repentance was complete. Francis said: "Please go to the Hofburg and ask any official you find there to send Francis of Lorraine and Maria Theresa ten guldens. You may use five of them to pay the fine and keep the rest for your trouble."

The keeper eyed him critically and burst into laughter.

"So you think I'm a fool!" he said. "Francis of Lorraine! Maria Theresa! ha! ha! For this you get yet twenty-four hours more in the bacon house!"

The door slammed and they heard the keeper's "ha! ha! ha's!" die away in the distance.

In the meantime an alarm had spread throughout the palace that the Queen and her Consort had mysteriously disappeared. Soon secret detectives were scurrying hither and thither through the city and country to find the missing monarchs. Before long some clever sleuth picked up the trail, and soon arrived with the keeper of the vineyard at the bacon house, where they found the very crestfallen Majesties patiently waiting for deliverance. The keeper was immediately arrested, and would have been severely punished but for the intervention of the Queen who boldly commanded, "Let the man alone; he did nothing more than his duty."

Later the keeper was loaded with gifts, and his vineyard exempted from future taxes. But the shrewd Maria Theresa did not stop with that; she had a monument erected on the spot where she ate the stolen grapes, and instituted an annual feast to commemorate the occasion. On the monument was chiseled the inscription, "Let every man do his duty." Thus this clever Queen converted a little incident, fraught with considerable danger to her good reputation, into a holiday on which all the winegrowers feasted and sang her praises for a generation.[4]

Another instance of her humor is related in connection with the great composer, Joseph Haydn. While the Palace of Schönbrunn was being built, she went there almost daily to inspect the progress of construction. One day she was horrified to see some youngsters doing all sorts of monkey tricks on one of the high balconies. She stormed at them and demanded that a certain *blond Buberl*, who seemed to be the ringleader, be brought to her. "Who are you?" she demanded, when the quivering lad stood in her presence. The guard who held the boy said, "Your Majesty, this is one of the boys from Kapellmeister Reuter's choir. You may recall that you were so pleased with the singing last Sunday, that you sent a permission for the boys to play here."

"So I did," she answered, "but I didn't tell them to go and kill themselves. Listen, sonny, don't do that any more, and next Sunday I will give you a new gold gulden. You understand me? You blond rascal! I saw how you were the leader of this crowd of rowdies. Remember, I am not joking!"

The next day when she made her rounds of the building, she was both horrified and outraged to witness the same group of youngsters, led by the same *blonde Buberl*, hanging like cats and bats from the same

---

[4] The authority for this story is Bermann, 519–523.

balcony. There was an imperial thunderstorm during which the angry monarch demanded that the guard take the ringleader and give him a sound spanking. "I promised him a new gold gulden to behave himself, but now I shall give the gulden to you as a reward for punishing him. Give the *blonde Dummheit* a full gulden's worth of spanking! He who will not hear and obey must feel!" The Queen did not leave until she saw her orders well executed.

Many years passed, and one day the Empress-queen was entertained by an orchestra from the castle of Prince Esterhazy. She was so delighted with the music that she asked the Prince to present the composer.

When he arrived she looked him over sharply and said, "Where have I seen you before?"

"You saw me when I was a boy," replied the composer. "I am the blond rascal who got a gulden's worth of spanking in Schönbrunn. I am now Joseph Haydn, the composer."

"What! Are you that little *blonde Dummheit?*"

"Yes, Your Majesty."

"Well, well, it was really worth a gulden to save you from breaking your neck, after all. Now let me see—I'll tell you what I'll do—I'll send you a nice *tabatière* filled with gold guldens. If the place where you were spanked still smarts, this may serve as a poultice!"

The *tabatière* filled with gold guldens arrived, and was always cherished as one of his dearest treasures by the celebrated composer. Many times he exhibited this memento and told the story to his friends.[5]

---

[5] Bermann, 542-544.

Once when Joseph, the Crown Prince, was an infant, Maria Theresa was walking with him and his nurse in the gardens of the palace, when she came upon a poor beggar with a baby. The woman was in rags and held an emaciated infant to her breasts, which were dry from lack of nutrition. "What have I done that I should be tortured with such a sad spectacle?" sighed the Queen as she handed the poor woman a gold coin.

The woman held the coin aloft, as if calling Heaven to witness its futility, and cried, "Of what use is gold to my starving baby?"

Maria Theresa was moved to tears, and on the impulse of the moment, took the child from its mother and began nursing it at her own full breast. The poor baby wiggled its toes over the rich milk, and the Queen noticing it burst into laughter. But Joseph soon began pulling at his mother's dress in jealous protestation, whereupon she exclaimed, "Never mind *Buberl*, there's plenty there for you too!"[6] Nothing but a victory over Frederick of Prussia could have given the Queen more joy than she felt on this occasion. She was a tender-hearted German *Frau*, as well as a great Queen.

III

From conversations with the Viennese one might easily receive the impression that Maria Theresa was a hypocrite in regard to sexual morality. We hear that she had *liaisons* with Count Silva-Tarouca, Kaunitz, and many others. If we attempt to defend her character, many Viennese smile and convey the idea that

---

[6] *Ibid.*, 582.

we are ignorant because we are foreigners. Not long ago, a guide who was conducting a large party of Americans about the city, was heard to say before the Queen's monument: "This is the great Maria Theresa who had sixteen children." Then lowering his voice, so as to make the remark all the more impressive, he added, "No two of them looked alike." [7]

Such intimations are absolutely contrary to authentic history; Maria Theresa's moral character was above the least reproach or peradventure of doubt, as can easily be shown by the testimony of numerous contemporaries and even by historical documents.

Wraxall, who visited Vienna during the latter part of her reign, wrote: "The Queen, who is very virtuous in her conduct, true to her marriage vows, and never has an impure thought, has but little patience with the indiscretions of others. She looks upon every grade of social vice with complete disapproval." Podewils, in one of his letters to Frederick of Prussia, said: "It would be absurd to think of Maria Theresa as a coquette, for she has no inclination whatever in that direction. Her love for her husband is true and honorable, and she watches his conduct toward other women with the most jealous care." Arneth, in his very reliable biography of Maria Theresa, said: "One point to which the Queen attached the greatest importance, was the preservation of public morals. Since she herself led such a blameless life, she demanded the same exemplary conduct of her subjects. She was intolerant of the prevailing immorality of the day, and seemed to have no sympathy for the frailties of mankind; this was

---

[7] Conversation overheard by the author.

indeed the only respect in which she was regarded as severe." [8] William Coxe, who wrote a monumental history of the House of Austria within a quarter of a century of the death of Maria Theresa, said: "She combined private economy with public liberality, dignity with condescension, elevation of soul with humility of spirit, and the virtues of domestic life with the splendid qualities which grace a throne."

When we search for some explanation of the frivolous reputation Maria Theresa seems to have among the people of her own city, we are very soon confronted with a most plausible one. It is the residue of a recoil from her vigorous action in suppressing vice. She caused so much annoyance to her subjects by her relentless war against social evils, that the people retaliated by circulating rumors that she did not practice what she preached. When individuals set themselves up as censors of public morals, they are very likely to find their own conduct carefully scrutinized and misrepresented. Under such circumstances the most harmless incident is often repeated from mouth to ear, and so distorted that white actually becomes black. It was probably thus that the stories of Maria Theresa's lapses from the straight and narrow path of moral rectitude originated, and they have grown to surprising dimensions.

In 1753 Maria Theresa founded a Chastity Commission,[9] whose activities remind us very much of some

---

[8] Arneth, IX, 399.

[9] The German word which we have translated into "Chastity Commission" is *"Keuscheitskommission."* Kaunitz was president of the commission, and nearly all the Queen's ministers held prominent positions on it.

of the governmental onslaughts against vice and intemperance witnessed today. It was a special department of the police which, as at present in Vienna, was under the control of the state. From the accounts of various contemporaries it seems there was some justification for this action on the part of the Queen. A very good description of the condition of society in Vienna at the time of the reign of Charles VI is to be read in one of the vivacious letters of Lady Montagu, of which we quote a part:

"Men look upon their wives' gallants as favorably as upon deputies that take the troublesome part of their business off their hands; though they have not the less to do, for they are generally deputies in another place themselves; in short, 'tis the established custom for every lady to have two husbands, one who bears the name, and another who performs the duties. And these engagements are so well known that it would be a downright affront, and publicly resented, if you were to invite a lady of quality to dinner without at the same time inviting her two attendants, a lover and husband, between whom she is to be seated in state. These submarriages often last for twenty years, and a lady commands her poor lover's estate even to the utter ruin of his family. . . . A man makes but an ill figure who is not in some commerce of this nature; and a woman looks out for a lover as soon as she is married, and as a part of her social equipment without which she could not be regarded as genteel; the first article of the agreement establishes her pension which remains to the lady although the man may prove inconstant. . . . I know several ladies of the first quality whose pensions are as well known as their annual rents, and yet no one esteems them the less; on the contrary, their discretion would be immediately questioned if they were suspected of being a mistress for nothing." [10]

It is very easy for us to understand that an invasion of such cherished rights by a monarch was very much resented by the Queen's liberty-loving subjects, especially since similar privileges were enjoyed in other lands, France in particular, where mistresses were received in the best society and often pensioned by the government. The people regarded this striving for social purity as only a chimera, and the silly whim of a woman who was piqued because her husband was known to be promiscuous with women.

The idea of suppressing vice became a passion with Maria Theresa, and led her to extreme measures which were hardly consistent with the good common sense she exhibited along other lines. She had five hundred officers in her College of Chastity, not to mention the hordes of secret agents and spies who prowled day and night through the streets of Vienna, raiding banquets, clubs, and even private gatherings, to arrest every one suspected of violating the social regulations of the court.

Not many of the Queen's official documents bearing upon this crusade are preserved, but here is one: "I have heard," wrote the Queen to the head of her commission in 1771, "that a man named Palm has taken advantage of a virtuous *danseuse* in the *Deutschestheater*, and, by means of false promises, has brought her to serve him in the same capacity as his wife. You will investigate this case and find out the truth. It was very

---

[10] Lady Montagu, I, 244, Letter of Sept. 20, 1716.

bad in Palm to be such a hypocrite, and also bad in the girl to injure him in this manner." [11]

At another time she wrote to Kaunitz to secure the extradition of a married Count who was living in adultery with a young Countess in Switzerland. The Queen expressed the "joy of a mother" when Kaunitz informed her that steps had been taken to bring the criminals to justice.[12] Apparently the punishment she intended to inflict upon this couple was to have the Countess placed in a nunnery for life, and the Count beheaded, but the fugitives managed to escape to Holland, where the Dutch were blissfully unmindful of the Queen's campaign to uplift morals. Upon hearing of this, Her Majesty was much overwrought, and determined that justice should not be completely swindled. She arranged to have the Count's effigy beheaded in public as an example for her subjects, but before this ridiculous show was staged, her sense of humor seems to have rescued her and she called the whole performance off, no doubt very much to the disappointment of the Viennese who intended to make a holiday of the occasion and attend *en masse*.[13]

According to trustworthy authorities the Queen's "Purity Squad" created a tremendous furor, under the influence of which vice buried itself in deep cellars, guarded by bolted doors and armed watchmen; passwords were required, and secret underground passages provided for escape when the alarm for a raid sounded. Any woman seen alone on the streets after dark, was likely to be arrested and carried before the commis-

[11] Arneth, IX, 401.
[12] *Ibid.*
[13] *Ibid.*, 401 seq.

sion for investigation; innocent gatherings were invaded, and foreigners suspected of having affairs with Viennese women were, in a few instances, expelled from the country.

We also read that the commission became corrupt, and that its members were guilty of accepting money for the protection of vicious clubs, and other places of ill fame. Under such conditions a seraglio of little girls thrived and made its owner rich. An archbishop was accused of being financially interested in a secret social organization for vice, and banned from the church. But such accounts are usually accompanied by the statement that, upon conviction of such crimes, the perpetrators were severely punished by the Queen.[14]

Especially prominent was a social society which flourished under the title of *Feigenbrüderschaft,* and met in hidden places several times a week; at such meetings the members, many of whom were very prominent in society, paired by a system of drawing numbers. In a raid of this organization, two sons of the Mayor of Danzig were taken, and along with others, sentenced to stand for months chained to the pillars of one of doors of the city, where they were heckled by passers and compelled to subsist upon whatever was offered by the public. But this method of punishment proved impracticable because the prisoners were too well-fed and received too much sympathy from the enemies of the commission. In the art shops of Vienna there are still old prints to be had showing such poor victims, with their ankles fastened to cannon balls and their arms chained to stone pillars, gazing sadly at the pave-

---

[14] Bermann, 786.

ment while taunted by passing men, women, and children.[15]

Still another order of this same character, known as the *Freidamenorden* (Order of Free Women), thrived, and was said to be under the patronage of a clandestine lodge of Freemasons. It also numbered among its members many women of "high society," more than a few of whom came from the Queen's court. This order was supposed to be protected by the police and was very exclusive and select. Each *Freidame* had a pseudonym known only to the order, so that the members could discuss one another rather freely, some said even in the presence of Her Majesty, without divulging their identities.

Wraxall drew a most interesting picture of the women of Vienna. He said: "The superstition of the Austrian women is amazing, but not at all inconsistent with gallantry; they sin, pray and confess; then begin all over again, never forgetting to attend mass. None of them eat meat on Fridays or Sundays, nor during the fasts of the church; they go to confession very often, not so much from principle as from habit. They seldom wear wedding rings, because they are too likely to lose them, so they send them for safekeeping to the church in Mariazell where there are more rings than Hannibal found in the Battle of Canna. The Viennese women do not allow their religion to interfere with their pleasure, but never become tangled in their conversations so as to reveal their secrets, only in their confessions do they really open their hearts."

But Wraxall also wrote: "In no other large city of

---

[15] *Ibid.,* 787.

Europe must one use so much care in approaching women. Such precautions are necessary because of the watchfulness of the Queen who is so severe in the punishment of social offences." [16] John Moore, an English traveller, in writing of his visit to Vienna during the reign of Maria Theresa, said: "I can imagine no city in Europe where a young gentleman would see fewer examples, or have fewer opportunities for deep gambling, open profligacy, or gross debauchery, than in Vienna." [17]

We may note that such letters contrast strangely with those of Lady Montagu, written during the reign of Charles VI, in which she describes Vienna as a "city of free adultery." We may be sure that under Maria Theresa, immorality was never flaunted in the faces of those who were not seeking it.

Should Maria Theresa return to earth today and stop in one of our modern cities, she would find much the same restrictions in vogue, and the same methods of evasion that characterized her own reign; she would be well qualified to head a vice commission in New York or Chicago, for she was one hundred and fifty years ahead of her time. One wonders what would happen should she chance to stroll along Kärntnerstrasse or the Graben at midnight under the enlightened government of the Austrian Republic.

But it is not customary for writers to give Maria Theresa very much credit for her severity in handling the social evil. It is generally put down as a brain storm brought on by her jealousy over the conduct of her husband. Even her most ardent admirers believe

[16] Quoted by Bermann, 785.
[17] *Ibid.*

she might have accomplished more had she been content to allow her own example, as a virtuous wife and devoted mother, to shine as a guiding lamp for the footsteps of her subjects. But what courage it must have required for her to face the public criticism occasioned by her unpopular, if not misguided, efforts to raise the moral standards of her day. How she must have been ridiculed in the profligate court of Louis XV, and in Frederick's little group of cynics at Potsdam.

Maria Theresa's high-minded endeavors were not restricted to the suppression of social vice. They extended into several lines where they were less criticized. One of the curses of her day was dueling, an evil which had been imported from Spain and France. At the beginning of her reign duels in Vienna were very frequent, and many prominent men of the nobility were killed in such combats. Nearly all the duels were fought in one little village just outside the walls. It was known as Josephstadt, having been named in honor of the Queen's son. The place had such a bad reputation that it was avoided by all good citizens except when they were engaged in dueling. It was in plain sight of the Hofburg and the commotion occasioned by the combats was often heard in the Queen's apartments.[18]

Maria Theresa was much disturbed by these contests, and resolved to end them by making all present at a duel subject to severe penalties. Very soon after she issued her edict against duels, one was fought in Paris by a nephew of one of her ministers, and in spite of the fact that the laws of France had not been

---

[18] *Ibid.*, 217–218

violated, she assessed a fine of one hundred thousand francs against the nephew, and made him pay it before allowing him to return to his native land.[19] Were Maria Theresa living today we may be sure she would have something very vigorous to say concerning the duels still fought by the students of the University of Vienna. We may also recall that at that time duels were not infrequent in the American colonies and throughout the civilized world.

Another twentieth century reform promulgated by Maria Theresa was the restriction of gambling. In this crusade she was obliged to contend with the bad example of her husband, who was passionately fond of playing cards for money.[20] He once acknowledged that he won, at Laxenburg, twelve thousand ducats in one night. This was almost the equivalent of thirty thousand dollars, and was regarded as a very large sum in those times. Probably owing to his influence the Queen finally consented to license faro tables, each table being held for a specified amount to be spent for Orphans' homes. The license was so high that only a very skillful player was able to pay it.[21] Personally the Queen seldom played cards, and refused to play for money.

The same year that saw the establishment of the Chastity Commission, witnessed the founding of a state lottery,[22] which has been continued almost without a break to this very day. The lottery was taken over by the state for the purpose of revenue. It was excused on the ground that such action was necessary

---

[19] Arneth, IX, 409.
[20] *Ibid.*, IV, 147 seq.
[21] *Ibid.*, IX, 407.
[22] *Ibid.*, IV, 70 seq.

to keep money from migrating to foreign lands, especially to France and Italy where lotteries were much in vogue.[23]

The story of how lotteries originated is most fascinating. In those times Genoa was governed by five senators and a doge, the former being chosen annually by placing the names of those eligible in an urn, from which five were drawn by a blindfolded girl. The list of eligibles was known to the public and the people were soon betting that certain names would be drawn. It was possible to bet against specified odds on any number of names from one to five, but it was soon discovered that certain ones were lucky because they were drawn more frequently than the others; very likely there was considerable fraud in connection with the drawings. Presently banks were formed to hold the stakes and the whole performance became systematized. A tremendous amount of money changed hands at each annual drawing of the senators.[24]

From this gambling over the drawing of senators came the enterprise of collecting money which, after retaining a certain percentage for the benefit of the institution promoting the lottery, was distributed by numbers. Lotteries sprang into existence in many lands, but in some they were soon prohibited by law. They flourished especially in France, which in this manner drew large remittances from surrounding countries. A huge sum from Vienna went annually to Paris for lottery tickets, in spite of all the warnings and prohibitions of the Queen's government. Maria Theresa probably concluded that, since the people were deter-

[23] Bermann, 618.
[24] *Ibid.*, 620.

mined to throw away their money in this manner, it might as well be caught in the coffers of the state, instead of dropping into the treasury of France to be spent in equipping armies to fight Austria. So a state lottery was established, and in ten years it yielded nearly four million guldens. Lottery tickets were purchased by many from patriotic motives, and in this manner revenues were provided with much less protest than by any form of taxation.[25] We may easily condemn Maria Theresa for her conduct concerning lotteries, but we must acknowledge that any system of raising money without taxation has a very strong appeal. We must also remember that at much later dates, greater evils were licensed—by supposedly better governments—for the purpose of revenues.

A fair consideration of the measures instituted by Maria Theresa for the improvement of public morals and the raising of revenues will bring us to the conclusion that they were nearly all based on good statesmanship, and framed for the welfare of state and society. Many of them indicated great courage backed by strong convictions—much more courage and conviction than was displayed by any of her predecessors or successors, with the possible exception of Joseph II.

IV

While Maria Theresa was a most zealous and devout Catholic,[26] she strongly resisted all encroachments

---

[25] Advertisements of lotteries are to be found in the *Diarum*, the official publication of the government at the time of Maria Theresa, and some of the notices state that tickets may be had in certain churches and monasteries.

[26] Gotthold Dorschel, 135-136.

of the church upon what she conceived to be the prerogatives of her state; she held Rome at arm's length, and never tolerated any undue familiarity from that quarter. The Catholic Church was never her master; on the contrary, she several times put it where she thought it belonged, by stern decrees, perhaps a trifle softened with wails of regret such as a fond mother displays when administering corporal punishment to her child.[27] During her reign the clergy found it as necessary to keep in good standing with the queen as with the pope. Several times she dictated the selection of abbots, bishops and archbishops who were known to be favorably disposed toward the monarchy rather than the pope.

In this connection the most notable act of her reign was the abolishment of the order of the Jesuits. There were two stories circulated as to what prompted her to this radical step. Both were probably true in part and are now so interesting that they are worth relating.

The Society of Jesus was the great missionary order of the Catholic Church, and as early as the time of Maria Theresa had carried Christianity into many of the remotest sections of the Americas, where it had converted the Indians and established fortified missionary posts. The Jesuits won the friendship of the savages and assisted them in many ways, one of which was in the art of defending themselves. The Jesuits of Portugal had introduced the Bible, and with it Portuguese weapons, into the southern part of South America, where one might imagine nothing whatever could happen that would in any possible manner affect

---

[27] Arneth, IV, 55 seq.; Steed, 11a.

the Austrian monarchy. But, at about this time, Pombal, the great despot of Portugal, heard that Paraguay was rich in gold, and determined to deport all the Indians from that country in order that they might not interfere with the operation of mines. He seems to have thought this would be a trifling task, and that the shortest way to accomplish it was to destroy all the Indian villages and slaughter any natives who offered resistance. He met with unexpected difficulties which he attributed largely to the influence of the Jesuit missionaries, but in spite of all opposition, completely depopulated Paraguay, with a cruelty compared with which the expulsion of the Acadians appears humane. We may mention incidentally, that when Pombal had emptied Paraguay of natives he also found it destitute of gold, and that the greatest result of his brutal conduct, as far as Europe was concerned, was the provocation of a campaign against the Jesuits, which began in Portugal and extended to Spain, France, and finally to Austria. Probably the reason other nations joined Portugal in attacking the Jesuits was that the order could not keep its fingers out of politics, and was continually hampering the various monarchs in the exercise of what they considered their rights. Portugal led off and other states followed in banning the order.[28]

In Vienna, the Jesuits were exceptionally well established in high places. Maria Theresa's religious instructor in childhood had been a Jesuit, her confessor was a Jesuit, and she had chosen a Jesuit to supervise the religious education of her eldest son Joseph. The Jesuits were in complete charge of the University of

[28] Arneth, IX, 91 seq.; Bermann, 840.

The Queen as a Woman 253

Vienna with its seven thousand students, of six other schools in the Archduchy of Austria, and twenty-three colleges in Hungary;[29] no one supposed the Queen would have the courage to join in a crusade against the order. But Kaunitz was opposed to the Jesuits and succeeded in convincing the Queen that they were infringing upon her monarchial rights. After some hesitation and a conspicuous flourish of regrets, she issued a decree removing them from all the institutions of the monarchy. "I cannot express the pain and regret with which I give this order,"[30] she said in her decree, but nevertheless she gave it and carried it out most thoroughly.

When Pope Clement XIII issued a bull in favor of the Jesuits she forbade its publication in her dominions, and when Clement XIV, in 1773, suppressed the order she promptly confiscated all its property. But she showed her devotion to Catholicism by encouraging the order of Piaristens, which, having had such an impressive object lesson, never became so obtrusive politically.

The other story of the origin of Maria Theresa's opposition to the Jesuits is not so well authenticated, but none the less interesting. According to this story, Kaunitz convinced the Queen that her confessor was writing out her confessions, and through a roundabout channel sending them to the pope. Nearly all the trustworthy historians dismiss this as a fairy tale but give it space in their works, proving that it was widely circulated at the time. One can easily imagine that even

[29] Steed, 113.
[30] Arneth, IX, 97; Gotthold Dorschel, 141. The Jesuits returned to Austria under Francis I, of Austria.

rumors of this character may have had a strong influence upon the Queen's mind, and caused her to join in the general outcry against the Jesuits.

Maria Theresa's intolerance of the Jews should be mentioned in this connection. In December, 1744, she called upon one of her ministers for an opinion as to whether or not she had authority to expel the Jews from her dominions, declaring it to be her intention to have them out of her domains by the first of January if she was invested with power to expel them. The minister investigated and declared that she possessed the necessary authority, but as there were some fifty thousand Jews in Austria and Bohemia, he recommended that the period for their departure be extended until the first of the following June. The order was made acccordingly.[31]

The result was consternation among the Israelites who hastened to invoke every possible influence to have the decree recalled. A prominent Jew, Solomon Koreff of Prague, rode to Vienna and begged for an audience with the Queen, which she refused at first, but granted later on condition that the Jew be separated from her by a screen. This interesting interview was actually held under such conditions. Solomon, not knowing how far he was from the Queen spoke loudly, whereupon one of the guards commanded, "Don't scream, Jew!" The suppliant paused for a moment and then exclaimed in great earnestness, "I am not screaming; it is the voice of the persecuted thousands, for whom I am

---

[31] Arneth, IV, 41 seq. This order was directed especially against the Jews of Prague who, as the Queen believed, had been disloyal to her in the Wars of Accession.

The Queen as a Woman 255

pleading, calling to Heaven for justice and mercy!" [32]

Maria Theresa soon changed her mind, if not her heart, concerning this decree. It was called to her attention that the easiest place for the Jewish men to migrate would be into the army of Frederick of Prussia. Then in a little while came protests from Holland and England, and probably glad to be provided with a reasonable excuse, she recalled the edict.

But again in 1777, merely because she was handed a petition to appoint a Jew to an important public office, the Queen gave vent to her hatred by issuing a most intolerant decree in which she said: "In future no Jew shall be allowed to remain in Vienna without my special permission. I know of no greater plague than this race which, on account of its deceit, usury, and hoarding of money, is driving my subjects to beggary. Therefore, as far as possible, the Jews are to be kept away and avoided." [33]

This exhibition of wrath may be looked upon as a puff of pent-up steam, for we notice that she left a wide loophole for escape by inserting the words "without my special permission." Very few Jews were expelled, and her anger subsided. In some instances, she showed considerable tolerance. Sonnenfels, who was so influential in the campaign against the torture of criminals, was a Jew, and we know she was not at all pleased with his propaganda. There were many Jewish money lenders who continued right along with their

---

[32] Bermann, 574.
[33] Maria Theresa several times showed intolerance toward the Protestants also. Religious tolerance was established during the reign of her successor, Joseph II

business, occasionally even offering assistance to the monarchy. Maria Theresa knew only too well that an expulsion of the Jews would bring down upon her much public condemnation, and give her enemies a great deal of material for use in turning the world against her.

One of the strange facts concerning the history of the Jews in Europe is that the race always seems to multiply most rapidly in the countries where it is persecuted. From that day to this Vienna has had a very large Jewish population, and many of its most prominent citizens have been Jews. If the Israelites were now expelled from the university, it would lose nearly half its faculty. Many Jews, probably to escape the wrath of the Hapsburgs, changed their names to others sounding more German, and in one instance, the Queen is said to have laughed when her attention was called to such a case.

V

In Austria the cruelest methods imaginable of punishing criminals were continued almost to the close of the reign of Maria Theresa, and in the end were abolished only because of the influence brought to bear upon the Queen by certain agitators, and by her son who was her co-regent. Maria Theresa would probably have felt insulted if any one had compared her morals with those of Frederick of Prussia or Elizabeth of Russia, yet during the first year of Frederick's reign he banned torture as a punishment,[34] and almost the first edict issued by Elizabeth abolished capital punish-

---

[34] Carlyle, III, 153-154.

ment. Strange as it may seem, this conduct on the part of Maria Theresa was not entirely inconsistent with her war against vice, dueling and gambling.

Maria Theresa was devoted to the idea of benevolent despotism, which she conceived to mean that as a monarch she should be a sort of schoolmistress to her subjects. She thought she should teach her people to shun evil, and that object lessons were very effective in training them to avoid crime, hence she had most of her punishments administered in public. She liked to have the violators of her social laws chained to the doors of the city where all could witness their degradation and shame. She stood thieves on platforms in public places and had their thumbs crushed with iron clamps; sometimes men were suspended by ropes attached to their arms, which had been tied together across their backs, thus dislocating both shoulders and crippling them for life; criminals were branded in the face, that they might become walking exhibitions of the evil consequence of crime, and many other revolting methods of torture were in vogue. Executions were, if possible, still more gruesome. It was the custom to lash criminals to a cross and hoist them before the people, often in pairs, one man on each side of an effigy of Christ on the cross, where they remained for days before being executed. In fact, they were usually kept on the cross until they prayed and professed repentence; then they were executed. In this manner two very benevolent ends were supposed to be served—the criminals were mercifully prepared to meet their God, and the public given a most impressive lesson in the consequences of crime. In the end some of the criminals were hanged or beheaded, but those guilty of the baser crimes expiated their sins in more painful deaths; sometimes their tongues were cut out, or their bodies thrust through with red-hot bars of iron. Such horrible punishments were not instituted by Maria Theresa; she merely continued them from the reigns of her predecessors.

To Joseph Sonnenfels, who today would be called an agitator, belongs most of the credit for abolishing the torture of criminals in Austria. When he began writing on this subject his works were not looked upon with favor by the Queen. She thought he meant well but was entirely mistaken as to the fundamental purpose of punishing criminals. He would rob the monarch of one of her most effective methods of educating the people. But Sonnenfels converted Joseph and finally the old *Landesmutter* was forced to yield.[35]

Only one point may be raised in defense of Maria Theresa in her attitude toward the punishment of crime; she conceived the end to be served in a criminal code was prevention of crime rather than reforming or disposing of criminals, and conscientiously believed her methods to be the most effective in attaining that end.

VI

Maria Theresa's domestic life is usually described as happy. She loved but one man and he was her husband. Her devotion to Francis of Lorraine began in the nursery and ended on her deathbed; like the eagle, she mated for life, and never entertained thoughts of an-

---

[35] Gotthold Dorschel, 117. Sonnenfels also waged a campaign against capital punishment, but did not succeed in having it abolished.

other marriage after the death of her husband when she was forty-eight years old.

Yet we may very well doubt if marriage brought her all the happiness she had anticipated. A terrible pall was cast over a most delightful romance when Charles VI demanded that Francis of Lorraine sign away his birthright and that of his family before receiving the hand of the Archduchess. From this act of injustice, Francis probably never completely recovered. He never liked Tuscany, and considered it but a poor compensation for his native Lorraine. The various sops handed him by his father-in-law, such as the appointment to be governor of the Netherlands, the promise of Archduchess Maria Anna to his brother Charles, and his own elevation to the chief command of the Austrian army in the war with Turkey, all turned to gall. Francis never got to the Netherlands, the command of the army brought him naught but disgrace, and Maria Anna died within a year of her marriage to Prince Charles.

As a bride, Maria Theresa looked upon her husband as the most wonderful man in the world; she thought he knew everything and could do everything. His travels had put him on intimate terms with all the great courts of Europe, and most of the coming monarchs were his brother Masons. She looked forward to the responsibilities of becoming queen of a great monarchy with calm complacency, because she would have Francis at her side. Francis knew all about politics and would guide her steps aright whenever the path seemed dark or uncertain.

The first blow to her idol fell when her husband made such a fiasco at Belgrade. The next came when he wished to make peace with Prussia at the expense of Silesia, apparently in part because he wished to win Frederick's support in the coming election of an emperor. The very thought of sacrificing one of the inherited dominions for an empty crown made her furious. In this case Francis yielded very quickly, but she knew the idea had been in his mind, and it made her realize that the task of holding the realms of her father rested primarily upon herself. Then came the various attempts of her husband to redeem his military disgraces in the Wars of Accession, all terminating in costly failures. She soon discovered that his ways were not hers, and conceived her own to be infinitely better.

Gradually Francis dwindled into little more than an official ornament, and in that capacity he was quite satisfactory in the main. He was a splendid cavalier, always ready to render his lady any homage from picking up her handkerchief to fighting a duel. No prince of the blood could have escorted her in public more faultlessly than did Francis. He was popular in Vienna because the Viennese loved an emperor who could shine on parade. Since she was bent upon doing all the work, and Francis was quite willing that she should, he was a fairly satisfactory consort.

Then too, Francis had streaks of heroism that filled the Queen with joy. There was the time, in 1744, when the lower quarters of Vienna were flooded by the Danube, and hundreds were standing on the roofs of houses crying loudly to be rescued, but no one had the courage to row a boat across the swift torrent. The Queen stood in one of the towers looking on in despair, when suddenly she beheld Francis launching a boat and rowing away to what seemed certain death. She

The Queen as a Woman   261

screamed and ran to the bank but he was gone, followed by other boats manned by heroes stimulated to bravery by the reckless example of her husband. Her heart was in her throat as she watched him directing the rescue and bringing the apparently doomed people to safety. Finally all were saved and the Queen wept for joy. She never forgot that great day.[36]

But the imperial family was not entirely free from jars. For one thing Francis continued his devotion to Freemasonry after it had been banned by the pope. The Catholic Queen did not like this and we may be sure there were several spats over the matter, for it seemed most inconsistent that the Emperor of the Holy Roman Empire, who was supposed to be the protector of the pope, should retain a membership in an order which the Church had banned. Francis continued his devotion to his lodge in spite of the Queen.[37] The lodges were raided at her order, but she could never catch Francis. It was reported that there were secret doors to the lodge room, and that the Emperor had an underground passage by which he escaped to the palace or a near-by *café;* at any rate, he always turned up smiling and serene after her raids.[38] Some said Maria Theresa even disguised herself as a man and attempted to enter the lodge, in order to see what her husband was doing there, but no one was certain that this was true.

But the worst skeleton in the closet of the imperial family was the infidelity of the husband to his marriage vows. Ever and anon this skeleton rattled its bones and

[36] Bermann, 580.
[37] Arneth, IX, 398.
[38] Bermann, 298-299.

the Queen shuddered in horror. There was the mysterious *danseuse,* Eva Maria Violet, who seemed to arrive from nowhere to set all Vienna agog with her beauty. Francis was stricken with her charms and completely carried away in adoration. Somebody—we are not saying it was the Queen—had the damsel dressed in boy's clothing and smuggled over to England, where she finally married David Garrick.[39]

Then Francis had many other affairs, or at least the Queen suspected that he had, and her jealousy knew no bounds. All the writers of the period, who knew Vienna well and were not intimidated, mentioned the fact that the Queen was very jealous of her husband, but his only real *liaison* firmly grounded in authentic history, was the one with Princess Auersperg. Over it Maria Theresa must have shed many tears.

Princess Auersperg, who was the daughter of General Neipperg, appeared at the court of Vienna in 1755, when she was in her seventeenth year. Her beauty was said to surpass all powers of description. Especial emphasis is placed upon her wealth of soft brown hair, and Francis seems to have had a weakness for soft, silky hair. Before long every one, with the presumable exception of the Queen, knew that the Emperor and the Princess were in love. She became his affinity, and remained so until his death, ten years later. When Francis formed this attachment he was either forty-six or forty-seven, and Maria Theresa was either thirty-eight or thirty-nine; the Emperor was apparently in the prime of manhood, but the Queen, especially in the form of her body, must have shown the effects of

---

[39] Mahan, *Famous Women of Vienna,* 251.

having borne either fifteen or sixteen children. Try as she might, the Queen could not appear as fresh and appealing as the Princess.[40]

At the funeral of Francis the Princess appeared, but did not mingle with the family as a mourner. Suddenly Maria Theresa surprised all by leaving her associates and approaching the Princess. All held their breath in fear of a tragedy, but the Queen merely grasped the hand of the Princess almost affectionately and said, "My dear, we have truly lost a great deal!"[41] That was all, but it was enough to cause amazement. Then, later, the Princess presented a note for a huge sum of money, signed by Francis. Maria Theresa's counsellors advised her to refuse payment, but she ordered it paid in full. Some have regarded this as a mark of greatness.

The Queen's troubles over this affair did not end with the death of her husband, nor with that of the Princess which occurred shortly afterward. In 1768 she received a letter from Bordeaux, signed by a young girl who claimed she was the daughter of Emperor Francis and Princess Auersperg. Naturally, the bereaved Maria Theresa was much disturbed by this letter, and appointed Count Philip Cobenzl to investigate the merits of the claim. At one stage of this investigation she seemed to be convinced that the girl was really the daughter of her husband, and wrote the Count a most touching letter dated, "In My Bed at Two O'clock in the Morning." In this letter she said, "This girl is a part of the one whom I loved best of all in the world," and begged that she be provided with

[40] Bermann, 767.
[41] Arneth, VII, 157.

everything she required, but later the Queen apparently altered her mind and expressed the belief that the girl's claims were absolutely false. Fortunately or unfortunately, just as the investigation was finished Count Cobenzl died, but on his deathbed he told a friend he was sure the girl was really the daughter of Emperor Francis. With that the matter ended and no one knew what became of the young woman.[42]

It is not improbable that in this instance Maria Theresa warped her judgment to the demands of expediency. She was capable of doing this, especially during the later years of her life. She may have thought it necessary to preserve the honor of her family. The extent to which this affair was known to her children is revealed by one of the letters of Maria Christina to her sister-in-law Isabelle. "The Emperor," wrote Christina, "is a very good-hearted father; one can always rely upon him as a friend, and we must do what we can to protect him from his weaknesses. I am referring to his conduct with Princess Auersperg; you may not know what a tremendous influence she has over him. He puts the greatest trust in her, and holds nothing from her confidence; the Empress is very jealous of this devotion."[43] Affairs were in a bad state when a young daughter wrote thus of her father.

All in all, we may say that Francis of Lorraine was entitled to as much sympathy as he has received at the hands of historians. Few men could have played the part of a husband to such a domineering woman better than he did. The manner in which he effaced himself is beautifully illustrated by the story, so often related, of

[42] Bermann, 774–779.
[43] Zwiedineck-Südenhorst, 98.

his remarks to some ladies of the court at one of the Queen's levees. He was sitting in a corner when the ladies approached and engaged him in a conversation. He begged them to be seated but they refused, because they said it would be impolite to sit in the presence of an Emperor. "Don't mind me," he replied, "I am only a husband; the Queen and her children are the court." [44]

Perhaps we may be allowed to add that the Austrian Monarchy might not have suffered additional ills had Maria Theresa listened a little more favorably to some of the suggestions of her husband. He was inclined to make a friend of Frederick of Prussia, even at the cost of Silesia, and many contend that in the end this might not have been a mistake—it is certainly a debatable question. Francis also opposed the alliance with France, another move which ended disastrously, but, when overruled by his wife and Kaunitz, swallowed his pride and served the court, politically at least, to the best of his ability. His weaknesses were merely those of most of the princes of his day, and may be looked upon with a certain degree of allowance.

What largely effaces all our sympathy for Francis of Lorraine is the indisputable fact that he was unfaithful to the great woman who, in the midst of such stupendous trials and tribulations, bore him so many children and never faltered in her wifely devotion. Many historians speak sympathetically of Francis, but invariably they give either open or veiled intimations of his infidelities, which in the language of the poet:

> "Like a cloud before the skies,
> Hid all his better qualities."

[44] Bermann, 311.

XI

THE QUEEN AS A MOTHER

I

MARIA THERESA'S record of motherhood is probably unequaled by that of any other great queen in history. She was married at nineteen, and when she was thirty-nine had given birth to sixteen children; seven were born during her long struggle to maintain her crown against the assaults of Frederick of Prussia and France, and one was born during the Seven Years' War. When we read the history of her wars we are prone to forget the difficulties under which they were fought, for she seems to have presented an unbroken line of activities. Behind the oft recurring statements that on such and such a date a child was born or died, there must be hidden volumes of grief and worry.

The first child came in a little less than a year after Maria Theresa married, and caused great disappointment because it was a girl. It died after one day's illness on the seventh of June, 1740.

The second baby was born during the second year of her married life, only to renew the disappointment because of failure to produce a male heir to the throne. This time all expected a boy and arrangements had been made to celebrate his birth, but the festivities were called off when it was learned that an unwelcome girl had arrived. Then after a little more than a year came another girl, completely blasting the hopes of Charles VI, who exclaimed, "Am I never to be permitted to look upon a male heir?" This question was answered in the negative by the Emperor's death the same year.

In January, 1741, while Maria Theresa was so excited over Frederick's invasion of Silesia, and striving with might and main to get together an expedition to meet the Prussians, her youngest daughter died, leaving her with only one living child, but expecting another in a month or two. On the thirteenth of March, just as General Neipperg was about to set forth to reconquer Silesia, a sixteen-pound boy arrived to gratify the twenty-five-year-old desire of Vienna to celebrate the birth of a Cæsar; but it was too late to cheer the heart of Charles VI. That was probably one of the happiest days of Maria Theresa's whole life; she expected her army to be victorious and she was the mother of a son.

Maria Theresa said she was never disappointed when she asked for divine aid through the medium of Saint Joseph, so she insisted upon naming the son Joseph, and prevailed in doing so over the protests of her mother, who thought the boy should bear the name of Charles Francis in honor of his grandfather and father.

Vienna's celebration of the birth of an heir to the throne was cut short by the defeat of the Austrians at Mollwitz, which seemed to forecast the downfall of the House of Hapsburg. In the hope of saving her throne, the Queen, when she had barely recovered from the birth of her son, undertook the strenuous ceremonies of her coronation at Pressburg, though it necessitated her departure from Vienna in May. She must have been glad to get through with this trying ordeal before entering the shadow of another confinement, but the shadow was there when she was obliged to appear before the assembly the following September and plead with the Hungarians to defend her family and her crown.

In May, 1742, while in the thickest of the fight with the French and Bavarians, Maria Theresa was compelled to retire for another confinement, but did not allow it to interrupt her work for more than a few days.

The next child was born August 15, 1743, disabling her for a short period in the midst of the excitement over the Treaty of Worms, when she certainly needed a cool head and a clear brain to meet the intrigues of the King of Sardinia and the King of England in settling questions that meant life or death to her monarchy.

The confinement which brought her a second son fell on the first of February, 1745. It was a period of great anxiety to the Queen, for Emperor Charles VII had just died, and all Europe was scheming over his successor. Maria Theresa's heart was filled with an ambition to secure the imperial crown for her husband, and she needed the full use of all her faculties in bargaining with the greedy electors for votes. When the time came to attend his coronation in Frankfort the following October, she was again embarrassed to appear in public on account of her condition. Shortly afterward, the French were sweeping all before them in Flanders, and the Queen gave birth to another baby.

In May, 1747, while the Austrians were losing in the Netherlands but gaining in Italy, Maria Theresa's third son was born. This was Leopold who, like Joseph, was destined to become an emperor. Then in September, 1748, in the midst of the Queen's fury at George II because she thought he had lost his nerve and was seeking to make peace with France while she wished to continue the war, came a baby who died the same day.

It was impossible for the Queen to have peaceful intervals for all these births during her Wars of Accession, for the simple reason that she was always in trouble and always having babies. Her two lines of endeavor had to be carried on simultaneously, and the amazing fact was that she never neglected either for the sake of the other.

Five children were born during the peace between her Wars of Accession and the Seven Years' War; the last of these was the celebrated Marie Antoinette who arrived while her mother was engrossed in getting ready for her second drive to humiliate Frederick of Prussia and recover her lost Silesia. Then just as she was getting this drive under way, she gave birth to her last child in December, 1756.

One might suppose that, since the mother was so pressed with important duties, the father relieved her of most of the care of the children, but such was not the case. Maria Theresa steered the family bark as well as the ship of state; nothing was settled in the household until it had been decided by mother. Had Francis been disposed to take charge of the nursery, which he probably was not, he would have been overruled.[1]

No doubt there were many little feuds among the

---

[1] Zwiedineck-Südenhorst, 190.

Queen's numerous fledglings, but only one has been much emphasized by authentic history. Joseph, being the "purple-born" because he was the heir to the throne, lorded it over the rest of the children, and as a consequence, won the hatred of Prince Charles who was the next son and only four years younger. Charles ridiculed his haughty brother and called the attention of the other children to the fact that Joseph, at birth, was the son of an archduke of Tuscany, while he, Charles, was born to an emperor of the Holy Roman Empire of the Germans. Since Joseph was so low-born, Charles meant to contend with him for the crown. The little family became a miniature Europe waging a war of succession, and the mother was unable to quell this ominous feud upon which she looked with great foreboding.

The war ended in a most unexpected manner by the death of Archduke Charles at the age of sixteen. The day the Archduke died Maria Theresa sat by his bed in tears, when suddenly the sick lad flooded her heart with mixed emotions by saying, "You should not weep for me, dear mother, for had I lived, I would have brought you many more tears!" [2]

This heart-rending death scene was interjected into the midst of Maria Theresa's heroic struggle to re-

---

[2] Bermann, 582. The feud between Archdukes Joseph and Charles is mentioned by several historians apparently on the authority of Count Batthyany who had charge of the education of both princes (see Arneth, IV, 178). Batthyany said Charles was the favorite son of his parents. The amusing feature of the story as told by Bermann is that Prince Charles was entirely mistaken; he was no more the son of an emperor than was Joseph. Charles was born in February, 1745, and his father was elected Emperor of the Germans the following September.

cover from the stunning defeat of the Austrians at Torgau. What self-control she must have had to pass immediately from this bitter experience and measure courage and strength upon equal terms with such an antagonist as Frederick of Prussia! Where in history shall we find another such woman as Maria Theresa?

II

Maria Theresa had scarcely finished giving birth to her younger children before she was confronted with the task of finding mates for the older ones. While she was getting Maximilian out of the cradle, she was doing her best to get Maria Anna to the altar. Her many marriage negotiations, like her confinements, had to be wedged in between the campaigns of her wars or the pressing duties of state during peace.

In her marriage negotiations Maria Theresa has usually been considered very heartless, for she sacrificed her children most ruthlessly upon the altar of her house and country, with little or no consideration for their future happiness. But the manner in which we regard her in this respect may be somewhat modified if we pause to consider her conduct in the light of the moral standards of her time and the traditions of her family, rather than the sentiments of the present day and the positions we occupy. Maria Theresa was a thoroughbred monarchist—the breed is now almost extinct—and regarded the interests of her monarchy as synonomous with those of her house. When she gave her children for the benefit of her dynasty, she also conceived it to be for the good of her country. Viewed in this light, her conduct appears both patriotic and noble. Such sentiments are difficult for us to appreciate because for a century and a half we have been inoculated with the serum of democracy while in her veins coursed the unmodified blood of sixteen generations of monarchs.

Ever since the days when Rudolph I gave a daughter to the Elector of Bavaria for a free passage to the walls of Vienna, and a son and daughter to a daughter and son of Ottacar to prevent loss of life in assaulting the bastions, the Hapsburgs had been taught to regard the sacrifice of children, especially daughters, upon the altar of state as justifiable on the ground of patriotism. By such sacrifices territory was often acquired, wars avoided, and the welfare of the people promoted with a minimum amount of suffering. The practice was, in reality, based upon sound statesmanship with due regard for the greatest good to the greatest number, and formed one of the corner stones upon which a great empire had rested and endured for centuries.[3]

[3] In 1273, Rudolph of Hapsburg, a rather obscure Swabian prince, was unexpectedly elected Emperor of the Holy Roman Empire. One of his first endeavors was to secure possession of Vienna, the metropolis of the Danube, which had been seized by Ottacar, King of Bohemia. To reach Vienna with his small army, it was necessary for Rudolph to pass through Bavaria whose powerful ruler was in alliance with Ottacar. Instead of attempting the apparently impossible task of fighting his way across Bavaria, Rudolph gave one of his daughters to the ruler's son in marriage, thus converting the father from an enemy to a friend and ally. So rapidly and secretly was the stratagem consummated that the new Emperor appeared at Vienna before Ottacar had heard of the wedding. Then, instead of assaulting the bastions of the city and thus arousing the enmity of the people he hoped to rule, Rudolph tricked Ottacar into a surrender through the artifice of a betrothal of a son and daughter to a daughter and son of Ottacar. That Rudolph was able to do all this indicates how desirable a union with a family of an emperor was regarded by the rulers of that time. The

We shall presently come upon a few of the Queen's outbursts of lamentation and protest over the manner in which she was sending her children into loveless and disagreeable marriages. She was keenly conscious of the fact that they were being sacrificed for their country, and sometimes she felt rebellious about it, but yielded because she conceived the interests of the monarchy to be at stake. We may be sure that she often smothered her feelings, for she was a woman who rarely displayed her emotions except when she thought it to her interest to do so.

When the time arrived for Maria Theresa to begin disposing of her children in marriage, she was convinced that the greatest enemy to her house was Frederick the Great, and with him she associated the King of England. She conceived that the best policy for her

---

Bishop of Basle, upon observing the shrewdness of the Emperor, exclaimed, "Now sit tight, Lord God, or Rudolph will take Your throne!" Thus, without shedding a drop of blood, was the House of Hapsburg established on the throne in Vienna where it remained in power for nearly six hundred and fifty years.

But when Ottacar returned to his wife in Prague, she scolded him most unmercifully for having allowed himself to be swindled out of the best city in his domains, and even went so far as to send Rudolph's daughter to a nunnery. Apparently his wife made life such a burden to Ottacar that he preferred to fight with Rudolph rather than quarrel with his spouse. Accordingly he returned to battle with the Emperor who had secured the backing of the Austrians and Bavarians and had the additional advantage of protection behind the walls of Vienna which had been built so high and strong during the time of Ottacar. In his first attack Ottacar was killed and Rudolph reigned supreme. Rudolph's scheme of sacrificing children upon the altar of state was faithfully followed by his descendants and became one of the fixed policies of the dynasty. Later a saying became current throughout Europe, and it may be translated as follows: "Happy is the House of Hapsburg, for the realms which Mars awards to others, Venus transfers to thee."

to pursue was to unite her house with the Bourbons, in order to form an irresistible combination against Prussia and England, hence she never looked in the direction of Brandenburg or Hanover when seeking matrimonial alliances. She even avoided Brunswick, the home of her mother, because of its intimate association with the ruling houses of Prussia and England. She meant to blend the Hapsburgs and Bourbons so intimately that their interests would be common and inseparable.

All the marriage negotiations of the imperial family, before the death of Emperor Francis, were largely influenced by his will. The idea that Maria Theresa was commander-in-chief of her household needs a little modification when we come to apply it to the marriages of her children; in this field her dominance was more apparent than real. She usually uttered the final decision, but in some instances contrary to her convictions and inclinations, because she was teased to distraction by the importunities of her husband. As Emperor, it was his prerogative to pass upon all marriage alliances in the empire, and Maria Theresa did not have the courage to completely override both his imperial and parental rights, but in the end, Francis usually unloaded upon their mother, the unpleasant task of communicating disagreeable news to the children.

After the death of Francis, Maria Theresa was greatly under the influence of Kaunitz, who had committed her to the policy of alliances with the House of Bourbon, especially its French branch. Next to her zeal for strengthening this union was her desire to bind to her monarchy the two strong German states of Saxony and Bavaria. We might add that, in the last analysis,

The Queen as a Mother

every marriage was planned with a view to making Austria capable of resisting Prussia.

The first marriage arranged by Maria Theresa was that of her sister Maria Anna, whom she gave to her brother-in-law Prince Charles of Lorraine in 1744. This marriage was entirely unrelated to those arranged later in life for her children, for it was merely a fulfillment of the promise of her father, though agreeable to her and to all concerned. She thought Charles merited the Archduchess for his conduct in war, and he and Maria Anna were much in love. It was a happy union but terminated very sadly. Prince Charles was made governor of the Netherlands, where his wife died in confinement during the first year of their marriage. The death of his young wife seemed to be such a severe shock to the Prince that he never fully recovered; his subsequent campaigns were conducted with much less efficiency than his preceding ones. An interesting incident in connection with the last illness of Maria Anna was that she was attended in part by the Dutch physician, Gerhard van Swieten, who so pleased the Queen that she summoned him to be her own medical attendant, and who later founded the school of medicine which has grown to such renown in Vienna.

The first marriage problem confronting the Queen in her own family was that of her eldest daughter Maria Anna, who, many believe, owing to exposure and improper nourishment on the flight to Tuscany during the late years of Charles VI, was never strong physically or mentally.[4] Her unattractive qualities were well known to all the courts of Europe, and Maria

[4] Arneth, IV, 153.

Theresa's efforts to attach her to the son of some prominent sovereign were met by excuses, the significance of which the Queen understood perfectly. The knotty problem was still unsolved when the Archduchess arrived at the dreadful age of twenty-seven; then the Queen hesitated no longer, but disposed of the spinstress by making her abbess of a convent in Prague. With much ceremony, after having fixed a large income upon Maria Anna, she was inducted into the order with the understanding that she need not reside in the convent.[5]

Next came Joseph, the son and heir to the throne, who must be married with great care, and surely to some princess well connected with the House of Bourbon. The most available one seemed to be Josepha, the daughter of the King of Naples who was almost sure to inherit the crown of Spain. As early as 1751, when Joseph was only ten years old, it was generally understood that he was to wed this princess. The prospective bride and groom were then so young that it was not considered necessary to announce the betrothal formally until later. What made this union especially attractive to Maria Theresa was that the crown of Naples seemed likely to pass to the heirs of this princess, and also the hope that the marriage might eventually lead to some sort of a claim to the crown of Spain, since male heirs were just then very scarce in that branch of the Bourbon family. But later it became noised about that the daughters of the King of Naples were not very attractive either physically or mentally, and the Queen was not pleased with the idea of having

---

[5] *Ibid.*, VII, 245; Guglia, II, 196.

her son, who was presumably destined to continue her line, make such a marriage. Then, in 1758, she was glad she had not snapped at Josepha, for Louis XV of France intimated that he would be pleased to give his granddaughter, Isabelle of Parma, to the Queen for her eldest son. Parma was not a great power, but since the request came from the court of Versailles, with which she was most eager to strengthen her alliance, it was considered a better union than a marriage with the Neapolitan princess.[6] Of much importance to the Queen was the fact that Isabelle was a beautiful girl and reputed to be very clever; of less consequence was the fact that Joseph, who was taking some interest in the matter, had seen the pictures of both princesses and expressed a decided preference for Isabelle. To avoid offending the King of Naples, Kaunitz suggested that a younger Neapolitan princess be shunted to Joseph's brother Charles, who was not so likely to become the father of future emperors. The Queen accepted this happy solution, and Joseph's betrothal to Isabelle of Parma, who was already old enough to marry, was announced immediately.

Until the arrival of Isabelle's picture, Joseph had taken but slight interest in his marriage, probably because he knew he would have little to say in the choice of his bride. It was generally understood in Vienna that he was not interested in women, and all expected him to be an indifferent husband. The wedding occurred in the autumn of 1760, while the Queen was still engaged in the Seven Years' War.

Very much to the surprise of his mother and all

---

[6] Arneth, V, 451.

Vienna, Joseph fell in love with his wife, and the marriage promised to be a most happy one, in spite of the fact that Isabelle had shown no enthusiasm whatever for the union. When notified that she had been chosen for the consort of a prospective emperor, she passed the subject by with the strange remark: "I am greatly flattered that the Queen has selected me from all the princesses of Europe to become the wife of her eldest son; I had not expected it. But I am convinced that this marriage will be in vain, for I am sure I shall not live long enough to fulfill the hopes of the Empress." [7]

When Isabelle arrived in Vienna, it was soon observed that she was the victim of a strange melancholy. Joseph was very affectionate and she pretended to be much in love with him, but continued her gloomy prophecies. In a year she gave birth to a daughter who was named Maria Theresa in honor of her grandmother, but Isabelle shocked the whole court by announcing that the child would never survive her seventh year. Shortly afterward, Joseph was elected King of the Romans and wished to have his wife crowned Queen, but she flatly refused, saying, "I am not interested in that; I have no desire to be Queen of the Romans." [8]

Very soon she renewed her forecast of her own death, and began spending all her time in contemplation of her departure from earth. The family tried to overcome this dreadful melancholy, but Isabelle refused to be comforted; she wished to die, and vowed she would die. In 1763 she was again an expectant mother, but blasted all hopes by saying that the child

[7] Bermann, 709.
[8] *Ibid.*

The Queen as a Mother 279

would be born dead and that she would not survive the confinement.[9]

Were we so disposed, we might make much of the conduct of Isabelle as an illustration of the power of mind over matter, but the strange fulfillments of her evil prophecies were probably only coincidents. It so happened that Maria Theresa's daughter Johanna fell ill with the smallpox, and Isabelle announced that her sister-in-law would die on a certain Sunday. Strange to say, this prediction came true.

In spite of all her despondency Joseph continued to love his wife, but Isabelle felt more affection for her sister-in-law, Maria Christina, than for her husband.[10] When Maria Christina was absent, Isabelle wrote her intimate letters expressing the most gruesome sentiments. Once she wrote: "I can say that death speaks to me in a distinct secret voice that rouses in my soul a sweet satisfaction; it gives me courage and a supernatural control over myself. For three days I have heard this voice, and it fills me with a joy that nothing else on earth can equal." [11]

In the summer of 1763, when Isabelle was returning from Laxenburg, just as she came in sight of Vienna she exclaimed, "Death is waiting for me there!" Then, during the night of November eighteenth, an alarm clock, owing to some defect, sounded continuously for several minutes. "That is my signal!" she cried. "It is my call!" She was then seized with a pain in the knee, but her doctor could discover nothing wrong. In a little while she became feverish and delirious, in which state

[9] *Ibid.*
[10] Arneth, VII, 46.
[11] *Ibid.*, 48.

she was delivered of a dead child, and in a few days it was discovered that she was suffering with malignant smallpox, from which she soon died.[12]

Isabelle's black prophecy concerning her first child also came true; it died just before it reached the age of seven. Thus four deaths were foretold by this gloomy princess, and they all came approximately as she predicted; it looked as though she killed her family and herself by her strange melancholy.

This psychopathic conduct of Isabelle would hardly be worth relating here except for the fact that it had a deep influence upon the mind of Joseph who was destined to become the ruler of a great nation. Joseph was crushed by the death of his young wife, but in some manner received the impression that her strange conduct was the result of a disappointment in love. He heard rumors that she had already given her heart to an Italian when she received the Queen's proposal, and that she was heartbroken over being compelled to abandon her first lover.[13] At times Joseph was overwhelmed with a fear that all her professions of wifely affection had been false; then at others, he pitied her and gave her great credit for having tried so hard to love a husband against the inclinations of her heart.

The modern psychologist sees in this love tangle the beginning of a mental disturbance which grew until it completely overcast the life of a prince who, under pleasant domestic surroundings, might have become the greatest emperor of the House of Hapsburg. Isabelle's morbid psychology eventually projected itself into the politics of Europe, and brought nearly all the good

---
[12] *Ibid.*, 61; Guglia, II, 205.
[13] Bermann, 713.

The Queen as a Mother 281

work of Maria Theresa's reign to naught through the erratic behavior of her son. How often keys to the mysterious actions of celebrated historical characters are to be found hidden in their relations with women.

Within a few months of the death of Isabelle, Joseph found himself with three fairly distinct concepts of her personality. One, the oldest of all, dated from the time he first saw and admired her picture, and it was rounded to completion when the beautiful young woman, bearing her bouquets of roses and orange blossoms, came as a bride to open the gate to his brief conjugal paradise. This image he cherished with an idolatrous veneration, and never allowed it to become separated from her name. Then, during their short married life, another notion arrived that naturally attached itself to his wife; it was that of a prophetess of death riding on black clouds of melancholy, and scattering sickness, bereavement and sepulchres. After her death, still another picture thrust itself unbidden into his mind; he saw a deceitful wife hiding behind a heavy veil of false pretensions of love.

Joseph began to examine, compare, and try to adjust these three images. The last two were so incompatible with the first that he could not apply them to the same personality, so he split his conception of Isabelle into two parts. One became the bride with whom he associated so much that was delightful, and to protect it he needed another personality to bear the evil qualities which he wished to remove from the one he held sacred. He disposed of the disagreeable attributes by attaching them to his conception of a wife, and soon spread them to cover wives in general. In this manner he preserved unmarred the image he loved, but created another that was horrible. He clung to his pleasant memories of Isabelle, but shrank in terror from the thought of having another wife. By such mental maneuvers Joseph extricated himself from the bog of cynicism and despair into which his bitter experience had plunged him, and got his feet on the solid ground of what seemed to be a much more normal attitude toward humanity, but he became quite incapable of marrying and becoming the head of a family to continue his line. All this may seem somewhat theoretical, but it supplies a much needed explanation of Joseph's character which is very hard to comprehend. It enables us to understand his aversion to marrying again—something which seems so foreign to his family and hereditary tendencies. That far we may go with certainty. With a little less assurance we may assert that this mental shock left him eccentric, and deranged the nice mental balance which was his by right of birth and training. Joseph's whole career was probably ruined by his first marriage. More distant sequences of this unfortunate marriage were a disastrous reign for the monarchy, and the shifting of all the future rulers of Austria to the line of a brother.

In the meantime Maria Theresa was very busy with projects for mating her other offspring. The marriage of Prince Charles to Princess Marie Louise, whose father had been promoted from the throne of Naples to that of Spain, was prevented by the untimely death of the Prince from a sequela of smallpox in 1761. Thus the ambitious Bourbon King was again robbed of his prospect of marrying a daughter to an archduke, but, like the ghost of Banquo, he kept coming up for another scion of the House of Hapsburg. The next one available was Archduke Leopold who was nearly two years younger than Marie Louise, but the King—now Charles III of Spain—offered to accept Leopold as a substitute for Prince Charles.[14]

At that time Isabelle was still living, and it was considered improbable that Leopold would ever be called upon to supply future emperors, so Marie Louise's rather indifferent qualities need not bar the Queen, who wished to deal honorably with the King, from accepting her as a bride for her son. Accordingly she dismissed the idea of marrying Leopold to a Princess of Modena, as she had already planned, and betrothed him to Marie Louise. Later came the death of Isabelle, but the Queen's sense of honor prompted her to keep her part of the agreement. (She probably comforted herself with the hope of continuing her line by a second marriage of Joseph.) Little did she think—little did any one think—that this ordinary Marie Louise would become the ancestress of more than a century of emperors. Marie Louise was a granddaughter of Elizabeth Farnese, the Termagant of Spain, who was so despised by Maria Theresa but who eventually became as much the mother of Francis Joseph, for example, as was the great Maria Theresa herself. How fortunate it was that the Queen could not penetrate the future.

Probably to convince the King of Spain that she was really in earnest, Maria Theresa agreed to wed Leopold to Marie Louise when he was but eighteen. Charles III said he did not wish Marie Louise to be married in Vienna, because he feared she might be

[14] Guglia, II, 197–198.

frightened by the noise of a great city; so it was arranged to have the wedding in Innsbruck.[15]

In July, 1765, the imperial family accompanied Archduke Leopold to the Tirols for his marriage. Of what was in store for the Queen on this never-to-be-forgotten trip, she had no more warning than the man who is destined to be instantly killed in an earthquake. The worst blow of the Queen's whole life came like a crash of thunder from a clear sky. While in Innsbruck Francis was coming down stairs with Joseph, when he fell as if shot through the heart, and died in his son's arms. The cause of death was given as apoplexy.[16]

At first Maria Theresa refused to believe that her husband was really dead; she was sure he was only asleep. When convinced of the awful truth she withdrew to her room and asked to be left alone. She bore the severest of all her bereavements with wonderful fortitude, and without any violent outburst of emotion. She seemed to be stunned and incapable of comprehending that Francis was really gone. Presently she recovered sufficiently to show her devotion and love in a most remarkable manner; it is said that she insisted upon preparing a burial robe and putting it on her husband's body with her own hands.[17] Her return to Vienna was unspeakably sad.

Later the Queen wrote in her prayer book: "Emperor Francis I, my husband, died on the evening of the eighteenth of August at half past nine o'clock. He lived 680 months, 2,958 weeks, 20,778 days, or 496,992 hours. Our happy marriage lasted 29 years, 6

---

[15] Bermann, 758.
[16] Zwiedineck-Südenhorst, 96.
[17] Guglia, 231.

months and 6 days, 1540 weeks, 10,781 days, or 258,-744 hours." It is said that when she prayed she repeated these figures and thanked God for having given her so many "pearls of joy." [18]

Immediately after the death of her husband the Queen made her son Joseph co-regent, and since he had already been elected King of the Romans, he also became Emperor. From that time forward, Maria Theresa transferred many of the burdens of state to the shoulders of her son, but continued to follow the affairs of the monarchy with keenest interest, several times overruling Joseph upon important matters of the government. She never delegated to him the power of conducting marriage negotiations for the family, probably because she was too fond of taking the part of a matchmaker. In this field she continued very much as if her son were not a co-regent, and disregarded the fact that as Emperor he outranked her in authority to form matrimonial alliances among princes and princesses.

But we must revert to the lifetime of Emperor Francis to resume the broken story of Joseph's unhappy domestic affairs. Isabelle died in November, 1763, and the next March found Joseph at Frankfort being crowned King of the Romans. Since a widower was being thus exalted, the coronation developed into a veritable scramble of kings and princes to present their eligible princesses to the young monarch's parents in the hope of having them chosen as his consort. The

[18] Our authority for these figures is Bermann, 764. We have been unable to find the prayer book for the purpose of checking them. Bermann makes no note of the errors in calculation they exhibit. However, we know Maria Theresa was famous for her mistakes in spelling and arithmetic. That she repeated erroneous numbers for fifteen years in her prayers is a rather fascinating thought.

market was glutted with representatives of prospective brides, in spite of the fact that Joseph had repeatedly said he did not wish to marry. He told his parents that, if he must marry, he preferred the sister of his departed wife, but this was not favorably received by the Emperor and Empress who thought the sister too young for Joseph. Besides, they had no desire to bring another prophetess of evil into the family.

Joseph's position at this time was pitiable. He sincerely felt his bereavement and wished to be left alone in his grief, but the tormenting diplomats allowed him no respite; one came on the heels of another to press the claims of one woman after another. He knew his parents were constantly receiving and considering applicants, toward none of whom he was in the least attracted.[19] While he was not always consulted, he realized he was on the block and likely to be knocked down to the highest bidder at any moment. One might suppose that such a man would never dictate a marriage to any one against his or her will, but we shall presently find him showing the same inconsideration that he was receiving.

Francis and Maria Theresa finally selected four princesses whom they were willing to consider seriously. They were Benedicta of Portugal, Elizabeth of Brunswick, Cunigunda of Saxony, and Josepha of Bavaria. Elizabeth, although a relative of the Queen's mother, was soon rejected because her house was too much entangled with that of Frederick of Prussia, and Benedicta was eliminated because Francis believed she would not have children promptly, and because her

[19] Arneth, VII, 89.

house was too favorably disposed to England. Having thus reduced the list to two, the Queen told her son he might take his choice between Cunigunda and Josepha, but that she preferred Cunigunda.

In reply Joseph said, "Well mother, I prefer not to marry either, but since you are holding the knife at my throat, I will take Josepha, because, from what I hear, she at least has fine breasts." [20]

But Maria Theresa still favored Cunigunda, and insisted that Joseph make a trip to Saxony to see her. The prospective lovers met on horseback, and Joseph was so displeased with the Princess that he seems to have ridden away without dismounting, much less proposing. While the meeting was apparently incidental, both Cunigunda and her father were well aware of its purpose. The Princess was eager to please the young King of the Romans, and very much chagrined because she failed. Joseph gave the Princess such scant attention that the Saxon court felt insulted.

Still undaunted, the Queen insisted that her son visit Josepha. He consented, probably because he was so distracted by the importunities of his parents, and went determined to propose regardless of his feelings. At this time Joseph was still mourning for Isabelle, and had formed the habit of opening his heart in intimate letters to his father-in-law in Parma. Of Josepha he wrote: "She is twenty-six years old, and has not had the smallpox; the very mention of that disease makes me shudder. Her figure is short and thick, and without any youthful charm whatever. Her face is covered with red pimples, and her teeth are horrible. I am not

[20] Bermann, 717.

tempted in the least to offer her the place so recently occupied by one who was quite the opposite, but I have put the matter before my parents plainly and asked them to decide what I shall do." [21]

If we may believe what Maria Theresa wrote in her letters, she was opposed to this union, but yielded to pressure from her husband and Kaunitz. Josepha was a daughter of the deceased Charles VII, who had caused the Queen so much trouble in the beginning of her reign, and the Elector of Bavaria was Josepha's brother, but had no sons. Francis and Kaunitz foresaw the death of the Elector without a male heir, and planned by this marriage to win at least a part of Bavaria for the Hapsburgs, hence they did their best to influence the Queen to put aside her objections on the ground of patriotism. Her views were stated in a letter to her daughter Christina, in which she wrote in part: "You have a new sister-in-law, and I have a new daughter-in-law; sad to say, she is the Princess Josepha. Against all my convictions and inclinations, I have been compelled to make this decision for my son, because of his father and Kaunitz. I had to give the command, because it would only have been obeyed when coming from me. My heart and my head were opposed to this union, and it was only with great difficulty that I brought myself to yield." [22]

The second marriage of Joseph was the worst farce of its kind in which the Queen played the deciding rôle. Even Josepha did not wish to marry Joseph, and is said to have regretted that her father was not living to

[21] Arneth, VII, 102.
[22] Guglia, II, 196.

deliver her from her fate. She was no less to be pitied than Joseph.

The wedding occurred in Vienna in January, 1765, under the most strained circumstances. To inject a little joy into the occasion, Maria Theresa found twenty-five couples who were willing to be married, and had their ceremonies performed at the same time, giving each couple a wedding present of two hundred guldens. Otherwise the whole ceremony would have been as sad as a funeral.[23]

Josepha was anything but pretty. She was two years older than Joseph, but many of the Viennese vowed she was old enough to be his mother, and some thought the Elector of Bavaria had cheated the groom by sending an aunt instead of a sister. The Viennese had no use for a Queen who was not pretty, and were unable to conceal their disappointment.

Wedding festivities were prolonged until June, but before they were finished, the bride and groom were very much bored and well on the way to a separation. Francis of Lorraine, who had promoted the match, did his best to make it a success, but in vain. Quite disheartened over the affair, he seemed glad when the time arrived for him to depart for Innsbruck, as it proved, to be brought back in a coffin.

Josepha withdrew to Baden, to take a cure and comfort herself as much as possible by entertaining lavishly at the best hotel of the place, where her table was rarely set for fewer than forty guests, but usually unhonored by the presence of her husband. All Vienna

---

[23] Bermann, 730.

knew the marriage was a failure, and the Queen was deeply grieved, but according to Wraxall, neither the Queen nor any of her daughters were cordial toward Josepha. He says: "Only Francis of Lorraine showed any interest in Josepha, and when she heard of his death at Innsbruck, she exclaimed, 'How unfortunate! I have lost my only friend!' Josepha's sisters-in-law avoided her, and the Queen treated her coldly, while the poor bride had so much disgust for Joseph that she trembled in terror whenever she found herself alone with him." [24]

But Josepha was not destined to annoy the imperial family very long. In the spring of 1767 she fell ill of smallpox and died in a few days. It was at the time the Queen had her awful attack of the same disease, and Joseph, being much worried over his mother, neglected his wife so that she died almost abandoned by the family.[25]

The manner in which Josepha was treated in Vienna was reported in Bavaria, and the court of Munich was very much offended. For years the Bavarians contended that Josepha was not dead, but that her supposed coffin, filled with stones, had been placed in the Capucine Church, while she was confined in some secret prison in Lower Austria. This idea was strengthened by the fact that Joseph refused to marry again, the explanation being, according to the Bavarians, that he was afraid his wife might be discovered and returned to confront him.[26]

The marriage of Archduchess Maria Christina, the

[24] Quoted by Bermann, 724.
[25] Arneth, VII, 326.
[26] Bermann, 724.

The Queen as a Mother 291

next of the family, was marked with both politics and romance. Maria Christina was very beautiful and had been fortunate enough to escape being marked by the smallpox.[27] She was also one of the cleverest of the daughters; none of the other elder archduchesses wrote such interesting letters as Maria Christina. Isabelle loved Christina and a strange attachment sprang up between them, resulting in the many letters from which we glean so much concerning the melancholy of Joseph's wife.

When Christina was nineteen, Prince Ludwig of Württemberg visited the court of Vienna and fell in love with her. They seemed to forget that they were prince and princess and became engaged like common folks. Then, in a little while, came Prince Albert of Saxony who also fell in love with Christina and succeeded in establishing himself as a rival.[28] Probably in a fit of jealousy, Prince Ludwig married a lady of inferior rank while he was campaigning in Saxony. Christina, upon hearing of this promptly gave her heart to Albert, but was presently most forcibly reminded of her rank by her father, who wished to give her to the Duke of Chablais, the son of the King of Sardinia by Francis of Lorraine's sister. Francis invited his nephew to Leopold's wedding at Innsbruck for the special purpose of presenting him to Christina, but it so happened that Prince Albert was there too. Christina stubbornly refused to yield to her father's will and the battle was being fiercely fought when Francis died. Knowing in what high esteem the Queen held the wishes of her

[27] Guglia, II, 198–199.
[28] Arneth, VII, 250–252.

husband, Prince Albert regarded his suit as lost, when to his joyful surprise, the Queen came to his rescue and presented him the hand of the Archduchess.[29] Albert was very grateful and from that day until her death was strongly attached to his mother-in-law. The truth was that the Queen considered Albert the better bargain of the two, because she was eager to bind the House of Saxony to hers as a check to Prussia. Thus it came to pass that there was one real love match in the Queen's family, and it proved to be the happiest marriage of all. Probably in order to have this happily mated pair near her, the Queen made Prince Albert commander of a division of the Hungarian army, and fixed his residence at the near-by city of Pressburg. The mother and daughter often visited back and forth, and the Queen regarded this son-in-law with as much affection as her own natural children.[30]

Elizabeth, the next daughter, was one of the most beautiful of all the archduchesses until she had the misfortune to be mutilated by a dreadful attack of smallpox.[31] It is said that when she found herself ill of that awful disease, she asked for a mirror in order that she might have a last look at her departing beauty. At first the Queen was disposed to give her to the Duke of Chablais who was still standing in line waiting for an archduchess in fulfillment of the promise of Francis of Lorraine, but progress was halted by an unexpected proposal from King Stanislaus of Poland. The King's qualifications were soon found to be far below the required grade; his country was too poor and his throne

---
[29] *Ibid.*, 256.
[30] *Ibid.*, 257.
[31] Guglia, 198–201.

too uncertain, but the Queen wished to avoid offending him.[32] She was much relieved when she learned that the union was opposed by Catherine of Russia, and availing herself of that excuse, sent the King a refusal. As she was about to turn once more to the Duke of Chablais she was seized with the idea of marrying Elizabeth to the King of Spain whose wife had just died, but as she was on the point of beginning negotiations, word came that Marie Leczinska, the wife of Louis XV, had died, thus bringing very much larger game into the field. Maria Theresa was enraptured at the prospect of getting one of her daughters into the Palace of Versailles as a Queen, regardless of the fact that the new wife would be facing keen competition from mistresses and concubines. Negotiations were opened with Choiseul, the French minister, and advanced so far that Louis XV sent a celebrated painter to Vienna to investigate Elizabeth's pockmarks, concerning which he had heard disquieting rumors. The artist's report was not given out, but Louis XV, who still had a sensitive eye for beauty, seemed to lose interest in the Archduchess and the whole project collapsed.[33] By this time Elizabeth had reached the alarming age of twenty-four, her pockmarks had been much advertised, and her marriage prospects so badly deflated that Maria Theresa hurried to dispose of her by making her an abbess in a convent in Innsbruck. So another daughter was piously given to the Church.[34]

[32] Had this marriage occurred, it might have prevented the partition of Poland which took place shortly after Stanislaus' proposal. The reader will doubtless recall that Catherine the Great had been Stanislaus' mistress.
[33] Guglia, II, 245.
[34] Arneth, X, 715.

The next archduchess to be put on the marriage block was the sleepy Maria Amalia, who fell in love with the Prince of Zweibrucken, a distant relative of the Elector of Bavaria. The Prince arrived in Vienna during the holidays at the close of the year 1767, when Amalia was twenty-one years old.[35] While he was not rich nor endowed with a very influential possession, he had a fair prospect of becoming Elector of Bavaria, since the present Elector was in poor health and had no direct male heir. Having such potential value, the Prince was very much surprised to have his suit for the hand of Amalia rejected with scant consideration. Kaunitz sneered at his proposal and pronounced it "comical, yes absurd." Kaunitz said the prince of such an insignificant realm could be regarded as but little more than a "private man." Also Joseph, who had advanced to the high station of Emperor and felt called upon to put in a few words now and then concerning the marriages of his sisters, was violently opposed to this union. Under such circumstances it is always well to search behind the scenes for hidden motives.

Sure enough, back of the Prince's rejection was an intrigue of which Kaunitz was probably the author. If the Elector of Bavaria died without a male heir, it was planned to annex a part or all of the Electorate to Austria, and the court wished to avoid disinheriting a member of the Queen's family. The bitter experience of Francis of Lorraine should not be repeated. Under such circumstances, the marriage of an archduchess to the Prince of Zweibrucken was bad politics, and must not be considered; Kaunitz undertook to manage the

[35] *Ibid.*, VII, 371.

Queen who had looked with favor upon the project.

When the full significance of the intrigue was unfolded to the Queen she yielded readily, and as usual, assumed the unpleasant task of communicating the sad news to the daughter. We have the authority of some of the Queen's best biographers for the statement that she did this against her own convictions and inclinations.[36] We may be sure that in persuading her of the necessity of vetoing this union, an appeal was made to her desire to gain some compensation for Silesia; this argument was to her almost irresistible.

To offset this love affair, the plan of marrying Amalia to the Duke of Parma, Isabelle's brother, was immediately proposed and pushed with great energy. The Prince of Parma's virtues were magnified to the Archduchess, and finally her consent to break her first attachment and resign herself to a loveless marriage was secured. She made the best of her fate, which proved to be a very hard one, and lived in her husband's dominion until deprived of it by the Napoleonic wars. Later it became the domain of Marie Louise, the wife of Napoleon.

The next daughter who lived long enough to be betrothed, was Johanna who at the age of twelve, was designated for the seven-year-old Bourbon King Ferdinand of Naples. This arrangement was made during the lifetime of Emperor Francis, and both he and Maria Theresa were very enthusiastic for the marriage, partly because the Queen was eager to have the fingers of the Hapsburgs once more feel the reins of the government of Naples—we may remember that this king-

---

[36] Guglia, II, 248-249.

dom was lost to Spain at the end of the War of the Polish Succession—and partly because the infant King was the son of Charles III of Spain, and might some day inherit the Spanish crown. The whole project withered to the ground when Johanna died of smallpox at the age of twelve, but it was presently revived by substituting Josepha for Johanna.[37]

How Maria Theresa regarded the young King of Naples is revealed in the now celebrated instructions given to Countess Trautmansdorff, Josepha's teacher, for her guidance in training the daughter for her position as wife of Ferdinand. From these instructions we translate the following:

"To you is entrusted the training of my daughter, who will soon be called upon to become the wife of a king whom she will make either happy or unhappy. Her husband will be a man who from childhood knew no authority but himself. I assure you I foresee the destiny of this union, and that my motherly heart is much disturbed by the vision. I consider Josepha a sacrifice to politics, and, if she fulfills her duty to her husband and her God, I shall be content. The King of Naples cares for nothing but hunting and the theater. He is childish, accustomed to follow only the inclination of his will, and there is no one who can or will teach him anything; such is the unhappy truth about this prince. I hope my daughter will not be selfish; she has a tendency in that direction. She is reserved, which is fortunate for her on account of the position she is to occupy, but it should not be carried too far lest she be misunderstood. We must train her to be gentle and pleasant in her dis-

[37] *Ibid.,* 201.

The Queen as a Mother 297

position, and to seek her happiness in herself by a devotion to art, music, and the like." [38] Can any one admire such a mother? Certainly, if we are sympathetic enough to believe that she was actuated by high motives of patriotism—the same motives which prompt mothers to give their sons to die for their countries on fields of battle.

The Queen's remarkable directions to Countess Trautmansdorff were entirely lost, for in the autumn of 1767, as Josepha, at the age of sixteen, was about to set forth to marry this undesirable king, she fell ill of the smallpox and died after a few days. A very sad feature of this death was that the Archduchess contracted smallpox in the Capucine Church where she had gone to pray, some say unwillingly, in compliance with her mother's demand. The disease was supposed to have come from the corpse of Josepha, Joseph's wife, whose coffin had not been properly sealed.[39] At that time the vaults of the Capucine Church were filled with dead bodies, but very much alive with the germs of smallpox. Fumigation and disinfection were little used or understood.

Most queens would have been so discouraged over the apparent opposition of fate to this union that it would have been abandoned, but such was not the case with the persistent Maria Theresa, who, along with the sad news of the death of Josepha, sent an offer to the King of Spain to substitute for Josepha her sister Caroline. Thus death and romance went hand in hand at the behest of honest politics and patriotism. This does not mean that Maria Theresa did not feel the

[38] *Ibid.,* 202.
[39] Arneth, VII, 332 seq.

grief of a fond mother over the death of her daughter; she wept bitterly, but said she considered it a point of honor to fulfill her promise of an archduchess for the King's son.

The King of Spain met this generous honesty by suggesting that perhaps it would be better to give the elder Amalia to Ferdinand, who needed the restraining influence of an older woman for a wife—at this time Amalia was twenty-one, Ferdinand sixteen, and Caroline fifteen. But Ferdinand preferred the younger archduchess and was allowed to have his way.

Two years younger than Caroline was Archduke Ferdinand, born in 1754. According to the Pragmatic Sanction, it became the policy of the House of Hapsburg to pass the unbroken inherited dominions to the eldest son. Hence it was not easy for Maria Theresa to find independent possessions for her younger sons. Francis of Lorraine arranged for Leopold by assigning him Tuscany, where he made a good record as a Grand Duke, until he became the head of the house at the death of Joseph in 1790. In order to provide for Ferdinand, he was betrothed to Princess Beatrice of Modena when he was fifteen years old. The marriage occurred when the Prince was seventeen. In spite of the fact that Beatrice was four years older than her husband, the union was a reasonably happy one.

Maria Theresa, as we have seen, now had the Italian Peninsula fairly well colonized with her offspring, and as long as she lived they held their dominions. She often spoke of her four treasured daughters in Italy, referring to Marie Louise, the wife of Leopold; Beatrice, the wife of Ferdinand; and her own daughters

Caroline and Amalia. Had the good *Landesmutter* lived two decades longer than she did, she would have seen her fledglings flapping their wings like flushed quail to escape from Italy upon the arrival of the conquering Napoleon.

There still remains to be mentioned the marriage of Marie Antoinette, the youngest and afterward the most renowned of all the daughters of Maria Theresa. The project of her betrothal with the dauphin of France arose when the Archduchess was ten years old, and was continued more or less precariously for a little more than four years, when it terminated in a marriage. Doubtless the Queen thought this union the most desirable one of her entire reign. She regarded it as the grand climax, the *chef-d'œuvre,* of all her marriage negotiations, and visualized a perfect weld of her house with that of the French branch of the Bourbons.[40] While the first proposal may have come from France, there is no doubt that it was joyfully received by the Queen, who saw in it a pleasant compensation for her failure to get Archduchess Elizabeth to the altar with Louis XV. The dauphin was one year older than Marie Antoinette, almost sure to succeed to the throne of France, and in every conceivable way, just the husband for the Queen's baby daughter.

When the betrothal was completed, the Queen sent for the French Abbot of Vermond to come to Vienna and train the future Queen of France for the exalted position she was to hold. That he did nothing but amuse

---

[40] *Ibid.,* X, 238. After Marie Antoinette's betrothal, Maria Theresa said, "Austria and France are now so firmly united that nothing can part them."

the child, with a view to making himself popular with the Princess for his own aggrandizement, was hardly the fault of Maria Theresa. In 1770 a marriage ceremony by proxy was held with much pomp and splendor in Vienna; then the fourteen-year-old maiden set forth to find her fortune at the foot of the rainbow which all Europe saw arched over Versailles. Of Maria Theresa's sixteen children, this daughter is the only one now missing in the vaults of the Capucine Church in Vienna.

It was Maria Theresa's custom to send her daughters away with written instructions for their guidance.[41] Many of these were very lengthy, but probably not carefully read by the brides who were naturally engrossed in the pursuit of their own happiness in their own way. She also watched over them through the eyes of the Austrian ambassadors to their various courts, sometimes secretly sending long letters of counsel and advice through the same channels. The Queen sacrificed her daughters ruthlessly, but did all in her power to make their lives as comfortable as possible in their new homes.[42]

The youngest child of the family was Archduke Maximilian. It was the Queen's intention to make a soldier of him, but he proved to be too tender and soft-hearted for such a stern occupation. He was more inclined to the church, and in the end, she decided to have him devote himself to religion. Naturally his rise in the church was rapid, and one of the last and sweetest triumphs of the Queen's life was experienced when, in

---
[41] *Ibid.*, VII, 434.
[42] The published letters of Maria Theresa to her children fill several large volumes.

spite of the opposition of Frederick of Prussia, she succeeded in having Maximilian made Elector of Cologne and Bishop of Münster. He never married.

Probably no queen in modern history surpassed Maria Theresa as a negotiator of political marriages. When she finished she had her house spliced with that of the Bourbons in half a dozen places, and had formed marriage alliances with the strong states of Saxony and Bavaria, although the one with the latter was a complete failure. She very nearly accomplished all that she had in mind at the beginning. That the union of the two great Houses of Hapsburg and Bourbon was only temporary was not her fault, but that of her successors.

It is customary to question the wisdom of the Queen's policy in attempting to combine the Hapsburgs and Bourbons against Prussia and England. Many contend that it would have been much better had she endeavored to consolidate the German race by marrying her children to German princes and princesses. It is much easier to discern past than present political follies. Maria Theresa was surely right in believing that the greatest enemy of Austria was destined to be Prussia, and it is doubtful if she could have held the other German princes against the rivalry of Frederick, who proved to be one of the most capable politicians of his day. Her plan may have been the wisest one possible at that time; its failure can be attributed largely to a lack of vision and judgment on the part of her successors.

Four of Maria Theresa's children lure us to follow them a little farther along their adventurous ways; they are Joseph II, Leopold II, Marie Caroline and Marie Antoinette.

Joseph II, who was Emperor from 1780 to 1790,

seemed inspired with the idea that he was destined to evangelize the world, but since he lacked the perseverance, discretion and common sense of his mother, he achieved only a small measure of permanent success. If his mother hated Frederick of Prussia and trusted the French too much, Joseph went to the opposite extreme, fell into the arms of Frederick, and revived the old hatred, which had almost subsided, between Austria and France. Joseph's emulation of Frederick degenerated into an awkward mimicry which, when compared with the lofty, independent spirit of Maria Theresa, almost moves us to pity.[43] Maria Theresa passed to her son the best hereditary possessions in all Europe, almost blended into a real nation in spite of differences in language and religion; Joseph, in only ten years, left his successor a nation very much in the same sad plight as the one his mother received from Charles VI. Upon his deathbed Joseph II exclaimed, "I would have engraven on my tomb, 'Here lies a sovereign, who, with the best of intentions, never carried a single project into execution.'"[44]

Leopold II, who was Emperor only from 1790 to 1792, was better known as Grand Duke of Tuscany than as a ruler of the Austrian dominions. His modesty and lack of presumption contrasted strangely with the disposition of his elder brother, but he accomplished much more. Sir William Coxe, in his excellent History of the House of Austria, written just after the close of Leopold's reign, said: "If we may judge from results, we cannot withhold the greatest praise from this sov-

---
[43] Gotthold Dorschel, 116.
[44] Whitman, 273.

ereign, who, within the short space of a single year, relieved his country from a foreign war and internal commotion, who baffled a great combination which threatened the destruction of his house, and firmly established a throne which at his accession was tottering to its very foundation." [45] Marie Louise, the Spanish Princess who was considered such a plodder, turned out to be an exceptionally true and helpful wife who always stood unflinchingly at her husband's side during life, and held him in her arms when he expired. She bore him sixteen children who, with two exceptions, survived both parents, and they and their descendants provided Austrian rulers until the end of the monarchy. Marie Louise and Leopold II deserve a higher rank in the House of Hapsburg than is usually accorded them.

Marie Caroline, commonly known as Caroline of Naples, was perhaps the most capable of the many daughters of Maria Theresa. She dominated her husband completely, and usually for his own benefit. Her adventurous life was interwoven with those of such renowned characters as Lady Hamilton, Lord Nelson, and Napoleon Bonaparte. The latter loved to ridicule her, but nevertheless it was Caroline's assistance to Lord Nelson that enabled the great English admiral to break Napoleon Bonaparte's back and blast his fond hope of conquering the world. Putting it in the style of "The House that Jack Built," we may say, it was Caroline who helped the British fleet, that won the Battle of Aboukir, that curbed the ambition of Napoleon. Nor is that all; it was Caroline who instilled into the heart

---
[45] Coxe, III, 727.

of her granddaughter Marie Louise the hate that finally brought the greatest warrior of modern times to complete destruction.

The renown of Marie Antoinette rests almost entirely upon the last scenes of her life, staged in prisons and on that horror of horrors, the guillotine of the French Revolution. Her husband was too weak to make the reforms—the very ones Maria Theresa did make in her monarchy—necessary to save his kingdom from the bloody uprising in which he met his death, which was soon followed by that of his wife. Marie Antoinette was indiscreet, but her fate arrived on the crest of a wave of racial hate which her mother strove with all her might to stem, only to have her successful endeavors nullified by a well-meaning but injudicious son. Few women of history met disaster and death with more courage than did Marie Antoinette; we imagine the plucky old Queen would have found much to admire in the way her baby girl played her last act.

By way of completeness, we append a brief summary of the important facts concerning the children of Maria Theresa.

1. Maria Elizabeth, born 1737, died 1740.
2. Maria Anna, born 1738, became abbess in Prague, died 1789.
3. Maria Karolina, born 1740, died 1741.
4. Joseph II, born 1741, became Emperor 1780, died 1790.
5. Maria Christina, born 1742, married the Prince of Saxony, died 1798.
6. Maria Elizabeth, born 1743, became abbess in Innsbruck, died 1808.
7. Karl Joseph, born 1745, died 1761.

The Queen as a Mother

8. Maria Amalia, born 1746, married the Duke of Parma, died 1804.
9. Leopold II, born 1747, became Emperor 1790, died 1792.
10. Maria Caroline, born and died 1748.
11. Johanna, born 1750, betrothed to Ferdinand of Naples, died 1762.
12. Josepha, born 1751, betrothed to Ferdinand of Naples, died 1767.
13. Marie Caroline, born 1752, married the King of Naples, died 1814.
14. Ferdinand, born 1754, became Governor of Lombardy, died 1806.
15. Marie Antoinette, born 1755, became Queen of France, died 1793.
16. Maximilian, born 1756, became Elector of Cologne, died 1801.[46]

III

A little study of the lives of great rulers shows that the narrow, precarious path to power stretches in one direction, and the broad, safe road to happiness in the opposite. This statement is abundantly illustrated by the lives of such celebrated characters as Alexander the Great, Julius Cæsar, and Napoleon Bonaparte; it also applies with equal force to the life of the less renowned Maria Theresa of Austria. Very few of the world's great rulers have enjoyed a peaceful, happy old age.

[46] This family record is derived from authentic documents. The reader will notice that the Queen repeated the names of two deceased daughters, but in the name of Maria Karolina, changed the spelling each time.

Prior to the death of her husband in 1765, the Queen's life was interspersed with glorious triumphs and heart-rending disasters, but after that date her path was almost continuously in the shadow of sorrows cast by real or imaginary misfortunes. Undoubtedly her greatest source of grief was her son Joseph whom she had made her co-regent, and who, unlike his father, was too spirited to submit to her will.[47]

The first serious outbreak between mother and son occurred the next year after the death of the father. Joseph, without consulting his mother, took upon himself the authority to write a scathing letter to a prominent member of the court, severely criticizing his conduct and that of Chancellor Kaunitz. It created a sensation, and upon hearing of it the Queen was very angry and wrote her son a letter from which we select a few quotations. "Do you think you can win men to your service in this manner? I fear you will fall into the hands of scoundrels who, in order to carry their points, may endeavor to please you by means no respectable person would use. And what worries me most is that you did not write this letter on the spur of the moment, but, after twenty-four hours of deliberate meditation, decided to thrust daggers into the hearts of those who would be your friends. It was not the Emperor, nor the co-regent who wrote such biting spiteful irony; it came from the very heart of my Joseph. That is what fills me with foreboding for the future of this empire and yourself. I have flattered myself that I will live in you after death, and that your family and state will thus be the gainer rather than loser by my departure. Can I

---

[47] Gotthold Dorschel, 113 seq.

still cherish this hope when you, in this manner, exclude your friends from your heart? Has Frederick the Great, the conqueror of whom you speak so often, a single friend? What a life it must be from which one's fellows are barred!

"A simple yes or no, or a decided refusal, would have been much better than this long ironical discourse in which you flail the air, and try so very awkwardly to conceal your real meaning. Take care not to become malicious. Your heart is not bad, but it may become so. It is time you cease to find pleasure in witticisms and sarcasms intended to make others appear ridiculous, but which in reality only offend them and drive those who are respectable away from you. You seem to be seeking your own ruin. You use clever phrases, which you read in your books, or hear from others, at your first opportunity, without any consideration of the appropriateness of the occasion. Your manner in this respect reminds me of the way Elizabeth tries everything of which she hears to restore her beauty." [48]

Joseph seems to have been completely squelched by this stinging letter, but only temporarily. In 1768, Maria Theresa again complained bitterly over Joseph's philosophy, which she said estranged him from all he met "in the theater, while hunting, dancing, or playing cards." She even went so far as to write to one of her daughters-in-law, cautioning her not to allow Joseph to make a philosopher of her husband. In 1771, she complained of Joseph's indifference to religion, which she feared had greatly increased since the death of his little daughter.[49] Another complaint was over the fact

[48] Letter of Maria Theresa to Joseph, Sept. 14, 1766.
[49] Gotthold Dorschel, 115

that it was necessary to consult Joseph, because he was her co-regent, concerning the affairs of the state and empire. "Public business is continually shuffled from one ruler to another, and Joseph degrades me until I feel as if I were only his empress. I cannot win him to my views, and I am continually losing ground. I hope the grief he is causing me is recorded to my credit in the next world, and that my unpleasant position may speedily come to an end." [50]

A little later she was rapturous with joy because Joseph had gone to confess. "My happiness over the return of my lost son is greater than I felt at his birth!" she exclaimed. But in a little while Joseph was "just as bad as ever," and she wrote, "He is again indifferent to his religion, and avoids me as much as possible." [51] By 1775 she was threatening to resign from the co-regency; she said, "My sight is failing, my hearing and perception are no longer good, and what I have feared all my life has come to pass; my resolution has failed." [52]

But Joseph and her ministers would not listen to her pleas to resign, because they feared the political consequences of an event which would so seriously emphasize the lack of harmony between mother and son—a state which was already too widely advertised for Joseph's

---

[50] Guglia, II, 256, quoting from a letter of Maria Theresa to Beatrice, the wife of Archduke Ferdinand.

[51] Gotthold Dorschel, 120, quoting a letter of Maria Theresa to Mercy.

[52] *Ibid.*, 124.

"I am as unnecessary to this government as is the fifth wheel to a wagon," wrote Joseph to Marie Antoinette in Nov. 1776.

"In spite of all the trouble Joseph causes me, I love him tenderly," wrote Maria Theresa the same month to Mercy. *Korrespondenz mit Mercy*, II, 621.

welfare. Whenever the Queen spoke of quitting, there was a love scene in which Joseph vowed, "I love my mother," and she said through her tears, "I love my son." That being settled, they again went at each other with "hammer and tongs" as before.

Joseph imagined himself very modern, and had a rage for innovations. At one time he started a campaign to dismantle the fortifications of the city, because he said they were no longer any protection against the newer forms of artillery, and were a great hindrance in consolidating the suburbs with the old city. To put a stop to this "nonsense," the Queen called her court together and said: "My son wishes me to dismantle the fortifications of Vienna. I am an old woman; I almost remember when Vienna was besieged by the Turks, and, unless the capital had been capable of withstanding a blockade until it was relieved by John Sobieski, the Ottoman hordes would have ravaged the hereditary dominions and overrun the empire. I myself have twice seen the walls of Vienna almost the frontier of my monarchy. Let Joseph act as he pleases when I am gone, but, while I live, the fortifications shall not be dismantled." [58]

Joseph's ideas were apparently correct; the fortifications were useless when Napoleon appeared before Vienna in 1805, and again in 1809. But the preservation of the walls proved to be of the greatest benefit to the city in a most unexpected manner. When they were torn down in 1857, the ground they occupied had become so very valuable that the city was able to dispose of a portion of it for such a large sum as to make pos-

---

[58] Arneth, *Briefwechsel mit Joseph*, II, 94—95.

sible the erection of the matchless public edifices now lining the Ringstrasse. Accidentally, through the stubbornness of Maria Theresa, Vienna, almost without cost to the municipality, became one of the most beautiful cities in the world.

Joseph was never able, as his illustrious mother had been, to reach the heart of his subjects. He was too stiff, formal and egotistical. One evening during the winter of 1768, a messenger from Florence arrived in Vienna with the news that Leopold had a son. Maria Theresa became so excited that, without changing her dress, she rushed afoot to the Burg theater where she arrived in the imperial box almost breathless. Then, without waiting for a pause in the play, she exclaimed twice in her broad *Wienerisch* dialect, *"Der Leopold hat ein Buberl! Der Leopold hat ein Buberl!!"* The whole theater broke into wild applause, partly because of the news, but perhaps more at the delightful manner in which it was announced.[54] Joseph could never have done that because he would have thought it beneath his dignity. In this picturesque and affable manner was proclaimed the birth of the Archduke destined to be the last Emperor of the Holy Roman Empire of the Germans.

The disputes—we really should say quarrels—between the Queen and her son continued, with a few intermissions, almost to the death of the mother. Only two months before her death Maria Theresa wrote: "Unfortunately it is well known that Joseph loves suspicion, and keeps himself thoroughly informed concerning everything of that nature; this makes our lives most unpleasant; we are constantly in an atmosphere of

---

[54] Felder, 33.

EMPEROR JOSEPH II

calumny from which there seems to be no escape." [55]

Undoubtedly there was much to be said in defense of Joseph in many of the quarrels, but most of the arguments in his favor are nullified by the simple fact that his mother achieved so much under adverse circumstances while he failed under conditions far more favorable. Perhaps this is putting the matter rather strongly, for there are some who contend that Joseph accomplished a great deal which was permanently beneficial to Austria.

Maria Theresa's other sons caused her very little worry. Leopold was successful as Grand Duke of Tuscany, and the others were never called upon to perform any conspicuous public service. Aside from Joseph, all the archdukes inherited enough of the easy-going disposition of their father to make them less ambitious and assertive.

But it was quite different with the daughters, over whom the Queen spent so many sleepless nights writing epistles filled with platitudes and admonitions. To begin with, she never ceased to worry over Maria Anna's health. Then Elizabeth's lost beauty haunted the mother to her grave. The misfortune of this daughter was so much emphasized by the refusal of Louis XV to marry her, that the poor Archduchess spent whole nights in weeping. She was not at all comforted by being made an abbess, but continued hoping against hope that some means of removing the dreadful scars might be found. Amalia who, as we have stated, was consigned to a loveless marriage by her mother and older brother, had a dreadful time with her husband,

[55] Letter of Maria Theresa to Ferdinand, Nov. 10, 1780.

who turned out to be dissolute and brazenly untrue to his wife. Amalia's husband was a brother to Joseph's first wife, Isabelle, and the Queen once said: "I cannot understand how the gentle Isabelle could have had such a brother. Some men love mistresses, others gambling, and others horses, but this one—"[56] There she stopped, apparently because she could find no words to express her disgust for Amalia's husband, or perhaps she suddenly remembered the circumstances of Amalia's marriage.

To Caroline of Naples who had the misfortune—or perhaps it was good fortune since she was so fond of ruling her husband—to be married to a man who appeared to be somewhat of a reversion to the type of our original ancestors, the Queen wrote volumes of letters in which she seemed to assume somewhat the attitude of a St. Paul writing to the Ephesians or Romans. But most of Caroline's troubles occurred after the Queen's death.

Marie Antoinette was the source of much anxiety to her mother, who seemed to have a premonition of the disasters in store for her. She spent many hours in writing admonitions and advice to her youngest daughter, cautioning her to keep out of politics and avoid the entanglements of the corrupt court of Versailles. Marie Antoinette, who inherited much of the mettle of her mother, sometimes answered with considerable spirit; perhaps her letters might be called saucy. This provoked the mother and she ended one of her epistles with this strangely prophetic warning: "If you will not be otherwise, some great misfortune will overtake you,

---

[56] Guglia, II, 270, quoting from a letter of Maria Theresa to her daughter Christina.

and then it will be too late." [57] The misfortune arrived and it was too late for poor Marie Antoinette. Once in a while Maria Theresa seemed to have the gift of prophecy.

One of Maria Theresa's greatest worries was that her children did not have babies fast enough to suit her. She wished them to multiply so that her seed might soon occupy all the thrones of Europe. Of Leopold and Marie Caroline she had no cause to complain in this respect, but she wished all the others to speed up before it was too late. At her death Maria Theresa had only about two dozen living grandchildren, and that was far too few to suit her. This explains her boundless delight at the news of the birth of her first grandson in the Pitti Palace in Florence. Then a few years later she had another burst of joy when the news came from Florence that Archduke Charles was born. No one will venture to say what the emotions of the grandmother would have been had she suspected that this boy would some day deliver a stunning blow to the French under Napoleon Bonaparte at Aspern.

The only daughter who seemed to please her mother without any interruption was Maria Christina who happened to marry the man she loved, and lived so near that the mother could see her frequently. Maria Christina enjoyed the complete confidence of her mother, and many of the statements made here are derived from information gleaned from the intimate letters of the Queen to her best-loved daughter.

On the whole we may say that Maria Theresa's family turned out very unsatisfactory to her, and blighted

---

[57] *Ibid.*, 264, quoting from a letter of Maria Theresa of Dec. 5, 1777.

her last years with a sadness quite ironical when we remember the manner in which she urged them into loveless marriages for political purposes. How often this has been true in the history of men and women of renown.

XII

THE SCOURGE OF THE HAPSBURGS

ENOUGH has already been told to indicate that smallpox was a veritable scourge in the families of the Hapsburgs. Joseph I, Maria Theresa's uncle, died of this disease, and it killed three of her children and two daughters-in-law, not to mention the daughters who were so blighted by scars as to render them objects of pity. In the worst epidemic of all, the one of 1767, the Queen fell ill of the disease and almost died. She had frequently been exposed to the infection, had always escaped, and believed herself immune, but in May she became seriously ill with an ailment that soon proved to be smallpox.[1] It was in a severe form and the court was almost paralyzed with terror; prayers for her recovery were offered continuously for days in all the churches.

In such dread was smallpox held that Kaunitz, who had had it in early life, feared to approach the Queen,[2] but her son-in-law, Albert of Saxony, insisted upon comforting her with his presence, and for his devotion caught the disease and barely escaped death.[3]

Gerhard van Swieten, who had the supervision of the health of the imperial family, was severely criticized for his failure to control smallpox, and there was

[1] Arneth, VII, 325.
[2] *Ibid.*, 329.
[3] *Ibid.*, 330.

almost an uprising against him. When we read of his treatment we are reminded that medicine had then made little progress toward its present high state of efficiency. The patients were kept in dark, closed rooms and wrapped in red cloth; the principal other treatment mentioned was bloodletting, which must have hindered rather than hastened recovery.[4]

Maria Theresa loyally defended her physician, but at the same time insisted upon trying some new means of limiting the ravages of such an awful pestilence. In casting about, she came upon reports of a method of inoculation practiced in England, and sent a request to George III for a physician skilled in the administration of the new treatment. The King sent her a Dutch physician named Ingenhouse of Leyden, and the first patients inoculated were the Archdukes Ferdinand and Maximilian.[5] Van Swieten looked upon this plan as a dangerous experiment, and opposed it; but the two princes had very light attacks of the disease and escaped with almost no scars.[6] This gave the new practice a tremendous boost, and won for it the ardent support of Maria Theresa. She had the children of the poor inoculated free, and even provided entertainments at Schönbrunn to induce the people to come and take the treatment.

We shiver when we learn just what was meant by this inoculation; it must not be confused with the vaccination which was introduced in England shortly after

[4] Van Swieten was at that time head of the medical faculty of the University of Vienna. Under his administration the medical school made great progress in anatomy and physiology, and thus laid the foundation for future advancement in medicine and surgery.

[5] Arneth, VII, 335.

[6] In honor of this event, Maria Theresa had *Te Deums* sung in the churches of Vienna.

The Scourge of the Hapsburgs 317

this period. The method practiced in the time of Maria Theresa was to apply pus from a mild case of smallpox to an abraded area on the arm or leg of the patient. In a few days the person thus treated became ill of smallpox which was usually mild but produced an immunity for life. There were many objections to this procedure, some of which were quickly apparent; occasionally the patients developed dangerous cases, and they were always capable of spreading the disease which might prove to be severe. There was still another risk which was probably not understood at that time; diseases of the blood could be communicated with the smallpox. But in spite of all these dangers, inoculation is said to have greatly reduced the number of deaths and instances of severe scarring. The Jennerian practice of vaccinating with cowpox was introduced in Vienna in 1802, and soon replaced the old practice of inoculation with the virus of real smallpox.

It is interesting to note that the method of inoculation, used in England and introduced into Vienna by Maria Theresa, came originally from China by way of Turkey. Lady Montagu, while residing in Constantinople with her husband, who was British Ambassador, saw it practiced among the Turks and was impressed with its benefits. She wrote home to England of her observations, and very soon the method was in vogue throughout the British Isles, and from there migrated to Holland.[7]

[7] Lady Montagu spoke of smallpox as a harmless disease among the Turks on account of their method of "ingrafting," which she described as follows: "An old lady comes with a nutshell full of matter (gathered from the pustules of a patient ill with smallpox), and asks what vein you please to have opened. She immediately rips open that you offer her with a large needle, and puts into the vein as much of the venom as

Maria Theresa of Austria

Nothing in the reign of Maria Theresa illustrates her progressive spirit better than her attitude toward this new method of fighting smallpox, although in the light of modern science, her conduct seems rather adventurous and hasty. It was rash for her to promulgate a new measure, intended to improve the public health, in opposition to the advice of her very capable physician van Swieten, but she thought the demands of the occasion justified the trial of anything offering hope of relief from such a dreadful scourge. Maria Theresa's behavior on this occasion reflects the advancement of science during the fifty years following the great epidemic of the plague in 1713. Charles VI regarded the plague as a curse sent from Heaven, and thought only of prayer, repentence, and vows, to end the epidemic. Maria Theresa was seeking some physical means of controlling a disease which she thought sprang from natural causes. It was this new attitude toward epidemics which gave science a strong impulse to seek causes and remedies outside the church, and laid the foundation for modern medicine and sanitation; it marked the dawn of a renaissance in the control of contagious diseases.

At the present time we can hardly comprehend what a curse the epidemic diseases were one hundred and

can lie on the head of the needle, and in this manner opens four or five veins."—Letter of April 1, 1717. Ye shades of Æsculapius! where was King Strepococcus in those days?

When the method was introduced into England, there were many fatalities, and Lady Montagu was severely condemned for having recommended it. She had smallpox when a child, and escaped severe scarring, but she was so impressed with its ravages to the beauty of young women that she wrote a poem on the subject, and it was published under the title of *Flavia.*

The Scourge of the Hapsburgs

fifty years ago. In those days smallpox was regarded as the twin sister of death. Frequently, in the German literature of the period, the words *smallpox* and *death* were coupled in a manner which now seems almost ridiculous. When the Germans wished to convey the idea that something was superlatively dreadful, they likened it to *smallpox and death*.[8]

[8] The Turkish method of inoculation was also introduced into Russia in 1768, and one of the first to be inoculated was Catherine the Great. She, like Maria Theresa, became a strong advocate of the method. Anthony, 217 seq.

XIII

LATE DIPLOMACY

I

SHORTLY after the Seven Years' War there began a series of events which terminated in what is generally regarded as the great crime of the reign of Maria Theresa, the partition of Poland. We might preface a discussion of this subject by remarking that similar crimes have been very common, even in the history of nations which set themselves up as models of fair dealing with the weak and helpless.

An especially bad feature of the Queen's crime was that John Sobieski, a Polish king, had rescued Vienna from certain destruction at the time of the great Turkish siege of 1683.[1] If any city ever owed a debt of gratitude to any country, Vienna certainly did, for this reason, to Poland.[2] How could a high-minded queen like Maria Theresa ever bring herself to the performance of such a base act? At the risk of being called facetious, we will say that here is an illustration of how a good girl—not too good, but certainly well-disposed—was led astray by associating with a bad boy. The bad boy was Frederick of Prussia who, when he had accomplished his evil purpose, ridiculed the Queen by saying, "She wept but she took, and the more she wept the more she took."

---
[1] Mahan, *Famous Women of Vienna*, 19–40.
[2] Coxe, III, 493.

Late Diplomacy

Poland was a very unhappy land. It had a peculiar form of government partaking somewhat of the characters of both monarchy and republic. Its kings were elected for life by a nobility made up of landowners whose holdings were sufficient to enable them to live without any occupation or profession; a man who earned his living was disqualified to vote for a king. Any nobleman might become king, but the choice was not limited to natives; princes of other lands were also eligible. Thus each election of a Polish king was an event in which all Europe participated, and one had been the occasion of a bloody war. In such elections the common people, who were held in a miserable state of feudal vassalage, had no part except to fight and die for their masters. Charles VI had made Augustus of Saxony king of Poland as a reward for a ratification of the Pragmatic Sanction, but not without a war with France which cost Charles his fair province of Lorraine.

In October, 1763, just after the close of the Seven Years' War, Augustus died and a contention arose over the choice of his successor. Maria Theresa felt that the House of Saxony had suffered much on her account, and regarded herself as under obligation to promote its interests by having the eldest son of Augustus chosen king of Poland. But before the election the son died, and she then espoused the cause of Augustus' second son Xavier.[3] Several natives offered themselves as candidates, but all finally withdrew in favor of one named Poniatowski, who was supported by Catherine of Russia because of her devotion to him and his mother, and

---
[3] Arneth, VIII, 33-44.

also because she thought the election of Poniatowski, who was a weak character, would enable her to dictate the policies of his government.[4] When Frederick, very much to his delight, saw a bitter strife rise between two headstrong women, both of whom he disliked, he was soon meditating how he might turn it to his own advantage. To him this quarrel offered both hope and amusement, and he determined to foster it to the extent of his ability by secretly urging the two spirited women into a war.[5]

Maria Theresa began issuing manifestoes declaring her intention to prevent an unfair election in Poland, and succeeded in enlisting the support of France, while Catherine pretended to adopt a policy of "hands off," which she thought would lead to the choice of Poniatowski. Thus the two stubborn females stood with their feet firmly planted on "rocks of eternal justice," shaking fists at each other and threatening to start a war between Austria and Russia, while Frederick sat back and chuckled because both were seeking his aid and he was pretending to be a friend to each.[6] Very soon the Russian and Austrian armies were hovering over the border of Poland, and secret agents of the two countries were everywhere in the kingdom, inciting the natives to uprisings and riots. In one of these disturbances several Poles were killed, whereupon Catherine's army entered the kingdom under the pretext of establishing

---

[4] Coxe, III, 493. Catherine's well-known intimacy with Poniatowski led many to believe that she meant to marry him, and thus unite Poland with Russia. Probably this, rather than a division of the country, was her original design.—Anthony, 199.

[5] Guglia, II, 183.

[6] Arneth, VIII, 40, 57.

order. Eventually Catherine's candidate was elected, and crowned under the title of Stanislaus Augustus.[7] Maria Theresa then recalled her minister from Warsaw and prepared to open hostilities, but seems to have halted as she remembered her dreadful experiences during the last war.[8]

Then another external factor was introduced. The Russians chased some Polish rebels into the Turkish town of Balta which was burned. On account of this, at the instigation of France, Turkey declared war on Russia and the Austrians found themselves fraternizing with the Turks, their traditional enemies; it was a strange situation, and unpleasant to both.

Next entered Frederick of Prussia to become a star performer. He solicited an interview with Joseph II, Maria Theresa's son and co-regent, by whom he was greatly admired, and the two rulers met at Neisse in 1769. It was at this meeting that Joseph greeted Frederick with the remark, "Silesia no longer exists as far as the House of Austria is concerned"; in reply to which Frederick must have thought, if he did not say, *"Gott sei dank."*

Joseph began by proposing that Frederick remain neutral in the impending war between Austria and Russia. Frederick replied by calling Joseph's attention to the incongruous position of Austria when allied with such a traditional enemy as Turkey and making war upon a good friend like Russia. Frederick thought it might be better to come to an agreement, in which he would be happy to join, looking toward permanent peace by partitioning Poland among Austria, Russia,

[7] *Ibid.,* 71.
[8] Guglia, II, 84

and Prussia. He volunteered to use his good offices to promote this enterprise with Catherine. While doing this, we may be pretty sure that he did all in his power to prevent the two women from arranging any peace between themselves.[9]

In the meantime war had been in progress between Russia and Turkey, and the latter had lost rapidly. Maria Theresa knew Russia would make heavy demands of territory upon Turkey, and was alarmed to see such an advancement on the part of an unfriendly neighbor; but the dreadful specter of war halted her from beginning hostilities against her former friend Catherine. Frederick's bait lured the Queen almost irresistibly; it offered some compensation for the loss of Silesia, to which she had never been reconciled, and it enabled her to keep out of war.

In 1770, there was another meeting between Joseph and Frederick at Neustadt in Moravia, and we are told that on this occasion a map of Poland was laid on the table before the rulers and the contemplated division marked out definitely. Frederick undertook to secure the coöperation of Catherine, and Joseph was to do his best to obtain the consent of his mother.

Undoubtedly Maria Theresa was wavering, but her conscience reasserted itself, and she made an agreement with Turkey to enter the war against Russia. Turkey was to pay a subsidy to Austria in installments, the first being due when Austrian troops were on the march to

---

[9] It was at this meeting that Frederick the Great uttered the following: "We are Germans. What do we care about America, the British Isles or France, or the quarrels of Turkey and Russia? So long as we two, Austria and Germany, are united, we have nothing to fear."—Arneth, VIII, 157. It required a World War to disprove Frederick's statement.

assist the Turks. Maria Theresa went so far as to put her army in motion and collect a payment of the subsidy, but the ghost of war rattled its bones and she paused.

Frederick kept parading this ghost to frighten both Maria Theresa and Catherine, and emphasized the blessings both might receive through a partition, even telling them that the partition would prove a benefit to the Poles by giving them stable governments and restoring order in their own land.[10] Catherine presently found herself in agreement with Frederick and the two united in an effort to make Maria Theresa see the error of her ways. Observing that the Queen was embarrassed because she had no excuse for taking a part of Poland, Catherine wrote her to search the archives of Austria for old claims; "Surely there must be some old claims that can be revived," suggested Catherine.

Finally Maria Theresa acquiesced; she was never convinced. It took her seven years to get the better of her conscience on this subject, but when she finally yielded and got out her scissors, both Frederick and Catherine were surprised at how sharp they were. She soon carved out about as much for herself as either of them had taken. The Treaty of Partition was signed in St. Petersburg on the fifth of August, 1772.[11]

---

[10] The first formal proposal for the division of Poland came from Frederick II, and was dated Feb. 20, 1771.—Arneth, VIII, 294.

Wraxall wrote: "I have little hesitation in asserting that the plan of this partition (speaking of the partition of Poland) originated with the King of Prussia; but so infamous was the transaction that each of the parties endeavored to place the blame on the others."—Wraxall's *Memoirs*, Letter 19.

[11] After Maria Theresa consented to the signing of the treaty of

The pact was held secret for a few months, during which the three powers stirred up as much contention and disorder in Poland as possible. Under a pretense of restoring order they then took possession of their respective portions and published the treaty. Thus, in spite of the Queen's reiterated statement that nothing on earth could ever induce her to enter into any sort of an alliance with the King of Prussia, she finally made an agreement with him which contributed materially to the enlargement of his domains and greatly increased his power. What was much worse, she received a blot upon her moral character which her most sympathetic biographers are unable, through excuses and apologies, to erase. The good girl went wrong because she played with a bad boy.

Many Austrians believe this addition of Slavs to the population of the monarchy proved a curse to the nation, because it gave that race too much preponderance over the Germans. It increased the centrifugal force which finally rent the monarchy asunder.[12]

---

partition, she said: "I sign this because so many great and wise men want me to do so; but a long time after my death, the world will witness the bad results of an act which is against all precedents of what is accepted as sacred and just."

[12] A glance at the map of Europe of this period will show the tremendous significance of the partition of Poland to Frederick II. Before this, his provinces of Prussia and Brandenburg were widely separated by a corridor of Poland containing the important city of Danzig. What he acquired from Poland consolidated his kingdom and increased its area almost twenty-five per cent. Also, both Silesia and the part of Poland gained by this partition, were settled principally by Germans, so there was a consolidation of race as well as territory. The reign of Frederick the Great saw Prussia first rise to the position of one of the leading powers of Europe.

II

From the very beginning of the American Revolution, France, known to be smarting from the loss of Canada to the British at the close of the Seven Years' War, was suspected of being disposed to aid the colonies. But whatever inclination Louis XVI had in that direction was not shared by Maria Theresa who was shrewd enough to discern that the colonies were, in reality, waging a war against the monarchial form of government. On this subject the Queen and her son Joseph, then co-regent, were in complete accord. When Joseph was asked for his views of the American contention he answered, "I am a royalist by profession."

Both Maria Theresa and Joseph expressed themselves openly as opposed to the cause of the colonists. In an audience given to the British Ambassador the Queen said: "I appreciate the very kind expression of your King's good wishes for my people. I am happy to learn that my prohibition of all intercourse between my subjects and the rebel colonies has impressed the King's mind." [13] Joseph also said to the Ambassador: "I am extremely concerned over the difficulties which embarrass your King's government. The cause which England is defending is the cause of all sovereigns, who have a joint interest in the maintenance of due subordination and obedience to law throughout their neighboring monarchies. I observe with pleasure the vigorous force the King is employing to bring his rebellious colonies into subjection, and I sincerely wish him success." [14]

[13] Coxe, III, 548.
[14] *Ibid.*, III, 548.

In 1777 Joseph made a trip to Paris, and one of the purposes of his journey may have been to warn his brother-in-law, Louis XVI, against forming any alliance with the American colonies. If such was his mission, it proved to be in vain; Louis XVI almost despised Joseph, but admired Maria Theresa.

Those who are disposed to condemn Maria Theresa for her attitude toward the colonies, are likely to concede that it was a very natural one from the standpoint of a monarchist. Her support of England did not prompt her to break with France, and she was not an influential factor in the American Revolution.

III

Just after Joseph returned from Paris, in December, 1777, an event occurred which both he and Kaunitz had eagerly anticipated for several years; the Elector of Bavaria died without a male heir. The time had arrived for Joseph to imitate the example of Frederick of Prussia in achieving fame through a seizure of foreign territory, and the young monarch immediately showed a disposition to improve the opportunity. In fact he put troops in motion upon hearing that the Elector was sick with smallpox, and before the news of his death arrived.[15]

Joseph thought the occasion a most favorable one. Russia was again at war with the Turks, England and France were both tied up in the American Revolution, and Frederick of Prussia, now past sixty-five, was too old to take the field—or at least Joseph hoped so. The moment seemed most auspicious, and Joseph rushed

[15] *Ibid.*, III, 521 seq.

like a hunter of big game for the quarry. But he was deceived concerning the decrepitude of Frederick of Prussia who immediately prepared for a war to prevent such an advancement of Austria.

Maria Theresa was greatly alarmed to see her son hurrying impetuously into a war of conquest, and raised her voice—which for some years, had hardly been heard above a whisper in the affairs of the government—in vigorous protestation. When the news of the Elector's death arrived, she demanded that Joseph and Kaunitz give her a few days for meditation and prayer before committing themselves irrevocably to an invasion of Bavaria. But Joseph and his Chancellor, making light of the old Queen's fright, went right along with their enterprise.

At the end of her period of isolation, the Queen appeared displaying what Joseph and Kaunitz thought was a white feather, or one which was at least a trifle pale; she still opposed the war but not very vigorously, and seemed disposed to yield to the judgment of her young co-regent. The truth was that neither Joseph nor Kaunitz had any idea of what was in the depth of the old mother's heart and mind.

While Joseph was with his army of one hundred thousand men on the march to Bavaria, the Queen did something which was afterward considered very strange. She dispatched a secret messenger with a letter to Frederick of Prussia, telling how she dreaded another bloody war, and begging the King to join with her in an effort to settle their disputes by peaceful methods.[16] This conciliatory letter of a war-wise old

---

[16] Arneth, X, 520.

woman to a grizzly warrior met with a favorable response.

We quote a part of the Queen's letter: "I perceive with extreme regret the beginning of a new war. My age and my earnest desire for peace are well known, and I cannot give a more convincing proof of my love for peace than by sending you this letter in this manner. My maternal heart is alarmed for the safety of two sons and a son-in-law who are with my army. I have taken this step without the knowledge of Emperor Joseph or Kaunitz, and I beg you not to divulge the contents of this letter. I am anxious to recommence and bring to a successful conclusion the negotiations hitherto broken off by Joseph to my deep regret. I entreat you to join your efforts with mine to reëstablish harmony between us for the welfare of mankind and our respective families." [17]

Then followed a proposition of terms for settling all disputes, and at the end a postscript, which read: "Having just received word that your army is advancing toward that of my son, I am all the more anxious to hasten this letter. I will also send a courier to Emperor Joseph with a message begging him not to begin hostilities, and I sincerely hope it will be heeded."

Frederick's age and experience seems to have prompted him to avoid rushing into a new war, for he answered: "It was worthy of Your Majesty's character to give such proofs of magnanimity. The tender anxiety you display toward the Emperor, your son, and the princes of your blood, deserves the applause of every feeling heart, and augments, if possible, the high

---

[17] Coxe, III, 531.

consideration I entertain for your sacred person. I have added some articles to your propositions, and assure you that, until I hear from you further, I will act with such caution that Your Imperial Majesty will have no cause for apprehension for the safety of your family, and particularly for that of your son, the Emperor." [18] Frederick used the same precautions, exercised by the Queen, to have this letter sent secretly.

When Joseph heard of this exchange of letters he was indignant, and Kaunitz declared such a secret correspondence was degrading to a dignified court like Vienna. Both the men did what they could to bring on another war with Frederick in spite of the protests of the Queen.[19]

While matters were in suspense, Catherine of Russia finished a war with Turkey, and since she had received a subsidy from Frederick, showed a disposition to pay him back by entering the contest on his side. She dispatched a formidable force in the direction of Vienna. Maria Theresa met this new menace by sending a letter to Catherine, imploring her to halt and make terms by friendly conciliation. Catherine was touched by this appeal from the woman whom she considered the greatest of her day; she answered by offering to mediate between the Queen and Frederick.

Finally, with what must have been a tremendous sacrifice of pride, and against the most strenuous opposition on the part of Joseph and Kaunitz, Maria Theresa succeeded in preventing any serious armed conflict. Bavaria was continued as an electorate, and a new elector named by an agreement known as the

[18] *Ibid.*, III, 532.
[19] *Arneth*, X, 521.

Treaty of Teschen, which closed what was one of the best wars in European history, because it was fought without battles, although it lasted nearly two years.

When the treaty was signed, Maria Theresa wrote: "I am informed with joy that the danger of war is past. I am not partial to Frederick of Prussia, but I must do him the justice to confess that he has acted nobly and honorably; he promised me to make peace upon reasonable terms and he has kept his word. I am inexpressibly happy to avoid this threatened outpouring of blood." [20]

The Queen's conduct on this occasion falls so much out of line with the character she showed during her long reign, that we may well search behind the scenes again for hidden motives. They are not very difficult to discover. She had no confidence in Joseph's ability as a commander. She knew he was a son of Francis of Lorraine and a nephew of Prince Charles, and she feared he would lead the Austrians to a dreadful disaster. She knew Joseph was no match for Frederick of Prussia, and she was willing to crawl in the very dust before her old enemy to save her son and her monarchy.[21]

---

[20] Coxe, III, 540.

[21] The following letter, written by the Queen in secret to Mercy-Argentau, the Austrian Ambassador in Paris, on the seventh of May, 1778, confirms this view: "We are at war. It is what I have been dreading ever since January; and what a war! With nothing to gain and everything to lose. The King (Frederick of Prussia) has entered Nachod (in Bohemia near the border of Prussia) in force; he will surround us, for he has forty thousand more men than we have. You can conceive my despair! God help us if this war ends as I foresee from the beginning! France has assuredly wrought us harm by her secret intrigues with the King. We have done her some wrong, but none that balances the shocking indifference that she now shows to our fate. I dare not

Late Diplomacy

Be that as it may, the Treaty of Teschen, which was signed the very year the Queen died and represented the final diplomatic act of her life, caused her sun to set in a matchless halo of soft mellow tints, and enables us to declare that the great *Landesmutter* died a pacificist.

insist too strongly with the Queen (Marie Antoinette) for fear of injuring her. Show her this letter, if in your good judgment you see fit. . . . I am overwhelmed. . . . I do not know how I can live. . . . Nothing but my faith sustains me, but in the end I fear I shall sink."

XIV

DEATH OF THE QUEEN

ALMOST all writers, who were in a position to know, declared that Maria Theresa completely recovered from her very severe attack of smallpox, but the modern physician who reads the story of her life after that illness is likely to doubt the truth of such assertions. After 1767 we hear much of shortness of breath, fatigue, distress due to lack of air, cough, difficulty in climbing stairs, fear of impending death, and inability to sleep; later she became dropsical and died of some trouble of the chest. During the last thirteen years of her life, the Queen presented almost a perfect picture of a woman suffering and finally dying of a leaky heart—just such a heart as often follows an acute infectious disease. Like Alexander the Great, Suleiman the Magnificent, and many other celebrated characters of history, her life was terminated by bacteria rather than age and exhaustion. Owing to lack of advancement in the art of diagnosis, the disabled condition of her heart was never discovered.

Every physician knows that insufficiency of the heart is accompanied by a corresponding depression of the mind, loss of courage, fretfulness and impatience. When we remember this we should not be too severe in our criticisms of the Queen's conduct during the last years of her life. Many of her outbursts of temper toward Joseph, and her scolding letters to her daughters, came from a sick woman. Her mental condition was also greatly modified by grief over the loss of her husband. Immediately after his death she had her hair cut short, painted her rooms black, draped them in deep mourning, and never appeared in public except in heavy black crape. On the eighteenth of each month, the day Francis died, she shut herself in her chamber and refused to see any one except her chambermaid; the whole month of each August, the anniversary of his death, was spent in the same manner.

She had her own coffin prepared and placed by the side of her husband's in the Capucine Church; it was fully inscribed, with the exception of the date of her death. Several times each week she went there and spent hours in silent meditation, tears and prayer. During her last years, she could no longer walk up and down the steps to her rooms, or the long steep stairs to the vaults of the Capucine Church. In the Hofburg she installed a crude elevator operated by a windlass, and she was let down into and drawn out of the vaults of the church by means of a chair placed on runners likewise operated by a windlass. On her last visit to the tomb of her husband the machine refused to work, when she called to be helped out of the vaults, and she became greatly excited, crying loudly, "Francis is holding me! Francis is holding me! I will come soon, Francis!" For thirteen long years Maria Theresa was sick physically and mentally, and sitting constantly in the imaginary presence of death.

As she saw the end approaching she was seized with anxiety lest she might show weakness at the last moment. She wished to die bravely—just as she thought a noble queen should—as Browne and Schwerin died, in action with their colors streaming over their heads. She wished the world to know that she fell while engaged in the performance of duty, and remained in the harness until her very last breath. Once she said, "I feel timid, but I really have no fear of death; may Heaven give me courage to the end!"[1] At another time she asked her physician if she should receive the last rites of the Catholic Church, and when he told her the hour had not yet arrived for that she sighed, "Then it must be terrible!"

To the very minute of her death, Maria Theresa carried the weight of the nation on her heart. This was not entirely due to her desire to die on duty, but partly because she feared the fate of the monarchy under Joseph, and was so anxious to give him detailed instructions for his guidance. She looked upon death as the departure upon a long journey, and felt that there were many things to be attended to before starting, so that nothing could go wrong during her absence. The day she died she looked out of the window and saw that it was raining. "It is a bad day to set out on a long voyage," she said, and turned her face to the wall. Since all was to be left in the care of Joseph she thought of much to discuss with him, and every little while something she had forgotten came to her mind and she hurried to tell him about it before it was too late.[2]

Only a few hours before her death she exhausted herself in giving parting instructions and admonitions

---

[1] Zwiedineck Südenhorst, 106.
[2] *Ibid.*, 104.

Death of the Queen

to Joseph.[3] Noting that she was having difficulty in breathing and that she was weary, Joseph said, "Now mother, try to sleep for a little while."

"What!" she exclaimed impatiently—it was the last spurt of ill temper the plucky Queen ever displayed—"In a few hours I shall be gone; would you have me spend them in sleep?"

A few minutes before her death she seemed to realize that it was time to start, and like a traveller entering a carriage, she rose from her chair, and almost without assistance walked to her bed. The exertion caused a severe attack of shortness of breath and she cried to Joseph, "Open the windows!"

"They are wide open, mother," he replied.

Then, just as if she had rehearsed the climax of her last scene, she stretched her arms toward Heaven and said distinctly, "To Thee I come!" When her arms fell she was dead!

When we realize how anxious the brave Queen was to die dramatically, we feel almost like breaking the silence with applause as the curtain drops.[4]

In view of the tremendous historical importance of this woman, we are surprised at the scant notice of her death to be found in the *Wiener Zeitung,* the press of other lands, and the documents of the Archives of Austria. Her passing was but inconspicuously mentioned in the first number of the *Wiener Zeitung* printed after her death. The *Zeitung* was the official organ of

---

[3] Arneth, X, 727.

[4] Of Maria Theresa's ten living children, only four were present to comfort her in her last illness: Joseph, Elizabeth, Maria Anna, and Christina. After their departures, the children seldom visited their mother.

the government, and we naturally expect to find this edition given over almost entirely to details of the Queen's last illness and eulogies of her character, but we are sadly disappointed. When the *Zeitung* finally printed her obituary, it was more heavily charged with praise for Joseph than lamentation for his mother.[5]

Later numbers of the *Zeitung* contain a few tributes copied from the foreign press. Frederick the Great was reported to have said, "Maria Theresa is no more! Now we shall have another order of things." Perhaps the most impressive eulogy was written by a Frenchman who said, "The death of Maria Theresa is like a bottle of ink spilled over the map of Europe."

On the second of December—she died on the twenty-ninth of November—her body was placed in its coffin by the side of her husband's in the Capucine Church, and her heart sealed in the same silver jar with his and put in its little place on a shelf in the Chapel of Loretto of the Augustiner Church, where it may now be viewed through a small iron grate by the curious tourists.

The sarcophagi of the Queen and her husband, prepared during her life, are the most magnificent to be found in the vaults of the Capucine Church. Surrounded as they are by the numerous coffins of her family, they make a most impressive group.

Her last will, dated October 15, 1780, disposed of her personal effects only; the inheritances of her children had been designated long before. Joseph was permitted to select what he wished from her objects of

---

[5] Zwiedineck Südenhorst, 106.

art and books, and charged with the task of dividing the remainder among his brothers and sisters, but she wished her son-in-law, Albert of Saxony, to have certain pictures and articles which she mentioned especially. She left full instructions for her funeral, requesting, among other things, that no eulogy be pronounced over her coffin.

Thus ended the life of the greatest ruler ever produced by the House of Hapsburg. Among the great queens of history Elizabeth of England is probably the most famous; Victoria, the most beloved; Catherine of Russia, the most brilliant; but for courage, intellect, and sincerity, none surpassed the great Maria Theresa of Austria; while as a wife and mother her record is scarcely approached by any other queen.

Vienna was none too prompt in erecting a suitable monument to the greatest ruler in her history. For more than a century after her death there was no appropriate memorial to Maria Theresa in the capital of Austria. It remained for the smaller cities of the monarchy to remind Vienna of her neglect. In 1862 Wiener Neustadt erected a splendid monument to the Queen, and in 1873 Klagenfurt followed with a similar one, but it was not until 1888 that the magnificent memorial, now standing in the beautiful garden between the two mammoth museums in Vienna was built. Strange to say, it was constructed from funds derived from the sale of ground occupied by the fortifications she saved from destruction at the hands of her son.

In this monument, most characteristically German in architecture, we see the proud Queen sitting with her Pragmatic Sanction on her lap, while all about her are grouped the men who contributed so much to make her reign eminent. She faces the straggling old palace of the Hapsburgs, as if still guarding the dynasty and capitol she loved so well.

```
Emp. Francis Joseph, 1916    Maximilian         Charles Louis
(Married Elizabeth of Ba-    (Killed in
varia, murdered 1898)         Mexico, 1867)
        |                                           |
    Rudolph                  Francis Ferdinand    Otto
   (Suicide, 1889)           (Murdered, Sarajevo
                              1914)
                                                 Emp. Karl, 1922
                                                 (Dethroned, 1918)
                                                        |
                                                 Otto, born 1912
```

¹ Roman numbers indicate kings, but not always emperors of the Holy Roman Empire of the Germans. The numbering is not consecutive, because emperors of other dynasties intervened, and the Hapsburgs sometimes began numbering anew at the accession of a different line of the same family. The Arabic numbers, unless otherwise stated, indicate the year of death.

² *Emp.* before a name means an emperor of Austria after the dissolution of the Holy Roman Empire of the Germans. Many Hapsburgs, not rulers, ancestors of rulers, or otherwise of special interest, are omitted from the table for the sake of brevity.

CHRONOLOGY

Year   Event

1700.—Emperor Leopold I and Louis XIV begin the War of the Spanish Succession.

1703.—Leopold I decrees the rights of succession for his two sons, Joseph and Charles, assigning to Joseph, the elder, the Austrian Monarchy, and to Charles, Spain and her dependencies; also providing that in the event of the deaths of both sons without a male heir, a daughter should inherit the domains of the Hapsburgs, the daughters of Joseph being given precedence over those of Charles. Joseph and Charles both sign the decree and swear to abide by it.

" Charles is crowned King of Spain in Vienna and sets forth to conquer and take possession of his kingdom.

1705.—Leopold I dies and Joseph becomes Emperor Joseph I.

1708.—Charles of Spain marries Elizabeth Christina, daughter of Ludwig, Duke of Brunswick.

1711.—Joseph I dies, leaving two daughters, Maria Josepha and Maria Amalia, but no sons. Charles quits Spain to take the throne in Vienna, and is elected Emperor of the Germans, King of Bohemia, and King of Hungary.

1713.—The War of the Spanish Succession ends with the Treaty of Utrecht. Charles VI relinquishes the crown of Spain, and is compensated by the acquisition of the Netherlands, Naples, Milan, Sardinia and Mantua.

" Charles VI announces the Pragmatic Sanction giving his own daughters precedence over those of Joseph I.

1716.—Son born to Charles VI and Empress Elizabeth, but dies the same year.

Year	Event
1717.	May 13, Maria Theresa is born to Charles VI and Empress Elizabeth.
1718.	Another daughter, Maria Anna, born to Charles VI and Empress Elizabeth.
1719.	Maria Josepha, the elder daughter of Joseph I, marries Augustus, Prince of Saxony.
1722.	Maria Amalia, the other daughter of Joseph I, marries Charles Albert, Prince of Bavaria.
1723.	Maria Theresa betrothed to Prince Clemens, son of Duke Leopold of Lorraine.
"	Prince Clemens dies of smallpox.
"	Leopold of Lorraine proposes to substitute his second son, Francis Stephan, for Prince Clemens. Charles VI, without definitely promising Francis the hand of Maria Theresa, permits him to come to the court of Vienna to complete his education and become acquainted with his prospective bride. Francis arrives at the age of fourteen and is assigned to quarters in the Hofburg.
1724.	A third daughter is born to Charles VI and Empress Elizabeth, but dies in 1730.
1726.	Charles VI secretly betroths his daughters, Maria Theresa and Maria Anna, to Don Carlos and Don Philip, the sons of Philip V and Elizabeth Farnese of Spain.
1729.	The betrothals are broken because of protests from the leading nations of Europe against the disturbance of the balance of power.
"	Leopold of Lorraine dies and Francis Stephan leaves Vienna to take charge of his realm, but without having received a promise of the hand of Maria Theresa from Charles VI.
1730.	Francis Stephan as the prospective consort of Maria Theresa visits Versailles.
1731.	In a similar manner he visits Holland and becomes a

Year	Event
	Freemason. Later, he visits the courts of England and Prussia.
1732.	Francis Stephan returns to Vienna and is welcomed at the Hofburg, but does not receive a promise of the hand of Maria Theresa.
"	Francis Stephan is named imperial governor of Hungary by Charles VI.
1733.	Charles VI begins a war with Louis XV to win the crown of Poland for the King of Saxony against the claims of Stanislaus Leczinska, the father-in-law of Louis XV. In this manner Charles VI hopes to compensate the King of Saxony, who is married to the elder daughter of Joseph, for a ratification of the Pragmatic Sanction.
1735.	Owing to ill fortune in war, Charles is compelled to sue for peace. Louis XV offers him the crown of Poland for the King of Saxony, but demands Lorraine for Stanislaus Leczinska. As a compensation, Francis Stephan is to have Tuscany at the death of the Duke of Tuscany who is the last of the Medicis. Charles demands that Francis consent to this arrangement in return for the hand of Maria Theresa. Francis consents conditionally and is betrothed to Maria Theresa. Later, Francis is obliged to sign still harder terms.
1736.	February 12, marriage of Francis of Lorraine and Maria Theresa.
"	April 20, death of Prince Eugene.
"	Francis of Lorraine is appointed governor of the Netherlands and his brother Charles is promised the hand of Maria Anna.
"	Charles VI begins a war with Turkey, ostensibly to aid Czarina Anne, but in reality to win territory to compensate him for Lorraine and other territories lost in

Year	Event
	wars or sacrificed in securing ratifications of his Pragmatic Sanction.
1737.	Charles VI makes Francis of Lorraine generalissimo of the Austrian army fighting the Turks.
1738.	Francis conducts a disastrous campaign, and is removed in disgrace from his command.
"	Francis of Lorraine and Maria Theresa retire in exile to Tuscany.
1739.	Francis and Maria Theresa return to Vienna.
"	Austria makes a humiliating peace with Turkey, suffering a heavy loss of territory with the important city of Belgrade.
1740.	The Austrian Monarchy is much degraded by unfortunate wars and quarrels at the court.
"	October 20, death of Charles VI and accession of Maria Theresa.
"	Coalition of France, Spain, and Bavaria to conquer and partition Austria and Bohemia.
"	December, Gotter arrives in Vienna with a demand that Maria Theresa cede Silesia to Frederick of Prussia. The demand is refused and Frederick invades Silesia.
1741.	March, Austrians set forth to dispute the possession of Silesia by Frederick.
"	March 13, birth of Crown Prince Joseph to Francis of Lorraine and Maria Theresa.
"	April 10, Prussians defeat the Austrians at Mollwitz.
"	June 25, Maria Theresa crowned Queen of Hungary at Pressburg.
"	July, England appropriates 300,000 pounds to subsidize Austria.
"	September, an invading army of French and Bavarians reach and capture Linz.
"	September 11, Maria Theresa makes her celebrated appeal for aid to the Hungarian Assembly.

Year	Event
1741.	October, Maria Theresa cedes Silesia to Frederick in the secret Treaty of Ober-Schnellendorf.
"	November, French and Bavarians capture Prague.
"	December, Frederick repudiates the Treaty of Ober-Schnellendorf and renews war against Maria Theresa.
1742.	With the assistance of the Hungarians, the Austrians drive the Bavarians from Austrian territory and invade Bavaria.
"	February 12, Elector of Bavaria elected and crowned Emperor of the Germans under the title of Charles VII. On the same day, the Austrians capture Munich.
"	May 17, Frederick defeats the Austrians at Chotusitz.
"	July, Maria Theresa makes peace with Frederick by again ceding him Silesia.
"	July, the French under Belleisle are shut into Prague, and Cardinal Fleury writes an humble letter to the Austrian commander, begging for peace. The petition is indignantly refused by Maria Theresa.
"	December 16, French under Belleisle escape from Prague which is immediately occupied by the Austrians.
1743.	May, Maria Theresa is crowned Queen of Bohemia at Prague.
"	June, Austrians under Prince Charles cross the Rhine to invade the Netherlands and restore Lorraine to Austria.
"	June 26, indecisive Battle of Dettingen between the French and English.
"	September, Treaty of Worms signed by Austria, Sardinia, and England.
"	December, treaty of alliance between Austria and Saxony.
1744.	Marriage of Prince Charles, brother of Francis of Lorraine and Maria Anna.
"	January, death of Field Marshal Count Khevenhüller.

Year	Event

1744.—February, France declares war against England and makes an unsuccessful attempt to invade the British Isles.

" March, Maria Theresa, threatened by a new war with Frederick of Prussia, again goes to Pressburg to appeal to the Hungarians.

" September, Frederick invades Bohemia and captures Prague.

" November, Frederick is compelled to abandon Prague and retreats toward Silesia.

" December, edict against the Jews for their disloyalty to the Queen during the occupation of Prague by the Prussians.

" During this year the Queen made satisfactory terms with King of Sardinia and fought a successful campaign in Italy.

1745.—January 8, new alliance of England, Austria, Holland, and Saxony.

" January 20, death of Emperor Charles VII in Munich.

" May 2, Treaty of Füssen, forming a defensive alliance between Austria and Bavaria. The new Elector of Bavaria agrees to support Francis of Lorraine in the coming election of an emperor.

" May 10 and 11, the French defeat the English and Austrians in the decisive Battle of Fontenoy. The battle was followed by the conquest of the Low Countries by the French under Marshal Saxe.

" June 4, Frederick defeats the Austrians under Prince Charles at Hohenfriedberg.

" June 16, an expedition fitted out by the English colonists in America, commanded by Sir William Pepperell, captures Louisburg on Cape Breton controlling the mouth of the St. Lawrence River and cutting France off from access to her colonies in Canada.

Year	Event
1745.	August 4, English Ambassador Robinson attempts to intimidate Maria Theresa by threatening to discontinue English subsidies unless she makes peace at any price with Frederick of Prussia.
"	August 26, Treaty of Hanover in which England guarantees the integrity of Prussia's territory, thus virtually underwriting Frederick's claim to Silesia.
"	September 13, Francis of Lorraine elected Emperor of the Holy Roman Empire of the Germans.
"	September 30, Frederick defeats the Austrians under Prince Charles at Sohr.
"	October 4, Francis of Lorraine crowned Emperor at Frankfort, taking the title of Francis I.
"	October, Czarina Elizabeth promises to send an army to aid Maria Theresa.
"	December 15, Frederick defeats the Saxons at Kesseldorf, and soon afterward captures Dresden.
"	December 25, Austria, Saxony, and Prussia make peace in the Treaty of Dresden, Frederick retaining Silesia.
1746.	February 25, Brussels captured by the French under Marshal Saxe.
"	June 3, Antwerp captured by the French.
"	July, Charleroi and Mons captured by the French.
"	July, death of Philip V of Spain and passing of Elizabeth Farnese from power. Accession of Ferdinand VI who was married to Barbara of Portugal, a relative and friend to Maria Theresa. The Queen relieved of Spanish pressure upon her Italian possessions.
"	During the summer, unsuccessful peace negotiations at Breda. French eager to sacrifice Austria in order to make peace with England and regain Cape Breton.
1747.	The Wars of Accession transformed almost entirely into a contest between England and France for world dominion.

Year	Event
1747.	Capture of Bergen-op-Boom, and defeat of the English at Langfeldt. Disputes between Austria and England over English subsidies and assistance furnished the English by Austria.
1748.	January 26, meeting of peace conference at Aix-la-Chapelle.
"	April, Maria Theresa protests vigorously against the terms offered her.
"	November, Wars of Accession terminated by the Treaty of Aix-la-Chapelle. All European territories returned to former owners with the exception of Silesia which is awarded to Frederick of Prussia. Cape Breton returned to the French.
1749.	Maria Theresa begins internal reforms with the assistance of Frederick William Haugwitz.
"	June 4, death of Count Harrach, the leader of the opposition to the Queen's reforms.
"	Union of Bohemia with Austria under a common *Directorium*.
"	Crown courts established in Austria and Bohemia.
"	Van Swieton becomes professor of medicine in the University of Vienna.
1750.	Founding of a system of common and high schools in Austria and Bohemia.
"	Count Kaunitz made Austrian Ambassador to France. Beginning of negotiations for the reconciliation of France and Austria eventually terminating in an alliance against Frederick of Prussia.
1751.	Maria Theresa goes to Pesth and makes an unsuccessful attempt to have Hungary join in her reforms.
1752.	Founding of gymnasiums to prepare students for entering the University.
1753.	Appointment of a commission to codify the laws of Austria and Bohemia.

Chronology

Year	Event

1753.—Count Kaunitz returns to Vienna and becomes Chancellor of the Austrian Monarchy.
" Founding of the Chastity Commission (*Keuschheitscommission*).
1754.—Founding of a school of engineering in Vienna.
1756.—Treaty of alliance between France and Austria resulting in an entirely new grouping of the powers of Europe.
" Frederick of Prussia invades Saxony and captures Dresden. Beginning of the Seven Years' War.
" October 1, indecisive Battle of Lobositz between Austrians and Prussians.
1757.—May 6, Battle of Prague. Prussian victory.
" June 18, Frederick defeated by Daun at Kolin.
" June 22, founding of the Order of Maria Theresa.
" November 5, Frederick defeats the French at Rossbach.
" December 5, Frederick defeats the Austrians at Leuthen.
1758.—June, Frederick besieges Olmutz.
" July 1, Loudon destroys Frederick's transports, compelling him to abandon the siege of Olmutz.
" October 14, Frederick defeated by Daun at Hochkirch.
1759.—August 12, Prussians defeated by Austrians at Kuhnersdorf.
" New alliance between Austria and Russia.
1760.—Partial conquest of Silesia by Austrians under Loudon.
" October 25, death of George II of England.
1761.—Austrians triumphant throughout. Frederick of Prussia reduced to lowest estate.
1762.—January 5, death of Czarina Elizabeth and accession of Peter III. Alliance of Russia with Prussia. Complete reversal of the fortunes of war for Frederick and Maria Theresa.
" July, dethronement of Peter III and accession of Catherine II. Russia declares neutrality and withdraws for the Seven Years' War.

Year	Event
1762.	July and August, reconquest of Silesia by Frederick of Prussia.
1763.	February, Treaty of Hubertsburg. End of the Seven Years' War. Complete restoration of European territories to the same ownership as at the beginning of the war. Frederick retains Silesia. But France cedes Canada to England in the later Treaty of Paris which closed the war between France and England.
"	October 5, death of Augustus of Saxony and Poland. Precipitation of another dispute over the accession in Poland.
1764.	Joseph crowned King of the Romans at Frankfort.
1765.	January, marriage of Joseph to Princess Josepha of Bavaria.
"	August 18, death of Francis I at Innsbruck.
1767.	May and June, severe illness of the Queen with smallpox.
"	Introduction of inoculation for smallpox in Vienna.
1769.	August, meeting of Joseph II and Frederick at Neisse.
1770.	July, second meeting of Joseph and Frederick at Neustadt.
1772.	August 5, signing of the treaty for the partition of Poland.
1777.	Joseph II visits his sister Marie Antoinette in Paris, probably partly to influence Louis XVI to abstain from assisting the American colonies in their struggle for independence.
"	December, death of the Elector of Bavaria without a male heir. Beginning of a dispute between Austria and Prussia over the accession in Bavaria.
"	December, Joseph II, opposed by Maria Theresa, prepares to invade Bavaria with the intention of annexing it to Austria.
1778.	Maria Theresa secretly appeals to Frederick of Prussia

Chronology

Year	Event
	to settle the dispute over Bavaria by peaceful methods.
1779.	Treaty of Teschen, ending a war with Prussia without a battle, and terminating the diplomatic career of Maria Theresa.
1780.	November 29, death of Maria Theresa.
1862.	Erection of a monument to Maria Theresa in Neustadt.
1888.	Erection of magnificent monument to the Queen in Vienna.
1930.	*Maria Theresian Austellung* in the palace of Schönbrunn at Vienna.

WORKS CITED IN THE TEXT

In the citations, when not otherwise indicated, Roman numerals refer to volumes and Arabic figures to pages.

Anthony, Catherine, *Catherine the Great,* New York, Knopf, 1926. Cited as "Anthony."
Arneth, Alfred von, *Prinz Eugen von Savoyen,* Vienna, Dittmarsch, 1858, 3 vols. Cited as "Arneth, *Prinz Eugen.*"
Arneth, Alfred von, *Briefe Maria Theresia an ihre Kinder und Freunde,* Vienna, Braumüller, 1881, 4 vols. Cited by names and dates.
Arneth, Alfred von, *Maria Theresia und Marie Antoinette ihr Briefwechsel während der Jahre 1770–1780,* Vienna, 1880. Cited by names and dates.
Arneth, Alfred von, *Geschichte Maria Theresia,* Vienna, Braumüller, 1863–1879, 10 vols. Cited as "Arneth." This is probably the greatest biography in the German language, and is a veritable mine of information concerning the life and times of Maria Theresa. It has not been translated into English.
Bermann, Moritz, *Maria Theresia und Joseph II in ihrem Leben und Wirken,* Vienna, Hartleben, 1881. Cited as "Bermann." This work of one large volume is especially valuable for the information it supplies concerning the intimate personal life of Maria Theresa. It has not been translated.
Bright, Rev. J. Franck, *Maria Theresa,* London, Macmillan, 1897. Cited as "Bright."
Bryce, James Viscount, *The Holy Roman Empire,* New York, Macmillan, 1897. Cited as "Bryce."
Carlyle, Thomas, *History of Friedrich II of Prussia, Called Fredrick the Great,* New York, T. Y. Crowell, undated,

8 vols. Cited as "Carlyle." This work furnishes very detailed and interesting accounts of the Wars of Accession and the Seven Years' War.

Coxe, William, *History of the House of Austria,* London, Cadell and Davis, 1807, 3 vols. Cited as "Coxe." This work is in two parts: Part I of two volumes, and Part II of one volume. The volume cited is really Part II, but, since it is the third volume, we have cited it as such. This is an extremely valuable work, written by an eminent historian who had access to the papers of Robinson (British Ambassador to Vienna at the time of Maria Theresa), the documents of the two Walpoles, and many others who made history of Europe at that period.

Dorschel, Gotthold, *Maria Theresias Staats und Lebensanschaung.* Gotha, Frederick Andreas Perthes, 1908. Cited as "Gotthold Dorschel."

Felder, Erich, *Kaiserin Maria Theresia,* Leipzig, Rothbarth, 1907. Cited as "Felder."

Goldsmith, Margaret, *Frederick the Great,* London, Victor Gallancz, 1929. Cited as "Goldsmith."

Guglia, Eugen, *Maria Theresia,* Munich, Oldenburg, 1917, 2 vols. Cited as "Guglia." This is one of the best of the recent German works on Maria Theresa.

Gürtler, Dr. Alfred, *Die Volkszählungen Maria Theresias und Joseph II,* Innsbruck, Wagner Verlag, 1909. Cited by name and title. This book deals especially with statistical facts.

Higby, Chester, Ph.D., *History of Europe, 1492–1815,* Houghton and Mifflin, 1927. Cited as "Higby." We have drawn upon this work for general historical facts concerning the period of Maria Theresa.

Karajan, *Maria Theresia und Graf Silva Tarouca,* Vienna, Wiener Academie, 1859. Cited as "Karajan."

Khevenhüller-Metsch, Rudolf von, *Aus der Zeit Maria Theresias,* Vienna, Adolf Holzhausen, 1907, 4 vols. This is a diary, and a very tedious one through which to search for historical facts. The author must not be confused with Field Marshal Ludwig Andreas Khevenhüller. Cited as "Khevenhüller-Metsch."

Mahan, Dr. J. A., *Vienna Yesterday and Today,* Vienna, Halm and Goldmann, 1928. Cited by name and title. This is a travel book of Vienna.

Mahan, Dr. J. A., *Famous Women of Vienna,* Vienna, Halm and Goldmann, 1929. Cited by name and title.

Montagu, Lady Mary Wortley, *Letters and Works,* London, Henry G. Bohn, 1859. There have been many editions of this valuable work. The letters are cited usually by names and dates.

Oesterreichischer Erbefolge-Krieg K. und k. Archivs, 1740 bis 1748, Vienna, issued by the *K. und k. Archivs,* Seidel und Sohn, 1896, 6 vols. This is a voluminous work, telling everything there is to be told about the Wars of Accession. Cited as *Oesterreichischer Erbefolge-Krieg.*

Silva Tarouca, Graf Franz, *Die Silva Taroucas in Oesterreich,* Vienna, Frick, 1899. Cited as "Silva Tarouca."

Steed, Henry Wickham, *The Hapsburg Monarchy,* London, Constable and Co., 1914. Cited as "Steed."

Walpole, Lord Horatio, *Memoirs,* edited by William Coxe, London, Longman, 1820, 2 vols. Cited by name and title.

Walpole, Sir Robert, *Memoirs,* edited by William Coxe, London, Cadell, 1798, 2 vols. Cited by name and title.

Whitman, Sidney, *Austria,* London, Fisher Unwin, 1898. Cited as "Whitman."

Williams, H. Noel, *Madame de Pompadour,* London, Harpers, 1908. Cited as "Williams."

Wraxall, Sir Nathaniel, *Memoirs of the Courts of Berlin, Dresden, Warsaw, and Vienna,* London, 1799, 2 vols. Cited as "Wraxall."

Zwiedineck-Südenhorst, *Maria Theresia,* Leipzig, Velhagen und Klasing, 1905. Cited as "Zwiedineck-Südenhorst."

INDEX

Accession, Wars of, 103 seq., 200
Aix-la-Chapelle, Treaty of, 165
Albert, Prince of Saxony, 291, 315, 339
Algarotti, Count Francesco, 198
Alsace and Lorraine, 147
Amalia, Archduchess, 298, 311
American colonies, contentions of France and England over, 96, 158, 162, 165, 219
American Revolution, 327
Anne, Czarina, 48, 92
Anne, Queen of England, 10
Archives of Austria, 6, 37, 337
Argens, at Potsdam, 198
Argenson, Marc Pierre de Voyer, Comte d', 139
Army, national, 176; reforms, 179
Arneth, Alfred von, quoted, 239
Auersperg, Princess, 262 seq.
Auersperg, Count Heinrich J. J., 38
Augustus of Saxony. *See* Frederick Augustus II
Austria, defeat and financial ruin at end of Charles VI reign, 51 seq.; the Monarchy, 61, 70 seq.; and the Holy Roman Empire, 66, 68; the new Empire, 71; reforms in the Monarchy, 170 seq.; converted into a real nation, 181; change in alliance from England to France, 184 seq.; chronology, 341 seq.
Austria, Archives of, 6, 37, 337

Barbara, Queen of Spain, 161
Barcelona, siege of, 10

Bartenstein, John Christopher, 47 seq., 57, 59, 112, 169, 190; ultimatum to Francis of Lorraine, 35, 37
Batthyany, Count, 270 n.
Bavaria, 71, 274, 290, 301; in the Wars of Accession, 113, 125 seq., 148, 159; in possession of Austria, 137, 141; efforts of Hapsburgs to acquire, 288, 294, 328 seq. *See also* Charles Albert, Elector of
Beatrice, of Modena, 298
Belgrade, loss of, 51
Belleisle, Marshal, 88, 90, 132, 134, 140, 168
Belvedere, palace of, 44
Benedicta, of Portugal, 286
Bertolli, Anton, 22
Bevern, Prussian general, 209, 210
Bibliography, 352 seq.
Bohemia, 12, 71, 73, 155, 179; in Wars of Accession, 125 seq., 148; Maria Theresa crowned queen of, 136; Prussian advance into, 205
Botta, minister to Berlin, 105
Bourbons, 144, 161; union of Hapsburgs with, 274, 282, 299, 301
Brandenburg, 274
Breslau, Treaty of, 175
"Brigand from Berlin," 204
Browne, General, 203, 207, 208
Brunswick, 5, 274

Cæsars, unbroken line of, 65
Canada, 158, 162, 165, 219

Cape Breton, 162, 219
Capucine Church, 297, 300, 338
Carlisle, Thomas, quoted, 134, 213
Carlos, Don, of Spain, 26, 101, 102, 164
Caroline, of Ansbach, 17
Caroline, of Naples, 297, 303, 305, 312, 313
Carteret, Lord John, 131, 145
Catherine II (the Great), Czarina, 93, 94, 293, 331, 339; takes throne: attitude toward Frederick, 221; partition of Poland, 321 seq.
Catholic Church, 70; conflict with Freemasons, 30; relation to the Holy Roman Empire, 62, 65, 66, 69; power, 74; attitude of Maria Theresa toward, 250, 253
Chablais, Duke of, 291, 292
Charlemagne, 65; Empire of, 66
Charles V, Emperor, 12, 68 n.
Charles VI, Emperor, 89, 91, 100, 101, 318; desire for a male heir, 3, 6, 13, 267; ancestry, 8; made king of Spain, 9; charms English court: conduct in Spain, 10; inherits Hapsburg dominions: elected Emperor, 12; alters father's decree: the Pragmatic Sanction, 13; builds Karlskirche: character, 15; marriage: devotion to Queen, 18; attitude toward his daughter, 21; betrothal of Maria Theresa, 24 seq.; secret pact between Elizabeth Farnese and, 26, 102; treatment of Francis of Lorraine, 32, 35, 40, 49, 50; difficulties and losses resulting from Pragmatic Sanction promises, 33, 54, 72, 84, 85, 88, 91, 102; loses war of Polish Succession: yields Lorraine to France, 34; recompenses to Lorraine family, 40; relations with Prince Eugene, 45; joins Russia in War on Turkey, 48; letter to Czarina, quoted, 52; despair and illness, 53; death: mistakes, 54; territory lost by, 72; social evils during reign of, 241, 246
Charles VII, Emperor (Charles Albert of Bavaria), 59, 70, 85, 88, 89, 118, 125, 129, 137, 138, 288; appeals for restoration of Bavaria, 141; death: career, 151
Charles III, King of Spain, 9, 282, 283, 293, 296, 298
Charles, King of Naples, 276, 277. *See also* Charles III
Charles, Archduke, 270, 277, 282, 313
Charles, Prince of Lorraine, 39, 40, 259; in command of army: Wars of Accession, 128, 129, 130, 135, 140, 147, 148, 150, 151, 168, 171; in Seven Years' War, 205, 207, 208, 211, 213; removed from command, 215; marriage: influence upon career, 275
Charles Emmanuel, King of Sardinia, 99 seq., 131, 139, 143, 159, 160, 161, 163, 165, 291
Chastity Commission, 240, 242, 243, 244
Châteauroux, Madame, 149 n., 198 n.
Chesterfield, Lord, 29
Chevert, General, 135
Choiseul, Étienne François, Duc de, 293
Chotusitz, Battle of, 130
Christina. *See* Maria Christina
Chronology of Austria under the Hapsburgs, 341 seq.
Clemens, Prince of Lorraine, 24
Clement XII, Pope, 30
Clement XIII, Pope, 253
Clement XIV, Pope, 253
Clergy, power of, 74, 76, 173, 179; oppose taxation, 176 seq.
Cobenzl, Count Johann Casper, 37
Cobenzl, Count Philip, 263, 264

College of Chastity, 198, 242. See also Chastity Commission
Conscription, 172
Constant VI, 64
Courts, uniform system of, 179
Coxe, William, quoted, 160, 240, 302
Criminals, punishment of, 256 seq.
Cunigunda, of Saxony, 286

Daun, Fieldmarshal, 205, 209 seq.; honored by Queen, 212; in command of army, 215, 216, 218, 219, 222
Denmark, 196
Dettingen, Battle of, 140
Diplomacy, European, 77, 145
Directorium, the, 179
Dresden, capture of, 157, 202
Dresden, Treaty of, 158
Dueling, 247

Educational system, 180
Electors of Holy Roman Empire, 61
Elizabeth, Czarina, 88, 92 seq., 109, 162, 192, 197, 198, 214, 215, 220, 256
Elizabeth, Empress, 73
Elizabeth, Archduchess, 292, 304, 311, 337 n.
Elizabeth, of Brunswick, 286
Elizabeth Christina, Empress, 3, 17 seq.
Elizabeth Christina, Queen of Prussia, 27, 31, 82
Elizabeth Farnese, Queen of Spain, 101, 161, 163, 283; secret pact between Charles VI and, 26, 102
Emperor, title of, coveted, 68
Empire. See Holy Roman Empire
England, during reign of George II, 95 seq.; contentions with France for world power, 96, 158, 162, 196, 200, 219; alliance with Austria, 97, 109, 131, 139, 145, 147, 152, 158, 166; in the Wars of Accession, 112, 126 seq.; subsidies to Austria, 112, 139, 143, 153, 167; beginnings of estrangement between Austria and, 142, 155; opposition to policies of George II, 145; attacked by France, 146; withdrawal of army from Continent, 160; peace negotiations, 163 seq.; alliance with Austria severed, 184 seq., 225; influence of Prussia upon, 188; alliance with Prussia, 191, 196; subsidies to Prussia, 223. See also George, King
Epidemic diseases, 318
Esterhazy, Count Joseph, 119
Eugene, Prince of Savoy, 24, 25, 42 seq., 115, 116, 128; quoted, 109
Europe, monarchial governments, 76 seq.

Farnese, Elizabeth. See Elizabeth Farnese
Faro tables, 248
Feigenbrüderschaft, 244
Ferdinand, King of Naples, 295 seq.
Ferdinand VI, King of Spain, 102, 161
Ferdinand, Archduke, 298, 305, 316
Finale, Marquisate of, 131
Fleury, Cardinal, 36, 48, 86, 151; plots against Maria Theresa, 88, 90; humiliated by Maria Theresa, 132; death, 139
Flood, Heroism of Emperor Francis during, 260
France, 109, 151, 152, 302, 322, 323, 327; War of Polish Succession, 33; under Louis XV, 86 seq.; contentions with England for world power, 96, 159, 162, 196,

200, 219; in the Wars of Accession, 113, 125 seq.; cabinet after death of Fleury, 139; attack on England, 146; advance through Low Countries, 147; conquests under Saxe, 160; desire for peace, 161; peace negotiations, 163 seq.; alliance with Austria, 184 seq., 265; weakening of Prussia's alliance, 191, 197; in Seven Years' War, 213, 214, 219, 225; lotteries, 249. *See also* Louis, King

Francis I, of France, 68

Francis II, of Austria, 71

Francis Joseph, 73, 181

Francis Stephan of Lorraine, 84, 113, 165, 171, 189, 191, 290; offered as husband for Maria Theresa: arrival in Vienna, 25; love of Maria Theresa for, 26, 32, 36, 38, 231, 239, 258 seq., 284, 335; takes charge of his realm, 27; visits to courts of Europe: reception, 28, 31; joins Freemasons, 29; treatment of, by Charles VI, 32, 35, 40, 49, 50; loses Duchy of Lorraine, 35; price paid for his marriage, 36, 259; betrothal ceremony, 37; letters of Maria Theresa and, *text*, 38; marriage, 39; appointed Governor of the Netherlands, 40; made commander-in-chief of army, 49; retires to Tuscany in disgrace, 50; interview with messenger of Frederick, 104; placed in command of army: replaced by Prince Charles, 128; candidate for imperial crown, 152; supported by George II, 154; election: rank, 157; fondness for women, 231; incident of stolen grapes, 233; fondness for card playing, 248; dwindling importance: heroism during flood, 260; continued devotion to Freemasonry, 261; infidelity to marriage vows, 261, 265 n.; affair with Princess Auersperg, 262 seq.; deserving of sympathy of historians, 264; political judgment: opposition to alliance with France, 265; influence upon marriage negotiations of children, 274, 288, 291, 295; death, 284; assigns Tuscany to Leopold, 298

Frederick II (the Great), of Prussia, 31, 168, 256, 301; reluctance to marry Maria Theresa, 27; on Prince Eugene, 45; influences European diplomacy, 77, 145; unscrupulous methods, 77, 107, 146, 172, 199; accession, 78, 83; childhood and youth, 79 seq.; family: inherited traits, 79; marriage, 82; character, 84, 85, 108; relations with Elizabeth of Russia, 93; a nephew of George II, 98; Silesian wars, 103 seq.; sends Gotter to make demands on Austria, 104; invades Silesia, 107; conduct at Mollwitz, 110; rejects peace terms: alliances against Austria, 113; Treaty of Ober-Schnellendorf, 124; enters into conspiracy with Maria Theresa, 126; siege of Neisse, 127; breaks Peace of Ober-Schnellendorf: second peace with Austria and deed to Silesia, 130; aids appeal of King of Bavaria, 141; relations with George II, 141, 154, 188; third war with Austria, 148; retreat from Prague, 150; aspires to be Emperor, 152; Treaty of Hanover, 154; retreat: Battle of Sohr, 156; third peace with Austria, 158; the real enemy of Austria, 188; frustrates Kaunitz in Paris, 190; change of alliance from France to England, 191;

opposed by female triumvirate, 192; preparation for new war, 194; political enemies, 196, 204; maintains court of scoffers, 197; Seven Years' War, 200 seq.; ruthless sacrifice of soldiers, 200, 206, 210; invasion of Saxony, 202; advance into Bohemia, 205; Battle of Prague, 206; defeated at Kolin, 210; defeats French at Rossbach: victory at Leuthen, 213; considered a great general, 219; despair: contemplates suicide: saved by death of Czarina, 220; end of resources, 222; necessity for peace, 223; Podewils' letters about Maria Theresa, 228 seq., 239; Emperor Francis inclined to make a friend of, 265; influence upon marriage negotiations of Hapsburgs, 273, 301; admiration of Joseph II for, 302, 323; partition of Poland, 320, 322 seq.; comments on Maria Theresa, 320, 338; prepares for war against Austria, 329; arbitration with Maria Theresa, 330
Frederick of Saxony, 68, 69 n.
Frederick Augustus II, King of Saxony and Poland, 33, 82, 85, 88, 90 seq., 92, 109, 130, 152, 155, 157, 197, 202, 203, 321
Frederick William of Prussia, 79 seq.; death, 83
Freemasonry, 29, 261
Freidamenorden, 245
Fuchs, Countess Charlotte, 22, 216
Füssen, Treaty of, 154

Gambling, 248
Garrick, David, 262
Genoa, 161, 165; origin of lotteries in, 249
George I, King of England, 79, 95

George II, King of England, 30, 95, 98, 139, 140, 143, 145, 160, 164, 167; an uncle of Frederick of Prussia, 98; relations with Frederick of Prussia, 141, 154, 188; aids King of Bavaria, 141; offends Maria Theresa, 142; arranges Treaty of Worms, 143; Treaty of Hanover, 154
George III, King of England, 316
German states, attitude toward Frederick, 197, 204
Germans, ancient, and the Roman Empire, 62, 67
Gotter, Grand Marshal, 103
Gregory X, Pope, 66
Guastalla, 102, 163, 165, 166

Hamilton, Lady, 303
Hanover, 96, 98, 145, 147, 165, 188, 192, 274
Hanover, Treaty of, 154, 157, 225
Hapsburg, House of, and Holy Roman Empire, 66, 69 n.; dominions, 70; heartless sacrifice of children to state, 272; union with Bourbons, 274, 282, 299, 301; policy in regard to inherited dominions, 298; family record of Maria Theresa's children, 304; chronology, 341 seq.
Harrach, Count Ferdinand, 57, 177
Harrach, Count Frederick, 57, 177, 178
Haugwitz, Frederick Wilhelm, 175, 178
Haydn, Joseph, 236
Henry VIII, King of England, 68
Hohenzollern family, 80, 84
Holland, 196
Holy Roman Empire, 12, 61 seq.; dissolved, 71; scramble for imperial crown, 152
Hubertsburg, Treaty of, 223
Hungary, 12; position in Austrian

monarchy, 71, 73; Maria Theresa's appeal to, 114 seq.; aid granted, 122; her second appeal, 149; taxation, 181; tariff against, 182

Indians and Jesuits, 251
Ingenhouse, Doctor, 316
Inoculation for smallpox, 316 seq.
Irene, Empress, 64, 65
Isabelle, of Parma, 277 seq., 285, 291, 312
Italy, Austrian possessions in, 34, 40, 72, 100, .102, 131, 161, 163, 164, 165, 166, 182, 249, 298

Jaquemin, Niklas, 37
Jesuits, 251; removal of, from Austrian institutions, 180, 187, 253
Jews, Maria Theresa's intolerance of, 254 seq.; in modern Vienna, 256
Johanna, Archduchess, 279, 295, 305
John III, Sobieski, King of Poland, 43, 320
Joseph I, Emperor, 6, 8, 18, 33, 45, 89, 91, 315; inheritance, 9; death, 12
Joseph II, Emperor, 183, 191, 250, 286, 294, 304, 336, 337, 338; bans torture of criminals, 256, 258; birth: name, 267; feud between brother and, 270; negotiations for marriage of, 276; marriage, 277; made King of the Romans, 278, 285; influence of wife upon the mind of, 280; aversion to marrying again, 282, 286, 290; made co-regent of Austria: becomes Emperor, 285; negotiations for second marriage, 286; wedding ceremonies, 289; objectives: results, 301, 309 seq.; characteristics, 302, 310; admiration for Frederick of Prussia, 302, 323; relations with his mother, 306 seq.; negotiations with Frederick concerning Poland, 323, 324; opposed to American Revolution, 327; prepares to take Bavaria by conquest, 328 seq.
Josepha, Archduchess, 296, 297, 305
Josepha, of Bavaria, 286 seq.
Josepha, of Naples, 276
Josephstadt, dwelling in, 247
Jülich-Berg, Duchy of, 84
Justice, department of, reforms, 179

Karlskirche, 15
Katt, friend of Frederick of Prussia, 80
Kaunitz, Count Maximilian Ulrich, 185
Kaunitz, Count Wenzel Anton, 97, 163, 164, 185 seq., 238, 243, 306, 315, 328, 329, 331; Ambassador to France, 189; Chancellor, 190; personality, 193; opposition to Jesuits, 253; influence upon marriage negotiations for Queen's children, 274, 277, 288, 294
Khevenhüller, Ludwig Andreas, 128, 129, 130, 150
Kolder, Count, 121
Kolin, Battle of, 210
Königseg, Austrian general, 49, 132
Koreff, Solomon, 254

Lacy, a soldier of fortune, 218
Laws, codification of, 180
Leczinska. *See* Maria Leczinska: Stanislaus I
Leo III, Pope, 65
Leopold I, Emperor, 8, 15, 24, 45, 69, 79; provision for his heirs, 9
Leopold II, Emperor, 269, 283,

305, 310, 313; as Grand Duke of Tuscany, 298, 302; as ruler of Austria, 302
Leopold, Crown Prince, 4
Leopold, Duke of Lorraine, 24, 25, 27
Leuthen, Battle of, 213
Liebenberg, Bürgermeister, 128
Liechtenstein, Prince, 6, 177
Liegnitz, Battle of, 218
Lobositz, Battle of, 203
Lombardy, 72, 100, 131
Lorraine, Duchess of, 39, 40
Lorraine, Duke of, 43, 46
Lorraine, Duchy of, 24, 147; yielded to France, 34; an endless cause of contention, 42
Lotteries, state, 248; origin of, 249
Loudon, Gideon, 217, 218
Louis XIV, King of France, 42, 139
Louis XV, King of France, 33, 86 seq., 90, 91, 139, 149, 152, 153, 164, 179, 189, 214, 277, 311; demands made upon Charles VI, 34; efforts to marry an archduchess to, 293
Louis XVI, King of France, 179, 299, 327, 328
Louisburg, Canada, 158, 162, 219
Ludwig, Prince of Württemberg, 291

Madras, India, 165
Maillebois, French general, 140
Mailly, Comtesse de, 87
Mancini, Marie, 42
Mancini, Olympia, 42
Maria Amalia, cousin of Maria Theresa, 89
Maria Amalia, daughter of Maria Theresa, 294, 305
Maria Amalia, sister of Maria Theresa, 26
Maria Anna, daughter of Maria Theresa, 271, 275, 304, 311, 337 n.
Maria Anna, sister of Maria Theresa, 23, 26, 40, 50, 136, 259; marriage: death, 275
Maria Christina, Archduchess, 279, 290 seq., 304, 313, 337 n.; quoted, 264
Maria Elizabeth, Archduchess, 292, 304, 311, 337 n.
Maria Josepha, Queen of Saxony, 33, 89, 91, 203, 204
Maria Theresa, birth, 3; baptism, 5; full name, 6; ancestry: inherited traits, 7 seq.; personal appearance, 20, 23, 55, 120, 228; education, 21; instructors: devotion to Countess Fuchs, 22; child pictures of, 23; betrothal, 24 seq.; love for Francis of Lorraine, 26, 32, 36, 38, 231, 239, 258 seq., 284, 335; betrothal ceremony, 37; letters of Francis and, *text*, 38; marriage, 39; friendship of Prince Eugene, 46; of John Palfy, 46, 115; in Tuscany, 50; accession to throne, 55 seq.; domestic tastes, 56; ministers of, 57, 59, 169, 171, 174, 231; preparation for her duties, 58; sets up first government, 59; disqualified to sit on throne of Cæsars, 67, 70; contemporaries, 76 seq.; early opinion of Frederick of Prussia, 79, 84; friendly feeling toward Czarinas, 93; Wars of Accession, 103 seq., 200; defies Frederick, 105; denied aid by friendly powers, 109; expedition against Prussians: defeat at Mollwitz, 110; urged to make peace, 112; appeal to Hungary, 114; ability to sway crowds, 116, 136; appears before Hungarian assembly, 117, 121; coronation ceremonies at Press-

burg, 119; speech before assembly, *text*, 121; signs Treaty of Ober-Schnellendorf: yields Silesia, 124; gratitude to friends, 124; gifts to John Palfy, 124, 150; unforgiving toward enemies, 124, 132; enters into conspiracy with Frederick, 126; places husband in command of army: substitutes his brother, 128; second peace with Prussia: again yields Silesia, 130; alliance with Sardinia: lauded in England, 131; humiliates Cardinal Fleury, 132; speech refusing terms of France, *text*, 133; coronation in Prague, 136; plans for conquests, 137; indignant at George II, 142, 155; Treaty of Worms, 144; second appeal to Hungary, 149; urged by England to make peace, 153; resentment over treaty of Hanover: defiance toward England, 155; secures election of Francis as Emperor, 157; Treaty of Dresden: third peace with Prussia, 158; regains Italian possessions, 161; alliance with Russia, 162; opposes peace terms, 163; dissatisfaction with Treaty of Aix-la-Chapelle, 165, 168; gains and losses: summary of relations with England, 166; summary of reign during Wars of Accession, 168; reforms in the Monarchy, 170 seq.; displeased with military commanders, 171; ideal of a benevolent monarchy, 174, 257; adopts Haugwitz tax plan, 175; struggle with nobility and clergy over taxes, 176 seq.; builds national army, 176, 179; establishes crown courts, 179; educational reforms, 180; presents tax plan to Hungarian assembly: converts Austria into a nation, 181; changes alliance from England to France, 184 seq.; influence of Kaunitz upon, 185, 187, 195; influenced by enmity toward Frederick, 188, 192; sends Kaunitz to Paris, 188; makes him Chancellor, 190; relations with Madame Pompadour, 189, 191; forms coalition against Frederick, 196; motives, 199; ridiculed by Potsdam scoffers, 198; Seven Years' War, 199 seq.; strengthens league against Frederick, 204; rejoices over defeat of Prussians, 211; founds Order of Maria Theresa, 212; grief over defeat at Leuthen, 213; removes Prince Charles: makes Daun Fieldmarshal, 215; difficulties with military commanders, 218; deserted by Russia and Sweden, 220; end of resources: necessity for peace, 223; successes and failures of the war, 224; aged, 225; as a woman, 227 seq.; capacity for work, 227, 231, 232; daily schedule, 227, 229; described in the Podewils letters, 228 seq., 239; sense of humor, 233 seq.; incident of stolen grapes, 234; meetings with Joseph Haydn, 236; feeds starving baby: moral character, 238; war against social evils, 240 seq.; criticized for its severity, 246; suppresses duelling, 247; restricts gambling: founds state lottery, 248; attitude toward Catholic Church, 250, 253; removal of the Jesuits, 251; intolerant of Jews, 254 seq.; upholds torture of criminals, 256 seq.; domestic life, 258 seq.; loss of confidence in husband, 259; pride in his heroism, 260; op-

position to Freemasonry: infidelity of Francis to, 261; jealousy, 262; attitude toward Princess Auersperg, 263; as a mother, 266 seq.; number of children, 266; when they were born, 266 seq.; arranges marriages of children, 271 seq., 285; heartless in the matter, 271; policy, 273, 301; reaction to death of husband, 284, 335; makes Joseph co-regent, 285; opposition to marriage of Joseph to Josepha, 288; summary of facts concerning children of, 304; sorrows of later years: grief over conduct of Joseph, 306 seq.; rushes to theatre with news of grandson's birth, 310; worries about her daughters, 311; attack of smallpox, 315; introduces methods of preventing smallpox, 316 seq.; late diplomacy: partition of Poland, 320 seq.; agreement to aid Turkey, 324; attitude toward American Revolution, 327; alarmed at Joseph's preparation for war: negotiates with Frederick of Prussia, 329 seq.; ill health, 334; mental condition: preparation for death, 335; death: notices and tributes, 337; burial: will, 338; place in history: monuments to, 339
Maria Theresa, daughter of Joseph II, 278
Marie Antoinette, Queen of France, 269, 299, 304, 305, 312
Marie Caroline. *See* Caroline, of Naples
Marie Leczinska, Queen of France, 86, 293
Marie Louise, Empress, wife of Leopold II, 282, 283, 303
Marie Louise, Empress, wife of Napoleon, 295, 304
Masonry, 29, 261

Masses, condition of the, 76, 173, 177, 178
Maupertuis, Pierre Louis Moreau de, 198
Maurepas, Jean F. P., Comte de, 139
Maximilian I, 68 n.
Maximilian, Archduke, 271, 300, 305, 316
Maxmilian Joseph, Elector of Bavaria, 152, 154, 157, 328
Mazarin, Cardinal, 42
Medical School of Vienna, 181
Metternich, Prince Clemens Lothar Wenzel, 100
Mistresses, 241
Modena, 165
Mollwitz, Battle of, 110
Monarchial form of government, 76, 159, 171, 327
Monarchy. *See* Austria
Montagu, Lady Mary Wortley, 37; quoted, 19, 44, 317; on Viennese society, 241
Moore, John, quoted, 246

Naples, 144, 161, 163, 164, 295. *See also* Charles, King of Naples
Napoleon Bonaparte, 68, 299, 303
Neipperg, General, 28, 57, 110, 171, 262
Neisse, siege of, 127
Nelson, Lord, 303
Netherlands, Austrian, 40, 72, 139, 159, 182, 191, 215
Newcastle, Duke of, 164
Nobility, power of, 74, 76, 173, 179; oppose taxation, 176 seq.

Ober-Schnellendorf, Treaty of, 124, 126, 127, 130
Odoacer, capture of Rome, 64
Order of Free Women, 245
Order of Maria Theresa, 212
Orry, French Controller, 139
Ottacar of Bohemia, 272

Palfy, John, 115; friendship for Maria Theresa, 46; appointed representative in Hungary, 60; aids Maria Theresa, 116, 119, 120, 149; receives gifts from her, 124, 150
Pandours, 217
Paraguay, slaughter of natives in, 252
Parma, 72, 102, 163, 164, 165, 166, 295
Parma, Prince of, 295, 311
Partition (of Poland), Treaty of, 325
Pelham, Sir Henry and Thomas, 145
Pelzel, on retreat from Prague, 134
Pepperell, Sir William, 158 n.
Personality, power of, historical instances, 123
Peter the Great, 92
Peter III, of Russia, 93, 94, 220, 221
Peterborough, Earl of, quoted, 10
Philip V, of Spain, 101, 161
Philip, Don, of Spain, 26, 101, 102, 163, 164, 165
Piacenza, 72, 163, 164, 165, 166
Piaristens, order of, 253
Podewils, Count, letters about Maria Theresa, excerpts, 228 seq., 239
Poland, 91, 109; war with Austria, 33; partition of, 293 n., 320 seq.; form of government, 321
Polish Succession, War of, 34
Pombal of Portugal, 252
Pompadour, Madame, 87, 198, 214; relations with Maria Theresa, 189, 191
Poniatowski. *See* Stanislaus II
Pope, relation to Holy Roman Empire, 65, 66, 69
Porter, Mr., on Charles VI, 53
Portugal, attack on Jesuits, 252

Portugal, Crown Prince of, 26
Potsdam "School for Slander," 198
Pragmatic Sanction, 13 seq., 59, 73, 109, 113, 114; difficulties and losses resulting from, 33, 54, 72, 84, 85, 88, 91, 102; attitude of Prince Eugene toward, 45; inheritance under, 298
Prague, siege of, 128, 132; evacuation, 134; coronation in, 136; captured by Frederick, 148; abandoned, 150; Battle of, 206 seq.; siege raised, 211
Pressburg, coronation of Maria Theresa in, 118; monument, 123
Propaganda, of historical characters, 136
Prussia, under the Hohenzollerns, 78 seq., 170, 172. *See also* Frederick II
"Purity Squad," 243. *See also* Chastity Commission

Queens, great, 339

Reforms in Austrian Monarchy, 170 seq.
Ringstrasse, Vienna, 310
Robinson, Sir Thomas, 37, 113, 135, 163, 167; quoted, 36, 53, 55, 120, 153
Roman Empire, 62 seq.
Rossbach, Battle of, 213
Rudolph I, 68, 272
Russia, alliance with Austria, 48; wars with Turkey, 48, 323, 324; under rule of the Czarinas, 92 seq.; alliance with England, 139; with Prussia, 220. *See also* rulers, Anne: Catherine: Elizabeth: Peter

St. Lawrence River, 158, 162, 165
Salm, Niklas, 128
Sardinia, 99. *See also* Charles Emmanuel, King

Saxe, Marshal, 147, 168
Saxony, 33, 274, 301; in the Wars of Accession, 113, 130 seq., 159; invaded by Prussia, 202. *See also* Frederick Augustus II
"School for Slander," 198
Schools, 180
Schwerin, Prussian general, 206, 207
Seckendorf, General, 27, 48, 57, 127
Self-interest, doctrine of, 98
Servia, 51
Seven Years' War, 199 seq.
Sicily, 144, 161, 164
Silesia, 71, 154, 155, 158, 163, 166, 168, 175, 199, 200, 221, 225, 323; invasion of, 103 seq.; ceded to Prussia, 124; second deed to Prussia, 130; reconquered by Prussia, 222
Silesian Wars, 103 seq.
"Silly Peter." *See* Peter III
Silva-Tarouca, Count, 227, 238
Sinzendorf, Count, 57; quoted, 35
Smallpox, prevalence of: treatment and prevention, 315 seq.; in Hapsburg family, 8, 279, 280, 282, 290, 292, 296, 297, 315 seq.
Sobieski, John. *See* John III
Social evils in Austria, 241; Queen's war against, 240 seq.
Society, Viennese, 241 seq.
Society of Jesus. *See* Jesuits
Sohr, Battle of, 156
Sonnenfels, Joseph, 255
Sophie Auguste, 93. *See also* Catherine II, Czarina
Spain, 72, 131, 161, 296; bestowed upon Charles of Austria, 9; siege of Barcelona, 10. *See also* Charles III: Elizabeth Farnese
Spanish Succession, War of the, 4, 8, 9
Stanhope, Philip Dormer, 29
Stanislaus I, Leczinska, King of Poland, 33, 34, 86, 91

Stanislaus II, Augustus (Poniatowski), King of Poland, 292, 321, 322, 323
Starhemberg, Count, 186
Subsidies, 144
Suleiman the Turk, 69 n.
Sweden, 196, 204, 221
Swieten, Gerhard van, 180, 275, 315, 316, 318

Taxation, 176, 180, 181; in Hungary, 181; in provinces, 182
Tencin, Cardinal, 139
Termagant of Spain, 101. *See also* Elizabeth Farnese
Teschen, Treaty of, 332, 333
Tindal, quoted, 10
Torture of criminals, 256 seq.
Traun, General, 128, 130, 149, 150, 151
Trautmansdorff, Countess, 296
Treaties, of Utrecht, 12, 96; Westphalia, 85; Ober-Schnellendorf, 124, 126, 127, 130; Worms, 144, 165; Füssen, 154; Hanover, 154, 157, 225; Dresden, 158; Aix-la-Chapelle, 165; Breslau, 175; Hubertsburg, 223; of Partition (of Poland), 325; Teschen, 332, 333
Triumvirate, female, of Europe, 88, 192, 198
Turkey, wars, with Austria, 24, 43, 48 seq., 320; with Russia, 48, 323, 324
Tuscany, 72, 102; deeded to Francis of Lorraine, 34, 40; Leopold as Duke of, 298

Ulfeld, Chancellor, 186, 190
Ulrich, Antony, Duke, 17, 18
Ulrike, Queen of Sweden, 196
University of Vienna, 180, 253
Utrecht, Treaty of, 12, 96

Vaccination, 317
Vermond, Abbot of, 299

Index

Vienna, as a medical center, 181; society in, 241 seq.; old fortifications, 309; beauty, 310; monument to Maria Theresa, 339
Vienna, University of, 180, 253
Violet, Eva Maria, 262
Voltaire, 82, 197, 198 n.

Wagenseil, George Christopher, 22
Walls of Vienna, 309
Walpole, Sir Robert, 131; quoted, 11
Wars, of Spanish Succession, 4, 8, 9; Turkish, 24, 43, 48 seq., 320; of Polish Succession, 34; of Accession: Silesian, 103 seq., 200; Seven Years', 199 seq.
Wars and their price, 159, 201
Westphalia, Treaty of, 85

Wiener Diarum, 6, 37
Wiener Zeitung, 337
Wilhelmine, of Prussia, 81, 83, 85
Wilhemina Amalia, Empress, 6
Winter Palace, 93
Women, in Viennese society, 20, 241, 245; denied throne of the Cæsars, 64, 67; female triumvirate of Europe, 88; opposition to Frederick of Prussia, 192; victims of his "School for Slander," 198
Works cited, 352 seq.
Worms, Treaty of, 144, 165
Wraxall, Sir Nathaniel, quoted, 120, 239, 245, 290, 325 n.

Xavier of Saxony, 321

Zweibrucken, Prince of, 294

www.ingramcontent.com/pod-product-compliance
Lightning Source LLC
Chambersburg PA
CBHW021846300426
44115CB00005B/29